On the Border

ON THE BORDER

An Environmental History of San Antonio

Char Miller, EDITOR

TRINITY UNIVERSITY PRESS
San Antonio

For
Benjamin and Rebecca

Published by Trinity University Press
San Antonio, Texas 78212

Paperback edition © 2005, Trinity University Press
Copyright © 2001, University of Pittsburgh Press

Published by agreement with the University of Pittsburgh Press, Eureka Bldg., Fifth
Floor, 3400 Forbes Avenue, Pittsburgh, PA 15260

Cover design by BookMatters, Berkeley
Cover art by W. C. M. Samuels (*West Side Main Plaza, San Antonio, Texas*)
Courtesy of Bexar County and the Witte Museum, San Antonio, Texas.

⊗ The paper used in this publication meets the minimum requirements of the
American National Standard for Information Sciences—Permanence of Paper for
Printed Library Materials, ANSI Z39.48-1992.

LIBRARY OF CONGRESS CATALOGING-IN-PUBLICATION DATA

On the border : an environmental history of San Antonio / Char Miller, editor.
    p.   cm.
Includes index.
    ISBN 1-59534-014-9 (alk. paper)
    1. Human ecology—Texas—San Antonio. 2. Human geography—Texas—San
Antonio. 3. Social ecology—Texas—San Antonio. 4. Water rights—Texas—San
Antonio. 5. San Antonio (Tex.)—History. 6. San Antonio (Tex.)—Environmental
conditions.   I. Miller, Char, 1951–
    GF504.T5O6   2005
    333.7'09764'351—dc22   2004058070

09 08 07 06 05   C   5 4 3 2 1

CONTENTS

ILLUSTRATIONS
AND TABLES

ACKNOWLEDGMENTS

On the Border has benefited greatly from the usual suspects. I am most indebted to the many contributors to this volume, who leaped at the chance to tell new stories in new ways. Librarians at Trinity University, including Craig Likness and Maria McWilliams, have also been remarkably supportive; Pat Ullmann, of Instructional Media Services, did splendid work on a number of the book's illustrations. As always, Eunice Herrington, senior secretary of the History Department, has been an invaluable aid and friend. My dependence on my colleagues in the department, and throughout the university, grows with the years; from them, I have especially learned how to think about the world through which we move. That environment, this San Antonio, would be considerably less compelling were it not home to three around whom my life so revolves: my wife, Judi Lipsett, and our two children, Benjamin and Rebecca. Although Benjamin is already off at college, and Rebecca will soon follow, I can only hope that what Frederick Law Olmsted touted as San Antonio's "odd and antiquated foreignness" will remain with them wherever their lives take them.

CONTRIBUTORS

Benjamin Bradshaw, a demographer at the University of Houston School of Public Health, has published extensively on the etiology of disease in San Antonio and South Texas.

Derrall Cheatwood is a well-published scholar in the areas of criminal justice and crime, and is a member of a national Homicide Study Group; he is a professor and division head of Social and Policy Studies at University of Texas–San Antonio.

Craig E. Colten is associate professor in the Department of Geography and Anthropology at Louisiana State University. He was coauthor of *The Road to Love Canal* (1996) and currently is working on a book on the environmental history of New Orleans. He also edited *Transforming New Orleans and Environs: Centuries of Change* in this series.

Jesús F. de la Teja is a member of the History Department at Southwest Texas State University, author of *San Antonio de Bexar: A Community on New Spain's Northern Frontier* (1995), and editor of *Revolution Remembered: The Memoirs and Selected Correspondence of Juan N. Seguín*, among many other works.

John M. Donahue is professor of anthropology in the Department of Sociology and Anthropology at Trinity University. Among his publications are *The Nicaraguan Revolution in Health: From Somoza to the Sandinistas* (1986) and a coedited volume, *Water, Culture, and Power: Local Struggles in a Global Context* (1998).

Lewis F. Fisher, an independent scholar and journalist, is author of *Saving San Antonio: The Precarious Preservation of a Heritage* (1996), and *Crown Jewel of Texas: The Story of the San Antonio River* (1997), among other books.

John Hutton, a member of the Art History Department at Trinity University, is the author of numerous articles on American and European art, and *Neo-Impressionism and the Search for Solid Ground* (1994).

David R. Johnson, whose most recent book is *Illegal Tender: Counterfeiting and the Secret Service* (1995), has written extensively on the history of San Antonio; he is associate vice-president for faculty affairs at the University of Texas at San Antonio.

Char Miller, chair of the History Department at Trinity University, is coauthor of *The Greatest Good: 100 Years of Forestry in America* (1999), and editor of *Fluid Arguments: Water in the American West* (2001), *Water in the West* (2000), and *American Forests: Nature, Culture, and Politics* (1997).

James F. Petersen is a member of the Department of Geography at Southwest Texas State University and has served as president of the National Council for Geographic Education. Coauthor of *Essentials of Physical Geography,* he is also coeditor of *First Assessment: Research in Geographic Education.*

Heywood Sanders, head of the Urban Administration program at the University of Texas at San Antonio, is coeditor of *Urban Texas: Politics and Development* (1990) and *The Politics of Urban Development* (1987), among other publications.

Jon Q. Sanders graduated from Trinity University in 1999 with an undergraduate degree in anthropology and a minor in geoscience.

Stephanie J. Shaw is a Ph.D. student in the Geography Department at Southwest Texas State University. She previously worked as an environmental consultant and as a natural resources planner with the U.S. National Guard.

Laura A. Wimberley, having completed her Ph.D. at Texas A&M University on "Sole Source: The Edwards Aquifer and South Central Texas, 1890s–1990s," has published a number of articles on this important topic. She currently serves as the assistant coordinator for Student Life Orientation at Texas A&M.

On the Border

Char Miller

Urban Nature

An Introduction

All he wanted was bait for fishing, but when the young man cracked open a mussel he had pulled up from the shallow waters of the San Antonio River he was startled to "discover a pearl imbedded in the unhappy bivalve." News of his discovery soon spread, launching a mad-dash effort to harvest the thick cluster of mussels the lad had unwittingly stumbled upon between Hot Wells Hotel and Berg's Mill, several miles south of downtown San Antonio. Within days, a swarm of prospectors had begun to excavate the site, and each freshwater, metallic-colored pearl they pried loose intensified the hunt to find more. Word that brokers for New York jewelers were offering top dollar for particularly fine specimens only added to the frenzy. "Scenes reminiscent of Klondike days," a newspaper later reported, "saw excited San Antonians 'panning' the river muck for the now valuable mussels." Soon the banks were littered with mounds of cracked, dried shells, a sign of the obliteration of the riparian beds. Although in subsequent years there would be "spasmodic revivals" of pearl fishing, none came close to replicating the excited, early-twentieth-century search for the river's gems.[1]

This small moment seems consistent with the larger history of resource exploitation in the American west. A valued commodity is identified, local labor begins its extraction, outside capital redefines the significance of the strike and reorganizes and hastens its expansion, ultimately leading to collapse of the rush. Gold, silver, and shellfish were of a piece: human avarice led to a thoughtless consumption of the natural, a confirmation of the sharp distinction between humanity and wilderness that since the early-nineteenth century has shaped American cultural expression.

Implicit in this Romantic sentiment about Nature, historian William Cronon argues, is the troubling notion that "the human is entirely outside the natural," that all of our actions within nature represent a fall from its pristine state; the "place where we are is the place where nature is not." Just how one-dimensional and inflexible this argument can be is revealed through a closer examination of the events surrounding the avid pursuit of San Antonio's pearls.

Like the gems themselves, which were generated within and shielded from view by the mussels' protective shell, there is a hidden element to this particular story that is reflected in the siting of the once-prolific mussel beds. When queried about their location, one of the "local pearl 'divers,'" Joe C. Bettencourt Jr., recalled that the "warm waters of this particular section of the river seemed to attract the mussels in unusual numbers." The heat source lay just upstream—the Hot Wells Hotel. In 1892 a 1,750-foot artesian well had been dug from which daily gushed hundreds of thousands of gallons of "sulphur water." Deemed unfit for human consumption, these 103° waters had other uses, entrepreneurs quickly realized. Over the next twenty years, a number of health resorts were built to take advantage of their alleged restorative power (these waters were said to cure "Rheumatism, Kidney, Liver and Skin Diseases"), and from which grew a substantial health-care industry. San Antonio's salubrious climate, and the scenic beauty of the riverside locale—with the baths, pools, and pavilions "embowered in trees"—helped generate national attention for these spas. "The Hot Wells is the prettiest place in Texas," one 1912 publication proclaimed. "Nature has done for it what man and money cannot do for any place."

However false a claim (plenty of human energy and capital went into the site's construction), the potential for rejuvenation through direct contact with the balmy south Texas environs led the celebrated and not-so-celebrated to take the plunge. Among those who reportedly benefited from immersion in the

Hot Wells spa, through which flowed 200,000 steaming gallons an hour, were political luminaries (Porfirio Diaz and Theodore Roosevelt), celebrated actors (Sarah Bernhardt and Rudolph Valentino), and even a fatally ill railroad magnate, E. H. Harriman; although he would die within eight months of his two-week stay at Hot Wells, Harriman, as he left town, publicly affirmed that bathing in the artesian sulfur water had extended his life.[2]

To the generative qualities of this water, the presence of the large mussel bed in the San Antonio River would also attest. The mussels directly benefited from the life-giving flow that first washed over human bodies and then was flushed into the nearby stream bed—an effluent amounting to 1,200,000 gallons per day in 1894; there it created a nurturing warmth in which the shellfish colony flourished. This symbiosis, in which human and animal made a shared, beneficial use of "nature," underscores the degree to which the wild and artificial can be so integrated as to lose their distinctiveness.

So, too, does weaving together San Antonians' simultaneous exaltation and exploitation of the natural world make for a more fluid, more accurate representation of the past. Certainly, that is the broader goal of On the Border, a collection of essays on the environmental history of what in 2001 stands as the ninth-largest city in the United States. By drawing upon an interdisciplinary array of authors and insights, it seeks to highlight the evolving interaction between humanity and the south Texas landscape, and make us a bit more sensitive to how changes in each shaped the other.

A crucial first step in this process is to establish the region's geological and climatological context. San Antonio, James F. Petersen argues in "San Antonio: An Environmental Crossroads on the Texas Spring Line," is situated at a point where the southern edge of the Great Plains, also known as the Edwards Plateau or the Texas Hill Country, meets the Gulf Coastal Plain. This "environmental bordertown" lies just east of another crucial boundary, that climatic transition between the humid east and the arid west. These, when linked with other overlapping zones of soil, topography, vegetation, and hydrology, increase "the geographical complexity of place" and have a profound impact on the character of life possible within this complicated bioregion. Nothing testifies to this more than the daily paradox surrounding water: there is either a surfeit or drought, and both deeply effect agricultural production, environmental sustainability, and urban development. But this does not mean that geography is destiny: "It is through human cultural practices, abilities, and technologies that the 'rules' governing environmental interactions are interpreted and acted upon," Petersen notes. As those skills and tools evolve, so have ecological challenges and human needs in a never-ending loop; neither "humans nor nature exert complete control on the environment."

The indigenous people, and later Spanish migrants, knew this full well. The Payaya, who migrated between semi-permanent settlements situated along the spring line to San Antonio's northeast and southwest, and the Tonkawa, who acted similarly within and beyond the higher ground of the Edwards Plateau, were among many bands of hunter-gatherers who adapted to and manipulated the often-harsh terrain. Reflective of their success over many millennia—carbon dating indicates some sites along the headwaters of the San Antonio River were in use over 11,000 years ago—was the wide range of their diet, their seasonal movements to insure access to flowing water, and the development of tools and social organizations that aided in the hunt. Although the Spanish had no interest in replicating indigenous folkways—that is why they were colonizers, after all—they were not blind to the success the Indians had in transforming, while living within, the regional ecosystem. Their regular use of fire, for instance, to maintain grasslands and the large mammals that browsed upon them also created the "range" on which the invaders dreamed of running large numbers of cattle, sheep, and goats; beefing up the food supply led both sets of people to think in new ways about the lay of the land.

It helped that for the Spanish everything about the south Texas environs seemed new, or at least new enough that they wrote down their observations. Their words are the heart of Jesus F. de la Teja's chapter, "A Fine Country with Broad Plains—the Most Beautiful in New Spain," which explores what they saw and how and why they responded as they did. The country's apparent plenty bedazzled them and led them to describe and catalogue the many possible uses of its varied flora and fauna: the *cíbolo* (buffalo) may have been a misshapen, "monstrous animal," one missionary reported, but its "meat is as savory as that of the best cow"; thick forests, and the lumber they contained, caught their eye as did the abundance of nuts, all of which "were more tasty and palatable than those of Castile." Yet south Texas was not Eden. Indians proved as independent and fierce as storms were unpredictable and damaging; the withering summer heat confounded agricultural ambitions that foundered as well because of the extended distance to viable markets. The Spanish came to live lightly on this land, de la Teja concludes, because in "the absence of precious metals" there was "little incentive to undertake the taming of Texas."

To domesticate the landscape on a larger scale required an amount of capital and population and more sophisticated forms of transportation, which would not be available in San Antonio until the mid-nineteenth century. That is why it remained a frontier outpost for Spain, Mexico, and the Republic of Texas, as well as for the United States, at least during the first decades after its annexation into the union. Tracking the interaction between these economic and social goods, and the alterations in the wider environment in which they developed, is the central thrust of my chapter, "Where the Buffalo Roamed." It assesses the slow transformation of the San Antonio River Valley (a segment of the Gulf Coastal Plain) and the Edwards Plateau as livestock replaced wildlife, and as Anglo-American settlers began in the mid-1830s to displace Indians and Mexicans. These demographic, ecological, and political alterations were magnified with the laying down of more efficient and rapid transportation systems. First mule-drawn wagon trains, and later railroads, reoriented historic trade patterns and established new ones; these broadened the city's economic reach, opened new markets, and expanded the territory devoted to agriculture and ranching. They even reconstructed the spatial design of the rapidly growing metropolitan center to such an extent that it would have been unrecognizable to those who had lived under the Spanish flag but a century earlier.

Many late-nineteenth-century residents of San Antonio professed their pleasure at these great changes and spoke of them as consequences of the civilizing power of the new age and republican form of government. For them, no better proof of this could be found than in the historic Spanish missions that lay along the river and that once had been the backbone of the regional economy. These dusty ruins offered mute testimony to the triumph of a more Progressive (and Protestant) era, wherein the "old missions of the pious Catholic priests look out upon the railroad station and gas-pipes run through streets still intersected by the irrigation ditches of the early Spanish settlers."[3]

With modernity came any number of pressing environmental dilemmas, some related to the city's continued dependence on that network of eighteenth-century *acequias* for the distribution of water. With a population of more than 20,000 in 1880 San Antonio had outstripped their delivery capacity, a situation compounded by a dangerous lack of sewers. Commercial sewage was diverted into the acequias, or flushed into the San Antonio River or local creeks, what one Alderman considered "sewers provided by nature." Most "liquid household wastes" and "human excreta" were run into cesspools or "privy-vaults," primitive and porous chambers whose contents leached into the soil and nearby wells, befouling the water supply. This was the source of some contemporary public health problems, which were expected to get worse as the city expanded: "the primitive means of . . . disposal answered while [San Antonio] was a village," the head of the West Texas Medical Association noted, but "such is inadequate to a population of 30,000, and cannot continue without disastrous effects." Not until the mid-1890s, after years of political wrangling, did a citywide sewage system go on line.[4]

Digging artesian wells also helped expand (and protect) the water supply: as a local paper enthused in 1893, following a successful attempt to tap the water table: "The fresh water supply of San Antonio is apparently unlimited. It has been increased three million gallons for each twenty-four hours by a splendid strike . . . on the property of Colonel George Brackenridge on Market Street." As this and other artesinal sources came on line, they sustained an ever-larger and, to some extent, healthier population, and yet gave rise to a new complication. Accelerating water consumption over time dropped the level of the Edwards Aquifer, thereby decreasing the natural flow out of the community's many bogs, springs, and wallows around which its parks had been platted, raising concerns about the long-term stability of the water supply and reducing the volume of the San Antonio River itself. Although spared the devastating industrial pollution then wracking other American metropolitan centers, by the early-twentieth century San Antonio knew something about the poverty of progress.[5]

Whether and how to mitigate these interrelated urban ills became part of the city's political agenda. Worried about the stress produced by rising population densities, for example, reformers in San Antonio, as elsewhere, championed the creation of more "breathing spaces"—parks. Their voices were rarely heard; there were three designated parks in 1880 totaling sixty-one acres, and for which the city budgeted a mere $500 for maintenance. The numbers and size of the city parklands grew slowly until 1898, when the 250-acre Brackenridge Park was purchased. It would not be until the early-twentieth century that the acquisition of a more substantial set of community parks occurred. As Heywood Sanders and I suggest, in "Parks, Politics, and Patronage," this spurt of interest revolved around the particular electoral needs of the then-reigning political machine. In exchange for votes, it distributed parks and other services to working-class neighborhoods, especially in the segregated, predominantly African American East Side. These parcels of open space were telling marks of a closed society.[6]

So was the incidence of disease and social pathology, from diarrhea to homicide. Making full use of a range of public-health indices, and plotting these on the physical layout of the city over a fifty-year period, has enabled David Johnson, Derral Cheatwood, and Benjamin Bradshaw in "The Landscape of Death" to determine the interaction between "public interventions in the infectious disease environment" and changes in the "patterns of specific infectious diseases, and homicide." One of their striking discoveries is of the correlation between the degree of political enfranchisement and the "city's pathological environment." Because of political patronage, which brought water and sewage systems to the East Side, these neighborhoods experienced a sharp decline in the per-capita rate of infant diarrhea. Similar gains were not recorded on the largely Hispanic West Side until the 1940s when federally funded housing, water lines, and other infrastructural changes were introduced, bringing infant diarrhea and tuberculosis under control. Social intervention, by contrast, did not alter the geography or incidence of homicide, a persistence that reminds how intractable some pathologies can be.

An antidote to murder and other urban miseries has been access to well-paying jobs. The explosive growth of San Antonio's five major military bases during World War II, and their continued expansion during the Cold War, provided considerable opportunity for employment. Among the beneficiaries was the Hispanic population that lived in and around Kelly, Lackland, and Brooks Air Force Bases, located on the city's West and South Sides; the numbers employed (government spending amounted to one-third of postwar jobs in the city), the work skills gained, and the rising level of pay helped elevate portions of the local Hispanic population into the middle class. While a good citizen, the military has not always been a good neighbor. As Stephanie J. Shaw and Craig E. Colten point out in "Battlefields," the sheer size of the installations, which cover more than 50,000 acres, has had a decided impact on the shape and character of urban development. That only has increased as the city grew out to, and now surrounds, these once-distant military enclaves. The close proximity of residential subdivisions, commercial nodes, and educational facilities has heightened concerns about threats emanating from soil erosion and runoff, air, noise, and groundwater pollution, the destruction of native habitat and the stress on sewage-treatment plants. These anxieties have been manifest more publicly since the mid-1990s when congressionally mandated base realignments and decreased Department of Defense spending led to the closing of Kelly; change of this magnitude has left vulnerable neighbors feeling at once "economically abandoned and environmentally violated."

Responding to and resolving that sense of violation, difficult though it may be, will not be as tense or as tangled as the efforts to negotiate the city's historic conflicts over the distribution and use of water. At the center of these debates is the Edwards Aquifer, a large limestone cistern that lies beneath the Edwards Plateau to the city's north and west, an easily tapped source of potable water.

Its undetermined size, when linked with the region's periodic droughts, has raised innumerable demands that San Antonio locate other, seemingly more dependable sources of water. That has been easier said than done. In "Empty Taps, Missing Pipes," an analysis of San Antonio's water policies of the mid-twentieth century, Heywood Sanders probes the business elite's curious inability to secure new streams of water to sustain the city's postwar economic boom. Committed to a cheap water regime, and therefore reluctant to raise taxes to fund the purchase of additional acre feet from nearby reservoirs, the City Water Board also avoided laying pipe out to the community's many poor neighborhoods. *Look* magazine in a 1951 article ripped San Antonio for its indifference to those for whom an "inside faucet is an item of envy," but its indictment had minimal impact. By "spending little, and keeping rates down," Sanders concludes, the City Water Board, the Chamber of Commerce, and the Good Government League, a reform machine then in power, had established a formula for "maintaining political control and avoiding political conflict."

They could not avoid a fractious brawl for very long. Questions about the quantity of the aquifer's water that had bubbled up during the devastating drought of the 1950s and a decade later were commingled with new fears about its quality. These anxieties were related to the very productivity of the Edwards, to its capacity to recharge rapidly following a storm, which left it vulnerable, according to Laura A. Wimberley, in "Establishing 'Sole Source' Protection," to pollution "from septic tanks, sewage systems, and surface run-off." To challenge damaging development over the recharge zone—including a proposed, federally funded planned community called Ranch Town—local congressman Henry B. Gonzalez attached a rider to the Safe Drinking Water Act of 1974 requiring EPA protection of aquifers, like the Edwards, that provided at least 50 percent of a region's water supply. Because the amendment placed restrictions on federal underwriting of projects threatening aquifer purity, Gonzalez and a coalition of environmental activists were able to scuttle the Ranch Town complex.

Their activism has not been able to halt the broader suburban surge that has fundamentally altered the city's physical size since the late 1960s. Making full use of a liberal statewide annexation policy, San Antonio has laid claim to large sections of Bexar County; in 1940 its political boundary encompassed thirty-six square miles, and sixty years later it had ballooned to more than 460 square miles. Much of this growth occurred to the north and west, absorbing the rolling hills under which the recharge zone is located. This expansion has insured that the struggle over the aquifer has dominated local politics for more

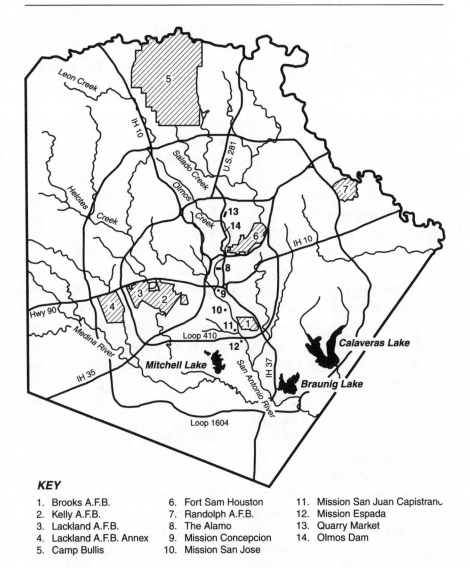

KEY

1. Brooks A.F.B.	6. Fort Sam Houston	11. Mission San Juan Capistranc
2. Kelly A.F.B.	7. Randolph A.F.B.	12. Mission Espada
3. Lackland A.F.B.	8. The Alamo	13. Quarry Market
4. Lackland A.F.B. Annex	9. Mission Concepcion	14. Olmos Dam
5. Camp Bullis	10. Mission San Jose	

Fig. I.1. Bexar County and San Antonio, Texas

than forty years. Over that time, the animosity and distrust that has built up between pro- and anti-growth forces have hindered the search for additional water supplies, argue John Donahue and Jon Sanders in "Sitting Down at the Table," something these opposing groups rarely managed to do. Tensions escalated in 1991, and again in 1994, when a disparate collection of grassroots organizations defeated at the polls city-backed propositions to construct the

Applewhite reservoir along the Medina River as it flowed through southwestern Bexar County.

Out of this debacle emerged the first real effort to develop a consensus on water. Under the aegis of the City Council, professional mediators and a committee comprised of many people involved on all sides of the Applewhite debates thrashed out many issues for six months, concluding in January 1997. The discussion broke out along two lines—whether the city had a water problem (that is, did it need a larger supply?) or a water-management problem (that is, was water mining and delivery flawed?). Less discussed was an older, but still relevant query about the aquifer's water quality. Still, the resolutions that emerged, and which the City Council accepted, offered a host of short- and long-term solutions, a unique demonstration of the capacity of a citizens' group to resolve some of the region's nagging water dilemmas.

It also took a powerful set of volunteers to identify and preserve elements of San Antonio's historic fabric. Most nineteenth-century visitors to the town had found it quaint, an out-of-the-way place that somehow had maintained physical reminders of its colonial heritage and frontier past; everything about the place, Richard Everett wrote after arriving on a mule train, "bespeaks a condition widely different from what you are accustomed to behold in any American town." Later, novelist Stephen Crane, who rode in on the rails, was appalled at the disruptive power that this engine of progress, and its urban offspring, the trolley, contained; these "merciless animals," he wrote, "gorged themselves with relics." Hoping to thwart this impulse and boost a nascent tourist trade, some late-nineteenth-century San Antonians fought to retain a semblance of the city's older form. Local activism, according to Lewis F. Fisher in "The Preservation of San Antonio's Built Environment," at once preceded and responded to national trends. The (second) battle of the Alamo was a case in point. News of Boston's successful efforts to save the landmark Old South Meeting House spurred a drive to buy the Alamo; lacking the necessary funds, supporters convinced the state legislature to underwrite the purchase. Subsequent generations may have sharply struggled with one another over the meaning imputed to the building—and Fisher sorts out who said what and why—but they also added to the site's property, buildings, and its mythic stature. In doing so, they turned the former hallowed 1836 battleground cum Army warehouse, into "Texas' most hallowed shrine," a site annually drawing millions of visitors.

The volunteerism that energized this and other early actions crystallized with the formation of the San Antonio Conservation Society (SACS) in 1924.

Since then, despite numerous setbacks, it has emerged as one of the city's most powerful lobbying groups as it works to save individual sites, neighborhoods, districts, and threatened landscapes. Nothing demonstrated its potency more fully than when in the early 1980s it pressed for and subsequently secured a Historic Preservation Office inside City Hall, one of the first in the country; headed by a leading SACS activist, the politics of preservation in San Antonio had gone professional.

However potent the local preservationist impulse, it is not omnipotent or fully embraced. The design and reconstruction of the Alamo Quarry Market, fashioned out of an abandoned cement factory, is illustrative of this point. Understanding why the much-anticipated rehabilitation project that opened in late 1997 proved to be, in one critic's eyes, "a planning disaster," requires a careful assessment of "city politics, decades of debate over reclamation, development, and tree preservation," and of the pressure "local developers and national chain stores" can bring to bear on "land-use patterns." The convergence of those factors, John Hutton argues in "Elusive Balance: Landscape, Architecture, and the Social Matrix," led to the creation of "an elite mall" that stands "in uneasy relationship with its historical predecessor." Dotted with mementos of its past—heavy machinery and locomotives, tall smokestacks and squat limestone blocks—these emblems are so divorced from their original context that the environmental ambiance is of kitsch, the shopping center as "nostalgic curio." Concluding that the "developers' failure of imagination reflects a broader problem," Hutton notes this paradox: San Antonio's hunger for prominence frequently has led it to spurn its formerly distinct architectural vocabulary in favor of a national speech pattern embodied in uniform megamalls and uninspiring office towers; what once seemed unique has since become mere analogy.

The attempt to understand what is particular to and common about San Antonio's environmental history is woven throughout *On the Border*. Collectively these chapters do not tell the whole of that past, nor were they intended to be comprehensive. But together they offer insight into the kinds of questions that can (and should) be asked of the manifold interactions of any city's climate and geography, demographic composition and social ecology, economic forces and natural resources. Nowhere will these relationships exist in the same ratio or balance, which is what distinguishes one urban landscape from another. But it is also true that each human community—large or small—has similarly struggled with an abiding, even healthy tension. The "human drive to control and impose order upon an unpredictable, unstable, and often recalcitrant environment," historian Andrew Hurley has written about St. Louis, is constrained by the "enduring power" of nature itself to channel "human choices" and shape "the precise contours" of urban development. That is just as evident in the American urban system, as it is abroad; St. Petersburg, which Peter the Great commanded be built in the Neva River swamplands, like Mexico City and Venice, stands on reclaimed, that is, shaky, grounds.

Even a Russian czar, Aztec tlatoani, Venetian doge, or American mayor would confirm that human agency, however imperial or democratic, has its limits. Conflicts between social groups and political interests often require negotiation that can deflect, revise, or halt urban development schemes. And should the haves run roughshod over the have-nots—about which, alas, San Antonio offers ample evidence—the disparity in power in time can be made visible, and the historical record used to challenge, if not fully correct, past inequities. Take flood control, a matter of great concern in the American Southwest (but not fully detailed in this volume). Although the region's many rivers and creeks seem of small flow and may even appear to be dry arroyos, should rain fall they can quickly fill, channeling a thunderous surge of water. Like Austin, Tucson, Phoenix, San Diego, and Los Angeles, the Alamo City has suffered extensive damage from a series of blockbuster floods, perhaps the greatest of which ripped through the community in September 1921. Early that month, a storm cell stalled over the San Antonio River watershed, dropping nearly seven inches of rain and generating a wall of water that built up as it swept down Olmos Creek and through the Olmos Valley; when it slammed into the central core, it tore apart streets and bridges and inundated innumerable businesses. The small creeks threading through the Hispanic West Side proved as fierce and more deadly: they blasted out of their banks, crashed through the shacks and shanties, killing scores.[7]

The city's response to the great loss of life and staggering destruction was revealing. Determined to protect the downtown, the citizenry voted to build a dam across the Olmos Valley. Once completed, the Olmos Dam not only stopped future high waters from washing through the central district but facilitated the construction to its east and west of a pair of suburban enclaves that sheltered the city's elite. The skyline also exploded upwards, as investors poured capital into the development of tall buildings on the former floodplain; and an old idea—a River Walk—was revived, and ultimately realized, now that flood controls were in place. For these reasons the Olmos Dam is arguably the city's most important public works project.

What did not happen was just as crucial. Social reformers may have clamored for flood-control projects on the West Side to elevate the waterlogged bar-rios and funding to build better housing for this most destitute of neighbor-hoods, but their appeals fell on deaf ears: on the same day that the city commissioners released $3 million for the dam's construction, they committed a paltry $6,000 to the widening and clearing of the Alazan and San Pedro Creeks, whose rampaging waters had killed so many. This remarkable dispar-ity in financial investment and flood-prevention technology would continue for the next fifty years; until the mid-1970s, when reenergized Hispanic voters gained political power, the management of San Antonio's flood waters cut along sharply etched ethnic divisions and class lines.

It is only appropriate, in a city whose history so hugs the shifting contours of its river, that this particular tale of environmental inequity helps illuminate a broader claim; it underscores the same, ineluctable connection between physical space and social structure that was evident when a young man, who wanted nothing more than to catch a fish, instead came up with a pearl.

ONE

Climate Controls

1

✳

James F. Petersen

San Antonio

An Environmental Crossroads on the Texas Spring Line

Poised at a cultural confluence, San Antonio is an urban bridge that links Anglo and Latin America. The city has a majority population of Mexican descent, and strong economic and cultural ties to Mexico as well as to its hinterland of south and southwest Texas counties that also have a Hispanic majority. In addition to this cultural and ethnic heritage, San Antonio is located on the edges of several physical-environmental regions. Climatic, geologic, topographic, vegetative, soil, and hydrologic zones all have regional boundaries in the San Antonio area, with attendant spatial changes in both environmental settings and in human uses of the land.[1]

Two of these boundaries, very different in their spatial and temporal expression, define major natural regions of North America and exert great local influence on the spatial distributions of other environmental areas. One boundary is geologic-topographic, spatially fixed, and the dominant landform feature of central Texas (see fig. 1.1). San Antonio is positioned where the southernmost section of the Great Plains (locally called the Texas Hill Country) meets the Gulf

Coastal Plain. Characterized by different geology and terrain, these two phys-iographic provinces are separated by the Balcones Escarpment. The other boundary, a statistical abstraction, approximates the mean position of an amal-gam of meteorological variables that indicate the degree of aridity for a place. Cutting through central Texas (as shown in fig. 1.2), this is a zone of signifi-cant climatic transition on the North American continent, marking where the humid east meets the arid west. Similar to the edges of most climatic regions, it is spatially gradational, and its position drifts in response to climatic change or annual meteorological variation. The presence of these two natural bound-aries, one geologic-topographic running roughly northeast-southwest, and the other climatic and trending north-south, exerts a strong influence on the envi-ronmental character of San Antonio and the central Texas region.[2]

Existing on the periphery of a region tends to increase the geographic com-plexity of a place. Rather than sharp delineations, regional limits tend to be transitional, with the boundary zones of adjacent regions sharing characteris-tics that are considered to be definitive of each other. Most regional boundaries

Fig. 1.1. Map of Texas. San Antonio's location in relation to the state and the Balcones Escarpment, which divides the Great Plains and the Gulf Coast Plain.

respond to environmental or cultural change by shifting their position over time. The delineation of regional borders is typically an imprecise proposition because geographically regions are analogous to fuzzy sets in mathematics. Although represented by discrete lines on maps, spatial-regional boundaries are abstractions and no more concrete, precise, or easy to define than the temporal divisions that historians use to divide time into convenient, meaningful segments. San Antonio's location at a crossroads of natural and cultural regions adds richness and complexity to local environmental analyses.

The ground rules for environmental interactions are set by the physical geography, the environmental setting of a place. It is through human cultural practices, abilities, and technology that the "rules" governing environmental interactions are interpreted and acted upon. The "rules of conduct" toward the environment shift in emphasis according to varying human needs and atti-

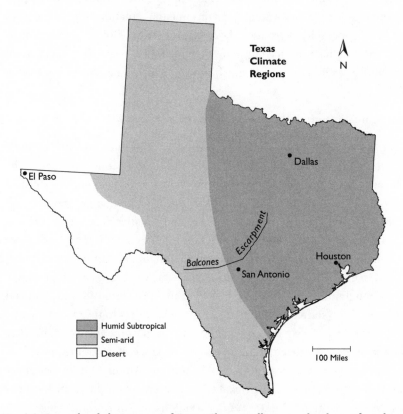

Fig. 1.2. Generalized climate map of Texas. This map illustrates the change from humid in the east to semiarid in the central parts of Texas, both north and south, and increasing aridity in the west. These climatic boundaries show their average position over the long term. (*Source:* Adapted from Wladimir Köppen's "Map of World Climates.")

tudes of the time. San Antonio's environs, like any terrestrial location, present environmental advantages as well as challenges and limitations to the local flora, fauna, and human inhabitants. Human and physical factors blend an urban setting with a natural one, with ample potential for both benefit and conflict. Neither humans nor nature exerts complete control on the environment, nor have they in the past, at least under "normal" conditions.

Understanding the environmental history of a site such as San Antonio requires some background knowledge about its physical geography, including landforms, geology, soils, water features, climate, weather, and vegetation-wildlife associations. These natural elements set San Antonio's environmental stage with an ecological richness that stems from the shared or combined characteristics of several physical regions. The city's long history of human-environmental interactions and modifications, along with the physical setting, offers a wealth of material for an environmental history. Water, however, provides the catalyst for San Antonio's environmental situation in terms of both history and geography. A paradox, however, is that the city is subject to challenges that stem from having not enough water over the longer term (droughts), as well as having too much (floods) in sporadic, short-term events.

San Antonio's Location: Where and Why There?

Locational descriptions, whether relative or absolute, provide the most basic geographic information and generally lead to other concerns, such as the significance and explanation for a location. Why was San Antonio established where it is? Questions of locational analysis deal with what geographers call *site* (location and characteristics of a place) and *situation* (changes in the significance or importance of a place over time). Jeffrey Roet has outlined three environmental factors that provide an explanation for San Antonio's location—water, topography, and ecotone. Each of these factors has retained an importance throughout San Antonio's history, but their relative meaning and significance have shifted over time. Briefly, *ecotone* refers to the environmental boundaries on which San Antonio is located as well as the increased diversity of natural resources offered at the spatial coincidence of several regional borders. *Topography* was important in establishing San Antonio on the periphery of the Hill Country along a beneficial route that exploited the relative ease of travel on the low-relief Coastal Plain. Elevations in San Antonio range from about 550 feet to higher than 1,000 feet above sea level in the Hill Country to the north and west. *Water* refers to the city's establishment, development, and nurture around sources of this essential natural resource—San Antonio has functioned as an oasis since its beginnings. These three factors have had great historic significance on the city's nature, and their influence continues today.[3]

The latitude and longitude of San Antonio (29.5°N, 98.5°W) exert an influence on its environmental character. Latitude affects atmospheric and earth-sun relationships that influence weather and climate. The city's "Sun Belt" climate is partly a function of its position, 6 degrees (about 400 miles) north of the Tropic of Cancer, nearer to the tropics than to Amarillo in the northern Texas Panhandle. San Antonio averages 111 days a year with temperatures of 90°F or higher. Longitude has a more abstract significance, because Greenwich, England, is an arbitrary reference point, not directly related to natural processes. In the Great Plains of North America, however, climatic transitions follow both zonal (latitudinal) and meridional (longitudinal) orientations. Regional climatologists have long used 99°W longitude as an approximate dividing line between the arid western and the humid eastern United States, a meridian that roughly coincides with the twenty-eight-inch isohyet for average annual rainfall. But it is the degree of moisture deficit in comparing yearly precipitation to evaporation that defines aridity rather than annual rainfall totals exclusively. San Antonio's existence on the boundary between arid and humid zones does not necessarily mean that the city enjoys moderate weather and a balance between these climate types. In one year San Antonio may experience desert-like conditions and in the next year receive a deluge of precipitation.[4]

The presence of reliable freshwater sources (groundwater, rivers, and springs) in an unpredictably droughty, warm-to-hot, semiarid-to-subhumid environment is paramount to the siting of San Antonio. The existence, nature, and geographic locations of these water sources are a function of geology, topography, and climate. The San Antonio River, freshwater artesian springs, and a major aquifer (bedrock groundwater source) have provided this necessity for life to prehistoric Native Americans, nurtured the establishment of Spanish missions and settlements, and have shaped and sustained the present urban setting. It is only in the last half of the twentieth century that this once-abundant resource has been threatened in terms of both quality and quantity.

The Climate of San Antonio

According to Wladimir Köppen's climatic classification, a widely used system for defining broad regional climates, San Antonio has a humid subtropical climate (Cfa, or moderate winter, with adequate precipitation and no dry season, and a hot summer), based on its seasonality of temperature and precipitation. This should be considered a *modified* humid subtropical climate, however, as it is drier than the typical climate of that type because the zone of subtropical semi-arid climate (BSh, or semiarid, with a dry, mild winter) abuts to the west.[5]

Mean monthly temperatures range from the 50s Fahrenheit in winter to 80s in summer, but it should be noted that those temperatures mask extremes by averaging the daily highs and the overnight lows of an "average" month. Winter days averaging below freezing are rare, although overnight lows reaching this mark are not unusual, and the summers are hot. The growing season (frost-free period) is lengthy, lasting about 270 days. What could be called "summer weather" lasts from May to October, well beyond the equinox dates that mark the end of spring and the beginning of fall. Gulf air intrudes the region during these warm-season months, and the humidity keeps overnight lows rather high during this lengthy "summer" season as the daily low temperatures generally exceed 75°F. Winters are mild and generally pleasant because of the dry, modified continental air that dominates this season. Climatic data for San Antonio indicate that during the "winter season" from October to May daily temperature ranges (the difference between the highest and lowest temperatures in a day) are greater because the drier continental air masses that dominate permit greater nocturnal cooling and daytime warming.[6]

Monthly and annual variations in precipitation can vary greatly and are generally unpredictable. Months-long droughts that dominate the climate of a particular year may end in torrential rainfalls, a situation that yields annual data suggestive of an "average" year. Annual rainfall totals can also experience extreme variation; for example, in 1996 San Antonio received 17.8 inches of annual precipitation, and in 1997 nearly double that amount at 34.0 inches.[7]

The average annual rainfall for San Antonio is about 30 inches, and, while variable, certain seasonal patterns exist. Mean monthly rainfall distributions over the year are bimodal, peaking in spring and fall. These seasons mark times of air-mass transition with the frontal clash of continental and Gulf air masses as they exchange seasonal dominance. This change in air mass is accompanied by a seasonal wind reversal that is basically a monsoonal effect. A wet season summer "monsoon" occurs as warm-humid tropical air is pulled in from the Gulf of Mexico by thermally induced low pressures in the hot interior of North America. The cooler, drier winter is dominated by modified continental polar air flowing southward to the Gulf of Mexico, out of the polar and arctic high-pressure systems. Wind directions, therefore, tend to be from the north in winter and from the south in summer.

Thunderstorms, particularly during the spring and fall transitional seasons, can be intense. The severity of these convective thunderstorms and the resulting flooding potential results from San Antonio's geographic setting. No world region can match the Great Plains for continuous low relief running north-south through climatic zones ranging from subarctic to subtropical, respectively. Polar and arctic air masses are channeled equatorward in an unobstructed meridional flow over more degrees (nearly forty) of latitude than in any other continental location on Earth. Fortunately for Texas, these air masses are moderated in temperature as they flow southward, but the arrival of a cold front is typically blustery, accompanied by winds locally called "northers," or "blue northers." The clash of air masses in this region can produce intense precipitation events, sometimes reaching world records in magnitude, particularly if tropical depressions, tropical storms, or hurricanes are providing the moisture-laden air. This combination of factors, flattish terrain, humid air, and the potential for frontal clash of unlike air masses, is what also produces optimal conditions for tornadoes and hailstorms. San Antonio is located on the southern edge of the infamous "Tornado Alley" region which extends to the north and east over the Midwestern plains of North America.

Orographic uplift of air masses along the Balcones Escarpment exacerbates the situation by increasing the rainfall potential. The modest local relief of the Balcones Escarpment (300 feet), would have minimal effect on orographic enhancement of precipitation in many other locations. Two factors, however, should be considered. First, the Hill Country north and west of the escarpment between San Antonio and Austin gradually rises to about 1,500 feet above the Coastal Plain (over a span varying between 25 to 50 miles). Second, air masses generated from the Gulf can be extremely unstable and humid, requiring little uplift and cooling to produce precipitation. Local meteorological factors can produce tremendous rainfall amounts in short periods of time, and flash flooding is a major problem. The climatic situation of central Texas was aptly characterized by Richard Earl and Troy Kimmel, who stated:

> Rather than having "intermediate" or transitional weather, the region tends to experience the extremes of interior North America as well of those of the tropical Gulf of Mexico. Hurricanes, tornadoes, Arctic blizzards, torrential downpours, flash floods, long periods of drought, and 38+°C (100+°F) temperatures are all

possible in the "normal" weather cycle of the region. Climatic statistics such as mean values of monthly temperature and precipitation can be misleading, as they portray winters as cool and summers as warm, with moderate precipitation over the year.[8]

The Geologic Past

The geologic history of the San Antonio region, as it is reflected in surficial rocks and landforms, begins in the Cretaceous Period of Mesozoic (140 to 65 million years ago) during the last period of the dinosaurs. At that time, present-day central Texas was inundated by a sequence of epicontinental seas that covered North America between the Rocky Mountain front and the Appalachians, extending northward well beyond today's Canadian border. Locally, climates were tropical and humid. Warm, shallow ocean waters in these tropical environments fostered deposition of limy muds on the sea bottom. Today, the lithified layers of these carbonate marine sediments form rock formations that dominate the Hill Country geology. Numerous marine advances and recessions are recorded in the Cretaceous rock strata with much evidence of ancient nearshore environments, such as small islands, reefs, lagoons, and tidal flats. Marine invertebrate fossils (particularly bivalves) are abundant, and dinosaur tracks are well preserved in the limestones of central Texas.

The last marine recession came in the late Cretaceous and was followed in the Tertiary (Miocene) by uplift in the Balcones fault zone. Seismic activity caused tensional fracturing of a crustal hinge between the Coastal Plain and the Great Plains along a set of discontinuous, roughly parallel, northeast-to-southwest trending faults. The Edwards Plateau was uplifted as the Balcones Escarpment developed along a sequence of faulted blocks of the earth's crust. Cretaceous rocks along the escarpment are fractured, tilted, and faulted in a sequence that steps down to the Coastal Plain. Rock strata north and west of the escarpment, in the Edwards Plateau, the southern part of the Great Plains, were relatively undeformed, maintaining a regional geologic structure of nearly horizontal layers of Cretaceous limestones.

The upper Cretaceous strata on the uplifted plateau side of the escarpment were removed by erosion to expose lower limestone units, most notably the Edwards and the Glen Rose Limestones. The Edwards Limestone, named for the plateau, is an aquifer (the Edwards Aquifer) that provides a critical water source to the central Texas region. A 400- to 700-foot-thick sequence of limestone rock layers, the Edwards Aquifer is porous, permeable, and cavernous.

The Glen Rose Limestone, a thicker formation of rock layers below, slightly older than the Edwards, also serves as an aquifer for wells north and west of San Antonio, particularly in rural areas. As uplift in the Balcones fault zone raised these water-bearing carbonate strata above the Coastal Plain, a gradient was created that caused both groundwater and surface streams to flow toward the escarpment. Groundwater flow exploits zones of rock weakness and follows broad stratigraphic up-and-down warps that trend roughly perpendicular to the escarpment. The permeability and porosity of both the Edwards and Glen Rose Limestones have been increased by solutional widening of faults, fractures, and bedding planes. These voids provide avenues for subterranean groundwater flow and where they are exposed at the surface they facilitate infiltration of rainfall and stream flow into the subsurface aquifer. The orientation, density, and distribution of faults and associated fractures in the carbonate rocks have strongly influenced today's topography, the directions and volumes of subsurface groundwater flow, the locations of springs, and the subsequent development of caverns.

The Texas Hill Country Landscape Today

In concert with uplift and faulting along the Balcones Escarpment, streams downcut the Edwards Plateau to form hills, canyons, and river valleys in the Hill Country. An active process today, this fluvial dissection is primarily responsible for the relief and topography of the Edwards Plateau in central Texas. The entire region was uplifted, and erosional sculpturing excavated valleys, leaving the hills as residuals. In other words, erosion and removal of material are the processes primarily responsible for the hilly terrain in the region. Without this erosion, which resulted from the uplift and the break in slope between the Hill Country and Coastal Plain, this region would have remained an extensive low-relief plateau.

The most highly dissected parts of the Edwards Plateau region have been referred to as the Balcones Canyonlands, a term that emphasizes the relative importance of the valleys and rivers rather than the hills. Most of the Hill Country's population, as well as the areas of highest land-use intensity, are located in the valley bottoms rather than in the hills. The hills, however, make a strong contribution to the scenic beauty of the region and exhibit a distinctive form that is related to the subsurface geology. Exposed at the land surface in wide areas of the Hill Country, the geologic structure of the Glen Rose forms a distinctive terrain resulting from numerous horizontal layers of resistant limestones interbedded with softer carbonate sediments (marls). Valley walls and hillsides display ledges and stairsteps that are distinctive topographic features of the Hill Country near San Antonio. The hills have flattish tops, resulting from structural influences of resistant caprocks and horizontal limestone layers that differ in thickness and resistance to erosion. Soluble in water, limestone dissolves in rain or runoff to expose bare expanses of Cretaceous bedrock that often forms little or no soil. Less-resistant layers of marl, a marine deposit of soft, powdery limestone mixed with clay, generally form slopes between the hillside steps. The marls also support more vegetation, produce better soils, and absorb more moisture than the resistant cliff-forming layers.[9]

Despite the Hill Country's strong ranching tradition, its rangelands are generally marginal, suffering from thin, highly alkaline soils and sparse vegetative cover. Historically, cattle, sheep, and goats have been grazed in the region, a ranching tradition that continues today. Overgrazing, excessive "cedar chopping" (cutting Ashe junipers for fencing materials and to improve range), and other acts of human neglect or degradation have resulted in considerable soil erosion from a landscape that can ill afford to lose any more of this scarce resource. Ranchers supplement their incomes by leasing rights on their lands for deer and bird hunting. The introduction of exotic game species (mainly African ungulates) has increased in recent years, resulting from an economic strategy that offers the advantages of higher income for a lease and the fact that exotic species are not regulated by state-imposed hunting laws, including seasonal restrictions, bag limits, or other regulations.[10]

With the exception of water, the Hill Country's most valuable natural resource is its scenic landscape. Craggy, white-gray limestone hills, divided by river valleys, are dotted with a sparse woodland (often referred to in the literature as "savanna," a term that is generally reserved for a grassland biome with scattered trees in a tropical climate) dominated by grasses, junipers, live oaks, other hardwoods, and prickly pear cactus. An invasion of Ashe junipers (*Juniperus ashei*, native trees, locally called "cedars") is ongoing, apparently a result of overgrazing and years of fire control. Ashe junipers proliferate beneath native hardwood trees in a dense understory that uses much soil moisture, crowds out competing species, and increases the severity and potential for major fire hazard. River bottom lands and floodplains provide the best conditions for Hill Country agriculture, partly because of water availability, but also because of the presence of alluvial soils deposited by flooding streams. Today agriculture in most of the Hill Country is dominated by grazing, partly because the lands along the rivers are prone to flash flooding and are confined to relatively narrow floodplains in plots too restrictive for large-scale commercial operations. Experimental ranching operations have tested the impacts of cedar removal, with the positive results of increased soil moisture, spring flow, stream flow, and general water availability. Removing Ashe junipers, however, also has several detrimental environmental effects. Mature stands of junipers provide prime habitat for the golden-cheeked warbler, an endangered songbird species. Cedar canopies and the organic litter from these trees greatly reduce soil erosion potentials according to William Marsh and Nina Marsh, who recommend against the widespread removal of Ashe juniper in the Hill Country.[11]

Many limestone caverns in the region are operated as tourist attractions, and others are closed except for limited scientific use in order to protect their natural beauty and local groundwater resources. Natural Bridge Caverns, near New Braunfels, is a beautiful cave that is highly decorated with a wide variety of speleothems (a general term for depositional cave features such as stalagmites and stalactites). Today cave features are still developing by carbonate deposition in this active cavern. A migration path for Mexican free-tailed bats follows the edge of the Hill Country. During the summer months a colony estimated at 20 to 30 million bats, which winters farther south in Mexico, occupies Bracken Cave north of San Antonio. The Texas Nature Conservancy has stated that this is the world's highest concentration of mammals (more than the famous Carlsbad Caverns in New Mexico) and that bats from Bracken Cave consume about 150 tons of mosquitoes and insects every night. It is interesting to note that the population of bats in this one cave exceeds the human population of Texas.[12]

Today the rugged Hill Country relief that was a barrier to travel in San Antonio's early days offers a scenic landscape for both tourism and residential development. The central Texas Hill Country's attractive landscape is further reinforced by its geographic location. Near the Interstate 35 urban corridor, the Hill Country is surrounded by regions of flat terrain and generally monotonous landscapes—the Gulf Coastal Plain and the northwestern Edwards Plateau. Texas has been traditionally referred to as "mile after mile of mile after mile," and the Hill Country offers a pleasant respite with its hills, topographic relief, clear flowing streams, and rural setting.

The Gulf Coastal Plain

From an elevation of about 600 feet at the base of the Balcones Escarpment, the Gulf Coastal Plain gently slopes to sea level at the Gulf of Mexico. Southeastern San Antonio and its suburban environs are located on the Coastal Plain. Both the terrain and the soils in this region are better suited to agricul-

ture than those of the Hill Country. Coastal Plain soils in central Texas are generally of two types, each related to their parent material. Dark clayey soils of
the Blackland Prairie form a broad belt that is roughly concentric with the Gulf
Coast. Expansion and contraction of these soils in response to fluctuating seasonal wetness and aridity create engineering problems in foundations constructed for roads and buildings. Sandy soils are found on sandstone rocks on
the Coastal Plain, and also on fluvial deposits along the floodplains of the generally southeastward-flowing rivers crossing the region to the Gulf. The presence of Hill Country rangelands north and west of the escarpment and Coastal
Plain agricultural lands to the south and east increases the environmental and
agricultural diversity of the San Antonio region.[13]

Low rolling hills with relief of 100 feet or less exist along the Coastal
Plain's interior edge, but the land is nearly level where it grades to the Gulf of
Mexico. Two particular types of hills exist on the Coastal Plain. Fault blocks
associated with the Balcones, tilted downward toward the coast, are exposed as
hills along the edge of the escarpment. Rock strata of the Coastal Plain have a
gentle coastward dip and are generally younger and less resistant to erosion
than those of the Hill Country. Coastal Plain rock units do vary in resistance,
however, and differential erosion has left the upward-tilted edges of more resistant strata exposed as cuesta ridges. Cuestas are ramp-like, asymmetrical
ridges with a gentle side and a steeper sloping side, each facing in opposite directions from the crest. The cuestas are oriented parallel to the coast with the
steeper side facing inland and the strata dipping coastward beneath the surface.
One rock formation that forms a prominent cuesta is the Austin Chalk, an
upper Cretaceous limestone that is also present in the fault zone. The Austin
Chalk is best known as a sequence of oil-bearing strata, but it has long been
quarried for building stone. The Alamo, other missions in the region, and
many buildings in San Antonio were built from this rock, which is responsible
for their distinctive buff color. The Austin Chalk has provided good building
stone, particularly during the time that the Alamo was constructed, because
the stone is hard enough for use in masonry block construction, yet also soft
enough to be easily worked and cut.[14]

The Balcones Escarpment: Texas's Spring Line

The Balcones Escarpment is the dominant landscape feature in San Antonio and the central Texas region. Dividing the carbonate rocks in the Hill
Country from younger, softer sediments that form the Gulf Coastal Plain, the

structural trend of the Balcones Escarpment runs northeast to southwest roughly from Waco to near Del Rio. Along the 200-mile escarpment is a zone of artesian springs (San Felipé, San Pedro, San Antonio, Comal, San Marcos, Barton, and many others) that have long functioned as critical oases to both travelers and settlers. Archaeological evidence near several springs indicates that perhaps as early as 11,000 years ago Native Americans were drawn to these waters.[15]

The escarpment was created as seismic activity in the Balcones fault zone raised the Hill Country rocks about 1,000 to 1,500 feet during a period of uplift that ended in the Miocene Epoch, around 10–12 million years ago. Today the fault is considered inactive. Erosion during and subsequent to the uplift reduced the escarpment's topographic expression to its present-day maximum of about 300 feet. The greatest relief exists between Austin and San Antonio, and the escarpment—relatively flat-topped along the edge—gradually becomes lower toward its northern and southern extremes. Spanish explorers gave the landform its descriptive name, noting its resemblance to a balcony. The Balcones Escarpment influences almost every aspect of the local environment: geology, topography, vegetation, soils, climate, stream flows, and land use, as well as water availability and quality.[16]

The Balcones Escarpment was not formed on a single fault but rather a system of subparallel, branching faults along a belt that varies from about five to twenty-five miles wide. This zone is one of complex groundwater flow and wide variations in permeability. General trends of groundwater flow in the Edwards Aquifer are oriented both along (northward and southward) and toward the escarpment. Limestone caverns, springs, and surface sinkholes provide additional avenues for rapid and multidirectional groundwater movement. The caverns in the region were produced, after the faulting and uplift, by solution along zones of weakness beneath the Edwards Plateau, particularly along fractures related to the Balcones Escarpment. Vertical faults and offset strata in the fault zone direct groundwater upward from subsurface aquifers to produce numerous natural seeps and artesian springs. Linear patterns of escarpment segments, rectangular drainage patterns, and limestone cavern passageways attest to the control of these landform features by fractures.

Peter Flawn has compared the geology of the Balcones Escarpment to that of the Fall Line, the boundary between the Atlantic Coastal Plain and the Appalachian Piedmont in the eastern United States. Many similarities exist between these two physiographic boundaries, as they each separate hilly regions from plains, and they divide older, resistant rocks on the interior side from more recent, less-resistant rocks that become increasingly younger toward the coast. The Fall Line forms the interior edge of the Atlantic Coastal Plain, and the Balcones Escarpment marks a similar division for the Gulf Coastal Plain.[17]

On the Atlantic seaboard, many towns and cities were established inland from the coast along the Fall Line, in part to take advantage of water power offered by rapids and falls on that boundary. In Texas an analogous line of settlements also exists along the Balcones Escarpment (or its structural trend), from north of Waco to the Mexican border. Towns along the escarpment that were located at the sites of groundwater springs include Waco, Austin, San Marcos, New Braunfels, San Antonio, Brackettville, and Del Rio. The springs and their locations are as strongly related to the Balcones Escarpment as the falls and rapids on the eastern seaboard are to the Fall Line. Ferdinand Roemer, a nineteenth-century German scientist and traveler, described artesian springs along the escarpment as sites of great beauty, with natural fountains of water. Noting the line of springs and their relationship to several central Texas rivers, Roemer had much to say:

> Several other streams of West Texas, such as the San Antonio and the San Marcos, are quite similar to the Comal in that they too issue forth as full-fledged streams from mighty springs. All begin at the foot of the mountain range [his reference to the Balcones Escarpment] which crosses Texas in a northwesterly direction, and which . . . is really only a slope of the higher rocky northwestern tableland extending to the lower undulating Texas.
>
> . . . the water was so clear that one could see the smallest pebble at the bottom. No better opportunity for bathing [swimming] could be found anywhere than the San Antonio River with its crystal clear water of equal volume and uniform temperature both in winter and summer.[18]

Certainly, the Balcones Escarpment and its line of springs has been as important to the settlement of central Texas as the Fall Line was to settlement on the east coast of the United States. Nationally, the Fall Line is both more widely known and discussed more in texts on history and geography. "Balcones Escarpment" is an appropriate, colorful name for this geomorphologic feature, but it does not evoke the same emphasis on its links to water and settlement as does the Fall Line. "The Texas Spring Line" has been proposed as a useful, complementary term for making reference to the important relationships between population and water along the Balcones Escarpment.[19]

Hill Country rivers receive considerable base flow from springs in their watersheds, and several rivers in the region have their source at major springs along the escarpment. In central Texas, the Comal (in New Braunfels), the San Marcos, and the San Antonio (now artificially fed) rivers are groundwater-fed from their source at springs on the escarpment. The waters of these rivers are typically crystal-clear because of low suspended load, except during times of flood, and they tend to maintain the same temperature all year long, about 68–70 degrees Fahrenheit, approximately equal to the local mean annual temperature. Comal Springs has ceased to flow in recent years during times of drought, shutting off the flow to the Comal River. Although drought may be blamed for the cessation of flow from the springs and in the river, the major factor involved is the increased water pumpage from the aquifer.[20]

The San Antonio River, which was once fed by natural artesian springs (San Pedro and San Antonio Springs), today maintains its flow from wells located at its former natural source. The springs now flow only during times of record precipitation and water-table levels. Two nineteenth-century observations provide a perspective on the changes that have occurred in these now-dry springs and the rivers they fed.

San Antonio Spring may be classed as the first water among the gems of the natural world. The whole river gushes up in one sparkling burst from the earth. . . . The effect is overpowering. It is beyond your possible conceptions of a spring. You cannot believe your eyes.

Two rivers wind through the city, flowing from the living springs. . . . One, the San Antonio, boils in a vast volume from a rocky basin. . . . The other, the San Pedro, runs from a little pond, formed by the outgushing of five sparkling springs, which bear the same name. This miniature lake . . . is one of the most beautiful natural sheets of pure water in the Union.[21]

The cessation of natural flow from springs in San Antonio has resulted mainly from groundwater withdrawal, and the drying up of these springs offers a rather ominous preview of what the future may hold for other spring-fed streams in the region. Aquifer water levels and spring flow respond directly to annual fluctuations in precipitation and groundwater withdrawal. Comal Springs in New Braunfels (about twenty-five miles north of San Antonio), the largest spring in the Southwest, yields an average 210 million gallons of water per second. San Marcos Springs discharges about half of that amount to the San Marcos River. Comal Springs flowed at a record rate of 350 cubic feet per second in 1973, but the springs dried up for the first time in recorded history in 1957 in response to drought. During a dry spell in the 1980s Comal Springs again ceased to flow. Directions of groundwater flow, in combination with the geologic settings of the springs, define a predictable sequence for the cessation of artesian spring flow in response to drought and water withdrawal. This scenario, having already occurred in San Antonio where the springs are now "normally" dry, would proceed toward the northeast to Comal Springs (dry only during droughts) and under severe drought conditions (or overpumpage) progress northward with San Marcos Springs experiencing them next and then Barton Springs in Austin. Linked to the cessation of artesian flow would be the drying up of the Comal and San Marcos Rivers, both of which begin at an artesian source at the base of the escarpment.[22]

The Edwards Aquifer

The springs in central Texas are a window to their source, the aquifers of the region, particularly the Edwards Aquifer, a major water-supply source for nineteen Texas counties and about 1.8 million people along the escarpment. The Edwards Aquifer is currently the only source for potable water in San Antonio, the largest city in the United States that uses groundwater exclusively for its public water supply. Most other towns and cities along the Balcones Escarpment (e.g., New Braunfels and San Marcos, as well as suburban areas south of Austin) use at least some water from the aquifer. Irrigation water for agriculture is another use for aquifer water, particularly to the south and west of San Antonio. In 1992 the Edwards was legally declared an "underground river" by the Texas Water Commission in an unsuccessful attempt (that lasted one week before legal challenge) to categorize aquifer groundwater under the same (and stricter) statutes that were written to preserve surface waters. Texas groundwater law follows the "right of capture," which permits virtually unlimited use of groundwater underneath the property of a private landowner.

The Edwards, like most karst (limestone) aquifers, operates much differently from "typical" aquifers that consist of clastic rocks, particularly because in the Edwards groundwater flow is so rapid and difficult to track in any detail. Clastic aquifers typically have low flow rates and filter the water as it passes through tiny voids. The Edwards has high flow rates, and the groundwater often flows through large conduits (in some cases, limestone caverns) that do little to filter impurities from the water. Responding rapidly to seasonal weather variations, the Edwards Aquifer rises in direct response to precipitation events but falls during times of drought, behaving in many ways like a surface reservoir. Recharge is rapid and the water-table level can change daily (annually, seasonally), up or down depending on weather conditions, spring flow, and pumpage. Aquifer water-table levels are reported daily in media serving the San Antonio area, and certain levels are employed as thresholds for enacting stages of water-conservation enforcement. In historic times, recharge amounts, spring flow, and water-table elevations have varied greatly with climatic conditions. Pumpage and artesian withdrawal have continually increased with the region's population growth.[23]

A remarkable episode that challenged Texas water law and local concern for water resource allocation occurred in 1991 when a huge artesian well (thirty-inch diameter), was drilled in southern Bexar County to supply artesian water for a catfish farm. Through artesian flow alone, as no pumping was required, this well issued 46 million gallons of water a day from the aquifer. This amount of groundwater was approximately equal to one-quarter of San Antonio's daily water usage. Not long after opening, the catfish operation was ordered closed by the state because of the effluent discharged from the farm ponds into the Medina River. As a result of the "right of capture" law, the amount of pumping was not a legal issue.

Management of the Edwards Aquifer benefited from this episode in at least two ways. First, this massive use of water by one user focused attention on the inadequacy of laws that were written to address the water needs of an earlier, smaller, and less urbanized population. Second, since then, San Antonio has renewed its previously stagnant efforts to secure alternative sources of water for the city.

Three distinctive hydrologic zones have been recognized that influence the operation of the Edwards Limestone as an aquifer: the artesian zone, the recharge zone, and the contributing zone, each related to and oriented roughly along the escarpment. The artesian zone is where the majority of springs are located, where water freely flows to the surface in response to hydrostatic pressure. The recharge zone is the region where the Edwards Limestone is exposed at the land surface, where precipitation, stream water, and runoff seep into and recharge the aquifer. The contributing zone is the watershed region upstream from the escarpment whose streams lose water to the aquifer as they flow over the porous and permeable Edwards Limestone, feeding the water table. Obviously, watersheds upstream from the recharge zone, those that feed water into streams that cross this zone, are an important part of the aquifer system, both in terms of quantity and quality of the water that they deliver to the Edwards Aquifer.

The recharge zone is the most environmentally sensitive area in Texas. The same properties that allow high rates of surface-water infiltration into the sub-surface also create a potential for rapid inflow of pollutants. The high porosity of bedrock in the recharge zone also creates an edaphic (linked to ground conditions) dryness, which, combined with the thin alkaline soils, presents a somewhat challenging environment for the growth of trees and shrubs and exacerbates the effects of grazing on the landscape.

Management and resource planning of the Edwards Aquifer and other local water resources are compounded by several factors, generally specific to the three aquifer zones. The recharge zone occupies land that is generally attractive for development, in a convenient location. Many former ranch lands are offered for sale in this area. Increasing numbers of septic tanks and sewage systems, as well as the use of pesticides, fertilizers, and other chemicals, are all causes for concern in the recharge zone. Hazardous fluids are transported across all three zones of the aquifer system via pipelines and trucks. The potential exists for a catastrophe that could pollute the groundwater and possibly cause long-term damage to the Edwards Aquifer. Water conservation and quality management plans in the region address the proper maintenance and potential problems for each of these three hydrologic zones. The contributing zone, the recharge zone, the Edwards Aquifer, the springs, and the rivers should be carefully managed in ways that will protect and enhance the quantity and quality of both surface- and groundwater resources.[24]

Flooding

Although not enough water is a continuing and growing concern, the meteorological and climatic fluctuations that San Antonio and central Texas are subject to can also create the opposite situation. Flash flooding in the region is a serious problem. San Antonio, like the rest of the cities and towns along the escarpment, has had its share of flood events. The severity of flood hazards in central Texas results from a unique combination of climatological, topographic, and geologic factors.[25]

The air-mass clash in fall and spring, combined with orographic enhancement of precipitation generated from humid, unstable air, can produce intense rainfall events. This climatic setting is reinforced by the potential for onshore movement of maritime tropical air, generated by tropical depressions, storms, or hurricanes, either from the Gulf of Mexico or from the Pacific coast of Mexico. Precipitation events with rainfall intensities at or near world records for time periods ranging from one to twenty-four hours in duration have been recorded in central Texas. New Braunfels received nearly 10 inches of rain in one hour in 1972, D'Hanis (west of San Antonio) received 22 inches in two hours, forty-five minutes in 1935, and in 1921 Thrall (near Austin) received 37 inches in eighteen hours. Although not quite up to these records San Antonio still is susceptible to torrential rainfalls. The city received a record of 13.35 inches of rain in twenty-four hours in October of 1998, and over 19 inches of rain in a thirty-day period (data from NOAA).[26] On the same day as the astonishing rainfall in Thrall San Antonio received about seven inches of rain, resulting in a flood that killed fifty people.[27]

Unfortunately, the natural beauty of the Texas Hill Country has a price. Many of the same factors that make this landscape attractive also generate high rates of runoff, moving fast enough so that most of the water does not infiltrate, even in the recharge zone. The Hill Country consists of steep, sparsely vegetated slopes, made of limestone bedrock or clayey marls. Each of these terrain conditions tends to increase runoff and decrease infiltration. The effects of overgrazing and the impermeable cover (concrete, roofs, asphalt) resulting from urbanization increase the problem.

Victor Baker has illustrated the topographic and stream factors that increase the severity of flash flooding in central Texas. Narrow canyons force streams to increase in velocity and the bedrock channels of Hill Country streams also encourage rapid flow. Streams in the Hill Country respond to heavy precipitation events by rising rapidly and then receding nearly as rapidly after the storm is over.[28]

The discharge of Hill Country streams in response to flood events can be astonishing. Normally dry arroyos can change from no flow at all to a rapidly rising, raging torrent in minutes. During one flood event in 1978 a storm cell associated with hurricane Amelia stalled over the divide between the Medina River and the Guadalupe River, splitting the precipitation between these two watersheds. The Medina River peaked at 281,000 cubic feet per second (cfs) of flow and the discharge on the Guadalupe crested at 240,000 cfs. To put this flow into perspective, some useful comparisons can be made to major world rivers. The combined total for these two normally small streams was equivalent to nearly five times the average flow of the Nile where it flows into the Mediterranean Sea (110,000 cfs), and about 85 percent of the average flow of the Mississippi above New Orleans (620,000 cfs). As S. Christopher Caran and Victor Baker noted, these values are amazing considering the small size of the basins that generated that amount of discharge.[29]

Flash-flooding hazard and potential in central Texas are among the worst in the nation, and perhaps the world. Although the statistics are highly variable from year to year, Texas generally has the highest annual death toll from flash flooding in the nation. Most deaths caused by flooding in Texas result from motorists trying to drive across "low water crossings," dips in the pavement designed to allow occasional floodwaters to flow over the road. In economic terms low water crossings are cost-effective (cheaper than building a bridge), but too often they tempt risk-takers who try to drive across the flooded road, sometimes by going around temporary barriers put up for their protection.

San Antonio has had a long history of problems with flooding. The flood of 1921 created a lake in downtown San Antonio that was nine feet deep. Businesses were inundated, and most of the areas along local streams were heavily damaged by rapidly rushing water. As a result of that flood in particular, today San Antonio has one of the best systems for flood control in Texas, although it still suffers from flash-flooding events. For the past sixty years or so, millions of local, state, and federal dollars have been spent on flood-control projects, especially in and around the central city, at least until recently. These projects have included dams, diversion channels, a gated bypass of the River Walk section, and two large (twenty-four-feet wide) tunnels under the city that carry stream flow and runoff from San Pedro Creek and the San Antonio River. Without these flood-control measures the record rainfalls of October 1998 (more than double that received during the 1921 flood) would have certainly caused disastrous flooding in the city, especially in the downtown sectors.[30]

An Oasis on the Texas Spring Line

Water resources and the environments that they sustain are critical to both life and the quality of life along the Spring Line in South and Central Texas. In fact, they are the primary reason why for thousands of years people have come to this environment and come to appreciate it. There is concern that population pressure on limited but precious resources will cause the springs, the groundwater-fed rivers, and perhaps even the aquifer to dry up some day. Wise water-conservation measures must not be ignored. The place of water in San Antonio's past, present, and future also presents an irony—the conundrum of recurrent, yet unpredictable and polarized, outcomes of flood and drought. Indeed, water will play a larger role in the future of Texas than oil has in the past. Whether Texas is receiving too much water in the form of floods, or not enough water as a result of drought or human use exceeding the available resource, water is a critical natural resource to the state. In fact, San Antonio's flood-control efforts could serve as a model for other cities—a fine example linking aesthetics with utility—much like the system of acequias the Spanish constructed. In what other city could one find that one of the major tourist sites, widely regarded as an attractive urban environment, is the concrete-and-stone-lined channel of the San Antonio River that once had been the natural centerpiece of the city, described as the "Crown Jewel of Texas"?[31]

San Antonio's nickname, "The Alamo City," is particularly apropos, not only for the namesake mission but because of the nature of *alamo,* the Spanish word for cottonwood tree (*Populus deltoides*). A phreatophytic (water-loving) tree that is common in many arid to semi-arid environments of North America, cottonwoods thrive in riparian habitats and are greatly dependent on the availability of water, much like the Alamo City itself. Throughout its existence as a place of settlement, the city has been intimately linked to its springs, rivers, and the availability of water resources that are critical in the climatic setting of south Texas. That will remain true: San Antonio's future will continue to be strongly influenced by the ecological relationships between its population, water, and the richness of the diverse regional environment.

TWO

Ground Movement

2

Jesús F. de la Teja

"A Fine Country with Broad Plains— the Most Beautiful in New Spain"

Colonial Views of Land and Nature

As in most fields, study of the Texas environment tends to begin with the advent of large-scale Anglo-American immigration in the 1820s.[1] The premise that Texas was "a howling wilderness" redeemed by intrepid, westward-moving pioneers leads to the conclusion that environmental change, significant change in any case, started with them. In the second of his two books on the state's environmental history, *At Home in Texas: Early Views of the Land,* Robin Doughty asserts that "Native American and Hispanic views of the environment are beyond the scope of this book." Although he quickly qualifies the statement with "this is not because they are unimportant," he never quite explains just why they are left out. At the beginning of chapter 2 it is quite clear that for Doughty—his protest to the contrary—the Hispanic experience is of little relevance to the story of Texas settlement.[2] A stagnant subsistence economy at the turn of the century remained so twenty years later when Stephen F. Austin arrived. This portrayal is, nonetheless, an improvement over Doughty's first book, *Wildlife and Man in Texas: Environmental Change and Conservation,* in which the possibility that the preexisting population of Texas when the Anglo-Americans arrived might have had something to contribute on these issues is not addressed at all.[3]

Limited as the Hispanic presence in Texas might have been before 1820, it left a rich record of observations about the natural world and interactions with it that challenges most evaluations of the significance of the interaction with the south Texas environment. Even if the impact of this population on the region's fauna and flora was limited, it went beyond the introduction of European livestock. The evidence makes clear that the Hispanic frontiersmen who came into the region in the eighteenth century made themselves as much "at home" as the Anglo- and African American and European immigrants who followed. In expedition journals, administrative reports, and a miscellany of other documents the Spanish colonial population of Texas has left us its impression of the challenge and potential that was Texas.

The land they knew as Texas, from just south of San Antonio to western Louisiana, was a well-watered region of rolling prairies and forests with much

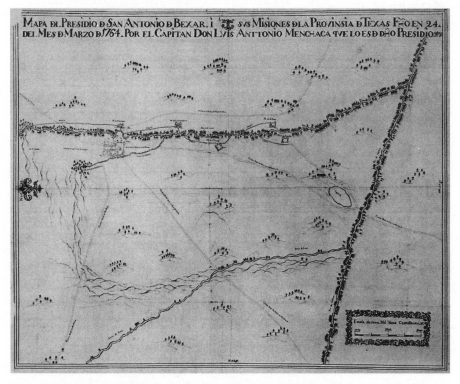

Fig. 2.1. Luis Antonio Menchaca's map of San Antonio, 1764 (*Source:* Courtesy The John Carter Brown Library at Brown University.)

promise for civilization.[4] It is this much smaller Spanish Texas, and how Spanish colonials dealt with it, that is the subject of this chapter. The emphasis on San Antonio, the largest center of Hispanic settlement and provincial capital after 1773, is natural because its record of human interaction with the natural world is the richest. Founded in 1718 as a waystation between the Rio Grande outpost of San Juan Bautista and the Louisiana border region, San Antonio quickly became colonial Texas's most successful settlement. Even during the fifty years before San Antonio became capital of Texas in 1773, governors often resided there for long stretches. In the last fifty years of the Spanish colonial period it contained about half of the province's population. Consequently, it was at San Antonio that Spanish colonials had the greatest impact on the Texas environment.

Texas offered a variety of landscapes that compared favorably with the rest of New Spain. The vast grasslands of the region from the Medina River to the East Texas forests evoked the word "beautiful" to describe their appearance. This judgment, by General Domingo Terán de los Ríos, governor of Texas between 1691 and 1693, was echoed by subsequent travelers through the region. Father Juan Antonio de la Peña, chronicler of the Marqués de San Miguel de Aguayo's 1721–22 expedition, described the Colorado River area downstream from Austin as composed of "some beautiful plains."[5] Spanish appreciation for the aesthetic quality of the landscape is no more clearly evident than in the following passage regarding the New Braunfels area from Fray Isidro Espinosa's diary of the 1716 expedition:

> May 18 . . . The waters of the Guadalupe [Comal River][6] are clear, crystal and so abundant that it seemed almost incredible to us that its source arose so near. Composing this river are three principal springs of water which, together with other smaller ones, unite as soon as they begin to flow. There the growth of the walnut trees competes with the poplars. All are crowned by the wild grapevines, which climb up their trunks. They gave promise already in their blossom for the good prospect of their fruit. The white and the black mulberry trees, whose leaves were more than eight inches in length, showed in their sprouts how sharp were the frosts. Willow trees beautified the region of this river with their luxuriant foliage and there was a great variety of plants. It makes a delightful grove for recreation, and the enjoyment of the melodious songs of different birds.[7]

Aside from the region's plentiful and impressive prairies, explorers and later travelers could also appreciate more rugged terrain—for better and worse. Domingo Ramón, leader of the 1716 *entrada* that established a permanent Spanish presence in East Texas, spoke of the country in present Dimmit County as containing "beautiful canyons." At the other end of the province, where missions, Indian villages, and Spanish Texas's first capital, Los Adaes, occupied clearings in the region's dense forests, Fray José de Solís described the site of the Nacogdoches mission as "situated in a small plain, surrounded by a great number of beautiful and shady trees."[8]

Travel through the dense forests of eastern Texas and along the coast was not necessarily a pleasant experience, however. The Marqués de Rubí during his 1767 inspection of the region named part of the route between Los Adaes and Orcoquisac "Purgatory" because it went "through a more dense forest of oaks, live oaks, and underbrush, with frequent hills, vales, and marshes, which made the going most vexing." Winter travel through this region of "ice, snow, and wind" led an exasperated Terán de los Ríos to comment, "I will not describe the character of the country, for no rational person has ever seen a worse one." In the coastal prairies it was not the terrain, but the summer climate that provoked travelers' ire. Francisco Alvarez Barreiro, engineer for Pedro de Rivera's 1727 inspection tour, was among the earliest commentators on the Texas summer. "In that season [the heat] is particularly oppressive on the coast which the province has on the Gulf of Mexico; and to this is added the plague of mosquitoes that is experienced greatly at that time."[9]

Despite the weather's ability to cause periodic discomfort or distress, the overall judgment of the province's climate was overwhelmingly favorable. Fray Morfi, exercising a considerable degree of hyperbole, addressed the issue as the second point in his general description of the province, commenting:

> Its climate is excellent, neither too cold nor too warm. Seldom is the sky covered with clouds for a whole day, though it rains abundantly at times. The heavy dews contribute to the fertility of the land, but it is not necessary to take precautions against their evil effect. In winter, snow and frosts are frequent, but neither one nor the other is so severe as to hinder the cultivation of the soil or molest the settlers. Storms and earthquakes have never been known in this country, and epidemics are very rare. The inhabitants are blessed with sound health and live to a ripe old age without suffering the infirmities of declining years.[10]

The vast variety of animals and plants that travelers encountered in Texas only served to highlight for them the prodigious fertility of the region.[11] Lions (cougar), and tigers (jaguar), and bears are mentioned prominently in expedition accounts, as are wolves and coyotes, foxes and badgers, beavers and otters. Alligators inhabited many Texas streams as far as the foot of the Balcones Escarpment. Although birds are mentioned less frequently and more generically, the presence of songbirds is noted, along with raptors and migratory species. The wild turkey stood out because it made good eating. Travelers also seemed impressed with the large assortment of fish to be found in Texas waters. Trout, bass, catfish, and some unidentified species are mentioned in numerous reports as providing good inland fishing. Along the coasts, shrimp, oysters, and other shellfish abounded.

Of all the animals to be found in Texas, none drew more comment than the American buffalo. Found from the Rio Grande northward in the late seventeenth century, the animal roamed both plains and forests. In July 1691 the Terán de los Ríos expedition encountered them in the woods in the Fayatte County area, "covered with ticks, red bugs and other vermin."[12] The *cíbolo,* as the bison was called throughout the colonial period, drew forth the most inspired descriptions from travelers. The best effort to capture the animal's uniqueness comes from the pen of Fray Peña:

> It is a monstrous animal; its horns are crooked, its back humped as
> that of a camel, its flanks lean, its tail short, and hairless as that of
> the pig, except the tip, which is covered with long hair. The entire
> skin, which is of a dark tanned color, resembling that of the bear,
> though not so fine, is also covered with long hair. It has a beard
> like that of a goat and, as the lion, its neck and forehead have hair a
> foot and a half long, that almost covers the big black eyes. Its feet
> are cloven, and its forehead is armed [with horns] as that of the
> bull, which it imitates in ferocity, although it is much more power-
> ful and swift. Its meat is as savory as that of the best cow.[13]

Except for its meat and its athletic ability, Domingo Ramón was less impressed with the animal, calling it "ugly." Among its shortcomings he counted the bison's "ill-shaped" forehead, long hair that obstructed its view, and that "the animal is very malodorous, does not hear well, and sees less on account of the mane of hair." The importance of the animal to the Indians was not overlooked, and Fray Morfi's description of the bison focuses on the varied uses the native peoples made of it: brains to soften leather; horns to make household items; shoulder blades for plowing; ligaments as bowstrings; hoofs ground down for glue; wool and hair to make rope, belts, and other ornaments; and the skin for all manner of leather goods and for blankets.[14]

The flora of Texas was no less outstanding. Diarists commented on the variety of useful plants to be found in seemingly limitless bounty. Aside from various species of oak (live and deciduous), pine, elm, and juniper (including cedar and cypress), willows, cottonwoods, and mesquite are reported throughout the province. As far as nut trees are concerned, use of the words *nogal* and *nuez* make clear identification difficult, but pecans, hickory, and walnut are all native to Texas. So, too, is the chinquapin, which the diarists referred to as *castaño* (chestnut). During the 1709 *entrada* Fray Espinosa commented that "the nuts are so abundant that throughout the land the natives gather them, using them for food the greater part of the year. . . . Not all the nuts are of the same quality, for there are different sizes and the shells of some are softer than others, but all of them are more tasty and palatable than those of Castile."[15]

As for useful plants, Texas offered an abundance of species with dietary and manufacturing properties. Observers noted the abundance of wild grapes throughout Texas. Even the taciturn Alonso de León, whose diary contains few references other than to direction, character of the landscape, and streams crossed, notes in his entry for May 21, 1690, the presence of fruit-bearing grapevines in the area of Houston County. During the 1716 expedition Domingo Ramón claimed to have "gathered some grapes as large as eggs." Blackberry (*zarzamora*), mulberry (*mora*), persimmon (*chapote*), and plum (*ciruela*) grew in much of the province. Other plants also showed dietary potential. For instance, Fray Solís wrote of finding "plants that looked like lettuce, and also some wild onions," in the Guadalupe River country. "These plants, prepared with vinegar and oil, make very fine salad."[16] Two staples of the Mexican diet, prickly pear (*nopal*) and wild sweet potato (*camote*), were so ubiquitous as to go almost without mention.

Texas also contained plants with commercial potential. By the time the Spanish entered Texas in a meaningful way in the late seventeenth and early eighteenth centuries, they had become acquainted with species of North American plants that had useful applications. The lechugilla root, for instance, provided a substitute for soap. Spanish moss, in reality a member of the bromeliad family, served as fodder in the absence of grass. Numerous expeditions mentioned flax and hemp growing wild in Texas. Regarding the latter Espinosa stated in his 1709 diary that it "was so flourishing that it seemed to be cultivated though it had received no other care than that of the liberal hand [of nature] that beautifies everything."[17]

The consensus among travelers was that Texas was prime agricultural country. Pedro de Rivera, who inspected the province in 1727, commented that "corn, vegetables, and other crops can be grown everywhere in the province. Even without the benefit of irrigation the land demonstrates its fertility and utility to the pagan Indians who cultivate it." Later in the century, Fray Morfi's observations, based on the accomplishments of the small Hispanic population, were even more enthusiastic: "The fertility of the soil exceeds all exaggeration. Wheat, barley, corn, beans, chick-peas, pepper, melons, watermelons, excellent potatoes, cotton, cane, all kinds of vegetables, and, in a word, whatever is planted yields abundantly."[18]

Spanish colonials, then, had a clear and deep understanding of the Texas environment. They recognized its variety, its potential, and the limitations of what they could do with it given the technology at their disposal. In humid East Texas, for instance, they did not try to build with adobe or stone, the traditional building materials of northern Mexico, but made use of the region's abundant timber resources. Fray Solís found the buildings of Los Adaes "suitable structures and well put together. The walls are of wood and the roofs are shingled."[19] The region's abundant rainfall and the presence of a large agricultural Indian population ensured the region's settlers of an adequate food supply. Still, with the intervening country between Los Adaes/Nacogdoches and San Antonio essentially unoccupied during the colonial period, East Texas remained an isolated and small establishment until it began to flourish as a center of Anglo-American settlement under Mexican rule.[20]

The coastal plains, on the other hand, challenged Spanish colonial agricultural practices. At the three different locations where the mission-presidio complex of La Bahía was located before 1750, gravity-flow irrigation was made impossible by the high banks of adjoining streams and the sandiness of the soil. As late as 1791, an experienced surveyor from San Antonio was sent to La Bahía to investigate the possibilities for irrigation, but he found neither the river nor five nearby streams suitable.[21] Consequently, agriculture at La Bahía frequently suffered from prolonged periods of little rainfall and high temperatures. An environmentally less attractive area, the Spanish colonial settlement of the vicinity remained limited to the presidio and a couple of neighboring missions.

From the very beginning of permanent settlement, what is today south-central Texas received the lion's share of attention as the most environmentally promising part of the province. Here the San Antonio River was fit for irrigation, there was plentiful timber and rock for construction, and abundant grazing land nearby. In 1709 Fray Espinosa had described the San Antonio River as capable of supplying "not only a village but a city, which could easily be founded here because of the good ground and the many conveniences, and because of the shallowness of said river."[22] On his return visit in 1716 Fray Espinosa was even more descriptive of the area's natural environment: "It is surrounded by very tall nopals [sic], poplars, elms, grapevines, black mulberry trees, laurels, strawberry vines and genuine fan-palms. There is a great deal of flax and wild hemp, an abundance of maiden-hair fern and many medicinal herbs." The missionary was no less encouraging regarding "its copious waters, which are clear, crystal and sweet. In these are found catfish, sea fish, *piltonte, catán,* and alligators. Undoubtedly there are also various other kinds of fish that are most savory."[23] Consequently, San Antonio de Béxar quickly became the largest of Texas's Spanish colonial settlements.

By the 1770s a presidio, small town, and five missions hugged both banks of the river. Fray Morfi's description of the settlement leaves no doubt of the continued fertility of the area, even after forty to fifty years of use:

> The trail is flat, with good footing and comfortable, and for the most part follows the margin of the San Antonio River and along a very thick wood of corpulent mesquite, pecan, live oak, oak, mulberry, wild grapevine, and many other trees and different plants. It is populated by various handsome birds, although owing to the inappropriateness of the season we found very few. The wild turkeys go about in flocks of 100 and 200. There are different species of squirrels, the prettiest being very blond with a red belly. On both sides of the trail can be found the missions' fields, and in my life have I seen such a multitude of ducks, geese, and cranes as I admired on this sown land, which had just been harvested, for I do not exaggerate if I say that they covered the entire plain. These fields are crisscrossed by ditches through which the water of the river is abundantly carried to irrigate an immense portion of the country. In them, when they are dried out in order to clean them, much fish is taken, and the eels are especially delicious.[24]

The very size and diversity of the agricultural enterprise at San Antonio allowed for a regular annual cycle to emerge in the course of the century. The census report of 1778 mentioned that very little wheat was cultivated in the

San Antonio area, which was planted in October or November and harvested in May and June. More important, the conditions allowed for two corn crops, an early one planted along with cotton, beans, and chiles in February or March and harvested from July to September, and a late corn crop planted with beans in late May and throughout June, with the corn harvested in December and January and the beans in October and November. January and early February were the months devoted to mending fences, cleaning irrigation ditches, and preparing the fields.[25]

San Antonio was well suited not only to crop agriculture but to horticulture as well. At the settlement's founding in 1718, Martín de Alarcón provided for "grapevines and fig trees and diverse fruit seeds, melon and watermelon as well as squash [and] peppers."[26] Vegetable gardens and orchards soon sprouted, both in the neighborhood of the presidio and at the missions, benefiting from the acequias (irrigation ditches), which were also made to run through the center of each population center. By the 1740s the presence of fruit trees on a lot was worthy of mention in land sales at San Antonio and added to the value of property.[27] Sugarcane did well enough to warrant the considerable investment that Francisco Delgado, one of the Canary Island immigrants, made in a sugar mill and associated processing equipment. Fray Solís claimed that the peaches of Mission San José, "which are grown in large quantities, weigh about a pound each."[28]

For the most part, farming and gardening in and around San Antonio provided for the subsistence needs of the population as a whole and the commercial aspirations of a few. The irrigation system normally mitigated the effects of droughts and other natural disasters to which the area was regularly subject, but there is evidence that at times the limited technological means available were inadequate. A year-long drought broke in April 1776, just in time to supply the needs of a plague of locusts and cause additional damage to new crops, "the said locust adding to the hunger that afflicts these inhabitants owing to the meager harvest of last year."[29]

During the 1780s conditions became particularly severe, not only causing damage to pastures, but to the irrigated farms of the settlement. At the end of June 1787 Governor Rafael Martínez Pacheco reported that a severe drought and harsh winter had finally broken in mid-March with abundant rains that had lasted until the middle of June and allowed for adequate corn, bean, chile, and cane crops to be harvested. Drought conditions soon returned, however, and reached such severity that in January 1789 Martínez Pacheco tried to institute price controls on corn and ban its export from the settlement. In March he had to inform visiting Comanches that he could not give them the usual gifts because the drought had kept the shipment from arriving.[30] The drought continued for another year, leading the governor to explain in June 1790 that "we have suffered from hunger to this day for lack of having harvested enough grain last year, so that in order to plant it [the farmers] have not eaten it." He went on to add that when the quartermaster was unable to purchase enough corn to satisfy the troop, he resorted to giving the troopers their corn ration in cash so that they might buy what they could from the mission Indians.[31]

While the level, well-watered land in the immediate vicinity of the settlement's presidio, town, and missions provided ample opportunity for agriculture, similar conditions in the rest of the San Antonio River basin made attractive ranchland.[32] After all, throughout this part of Texas immense bison herds roamed when the Spanish first arrived. On reaching the San Antonio area in June 1691 the Terán de los Ríos expedition encountered "so many buffaloes that the horses stampeded and forty head ran away."[33] Soon after Missions San Antonio de Valero (1718) and San José y San Miguel de Aguayo (1720) were founded, the friars started herds of cattle, sheep, and goats. In the early 1730s the other missions, which had relocated from East Texas, followed suit, and the first of the civilian ranches was claimed. By the 1770s the area between Ecleto Creek to the east and Hondo Creek in the west was almost entirely taken up with ranch claims.

Although Bexareños (residents of San Antonio de Béxar) and the missions established herds of cattle and flocks of sheep, the former dominated the commercial landscape throughout the eighteenth century.[34] Environmental conditions, which residents were well aware of, prevented colonial Texas from becoming an important sheep-raising region. As a 1789 report on the Texas missions by the Franciscan in charge, Fray José Francisco López, makes clear, "sheep increase very slowly in this country for many reasons, but especially because the land, being thickly wooded, abounds in wild animals that destroy them. Also many are lost in the brush." Fray López also went on to blame the carelessness and laziness of the Indian shepherds, but the available numbers suggest that the civilian population had little better luck.[35]

Cattle and horses stood a much better chance of successfully adapting to frontier conditions. Heavily wooded stream banks, patches of oak and mesquite wood, and a sparse population combined to give cattle the run of the country. One hint at the success that large stock had in going feral can be found in Fray Solís's comment that "in the woods between La Bahía and San Antonio there are a few lions and a great number of cattle, horses, deer, wolves, coyotes, rabbits, wildcats and boars." A decade later Fray Morfi's observations led him to conclude, "Nothing proves the fertility of the land and the richness of the soil more than the incredible number of wild horses and cattle found every-where."[36]

Given the open-range situation, much of the cattle in the San Antonio re-gion came to be treated as simply another product of the land. Until the 1770s harvesting of wild cattle most often took the form of slaughters, resulting in the production of dried beef and tallow. In the 1770s roundups of large num-bers of feral as well as branded cattle and drives to the interior of New Spain and north to Louisiana became common. The fecundity of the stock suggested to Bexareños that there was an inexhaustible supply. Although the arguments over ownership of this unbranded stock are beyond the scope of this chapter, it needs to be pointed out that missionaries and civilians both laid claim to the feral stock. For instance, in 1777 Francisco Xavier Rodríguez claimed that since his father, one of the settlement's founders, had lost cattle in the brush, he was entitled to collect unbranded stock. Some Bexareños with no rural property at all also participated in illegal cattle harvests, despite the efforts of officials.[37]

The supply of cattle was not, of course, inexhaustible. The indiscriminate slaughter of cattle both by raiding Indians and Bexareños, failure to control or improve pastures, and the latter's driving of large numbers to market consti-tuted a real threat to the viability of the cattle population. Warnings regarding poor pastoral practices are evident as early as late 1758. In a letter complaining of the behavior of the townspeople, Fray Mariano Francisco de los Dolores stated that as soon as they set up ranches next to those of the missions, the lat-ter's herds suffered dramatic reductions. "The cause being the continuous slaughters that they practice at their ranches, from which they not only supply themselves, but also send loads of lard, tallow, and meat to the presidio and town; the large number of cattle they scare away in their roundups being most deplorable." In regard to cattle, a comment in the census of 1778 presents a more ominous problem: "In the last few years there has been a considerable ex-traction of cattle, very disproportionate to the reduced means of the inhabi-tants. . . . And, extracting of it many females, it will become extinct, to which the Apache nation effectively contributes."[38]

The result of these practices was implementation of the first environmen-tal legislation in Texas history. Commandant General Teodoro Croix, on his 1778 visit to San Antonio, heard the complaints of Bexareños, missionaries, and the governor regarding ownership, depletion, and jurisdictional questions. He quickly instituted a licensing system for cattle exports, imposed a tax on the capture of unbranded stock, and issued a ban on the slaughter of wild stock "in order to stop the abuses committed in the field against the wild cattle, which is property of the king, because they are killed in the field and left there, only the tallow used for soap being taken." In 1780 Governor Domingo Cabello imposed a further restriction, banning the export of breeding cows. These and other measures met with the ire of the Bexareños, who launched a seventeen-year litigation effort to claim ownership of all unbranded stock. In 1795 the royal government issued its final decision: while all taxes due since 1778 were forgiven, stockmen had one year to round up whatever cattle they could manage, after which time unbranded stock belonged to the crown and became subject to taxation.[39]

Reckless slaughter was not the only threat to the feral cattle population; the weather played a crucial role in the late-eighteenth-century decline. During the drought of 1775–76 Governor Ripperdá reported that he had had to move the presidio's horse herd to La Bahía, where the grazing was better. At Béxar, he commented, the pastures were so bad "that even the cattle have left the area, so that this year the branding could not be made." The droughts of the late 1780s did even more damage. In 1787 Governor Martínez Pacheco explained that local stockmen paid cowboys one peso per day for more than a month, sometimes without catching any. Two years later, Martínez Pacheco was forced to defend himself from the commandant general's order for 500 head of cattle and other cattle products for a campaign against the Lipan Apache by seeking an affidavit from San Antonio residents that "the strong snows and ices which fell on those making the dried beef resulted in the loss of much of their horse stock," and that "the drought which has lasted to this month has not impeded the collection of cattle and beef."[40] Even the return of regular rainfall in the 1790s could not undo over two decades of damage. Governor Manuel Muñoz reissued a ban on the slaughter of breeding cows in 1794:

> Keeping in mind the reports of *vecinos* on the great shortage of livestock, which is evidenced by the inability to provision this garrison with meat from December 9 to this date, or to provide for the visiting Indians, or the inability of *vecinos* to capture many livestock in spite of the many licenses issued, [for] what does exist is in the brush and canyons, making roundups impossible and forcing the *vecinos* to shoot what they can, which is much effort spent on very little.[41]

In 1796 Manuel Delgado asked for permission for himself and others to go as far as the Colorado River "in search of cattle."[42] Owing to continued Indian depredations, and hostilities during the second decade of the nineteenth century, conditions would not markedly improve for cattle until the period following Mexican independence.

The extractive nature of the Texas livestock economy points out the significant degree to which Bexareños depended directly on nature's bounty. Béxar's town council put it well in a 1772 complaint to the viceroy when it declared that it was "impossible to live in this province without going into the country."[43] Just what they got in the countryside, aside from cattle and horses, Bexareños made clear in a 1788 complaint against the tithe collector, who demanded that wild livestock captured by Bexareños be tithed: "buffalo, bear, deer, turkey, and the other wild animals and fruits of the fields."[44] There is considerable evidence in the colonial records that as the eighteenth century progressed San Antonio's population went farther afield to obtain food stuffs and building materials. The evidence also makes clear that in carving out their home in the wilderness Bexareños had a significant impact on the regional environment.

The buffalo, on which some of the population had a dietary dependence in the late eighteenth century, is a good example of the effect of even such a small-scale settlement as Béxar on the landscape. Cíbolo Creek, named for the bison when the animal was so abundant in the region in the late seventeenth century, was no longer its home by the mid-eighteenth century. Instead, as cattle and horses became the dominant grazers throughout the San Antonio River watershed, those seeking to hunt bison had to go farther afield. Evidence from the 1770s suggests buffalo had to be sought on the Guadalupe and San Marcos Rivers and even the Colorado River, more than seventy miles north of San Antonio.[45] In the 1790s the Pedernales was among the destinations mentioned in petitions for buffalo hunts.[46] By this time a pattern of semiannual bison hunts had become the norm and, according to Governor Juan Bautista Elguézabal in 1803, if these slaughters that took "place in the months of May and October did not in a measure relieve the misery, the majority of the families would no doubt starve."[47] Not that Bexareños exterminated the buffalo in the San Antonio area, for there is no evidence for the export of such large numbers of hides as would indicate the kind of wholesale slaughter seen on the Great Plains the following century. Rather, it seems that the native grazer was displaced by "weed species"—cattle and horses.

Evidence also makes clear that Bexareños exhausted the better timber resources around San Antonio fairly quickly. As early as 1744 Governor Tomás Felipe de Winthuisen reported to the viceroy that the failure to finish construction of the presidio was not for lack of stone, but for a shortage of timber, which was located "far away, and its cutting and transport requiring an escort" because of the presence of enemy Indians.[48] By the late decades of the century it had become "customary" in January or February of every year for a group of Bexareños to make carts and cut timber at the Guadalupe or San Marcos River.[49]

Another product harvested by Bexareños for sale outside the province was pecans. The quality of the Texas nuts had been admired by members of some of the early expeditions, and as Indian populations in the region collapsed the potential harvest increased. Among the goods of petty merchant Tomás Travieso confiscated in 1777 were "some San Antonio nuts."[50] In 1791 Antonio Baca took sixteen mule-loads of pecans out of San Antonio for sale in neighboring provinces.[51]

Baca and the handful of fellow Bexareños who fancied themselves merchants and businessmen also dealt in other commodities that had their origins in the wild. Some no doubt were the product of the hunting and gathering activities of Bexareños themselves, and others were acquired from the Indian peoples who came to San Antonio to trade and receive government gifts. The most important of these products, buffalo hides and deer skins, were transported to the interior of Mexico in mule trains that also carried dried beef, cowhides, tallow, soap, pecans, and, on occasion, corn. Much work remains to be done to discover the range and size of this trade, however.

At the end of the colonial period San Antonio and Texas as a whole remained a land of promise. Spanish colonials themselves realized that in almost a century of Hispanic occupation and settlement the region's rich potential had yet to be fully tapped. Miguel Ramós Arizpe, native of Coahuila and deputy to the revolutionary Cortes in 1811–12, reported on Texas that

> it was previously covered with millions of undomesticated bovine and equine stock, or as they are called there, *mesteño*. For lack of regulation, which allowed its disorderly extraction and slaughter in the paltry interest of a half-peso per head, today it does not have enough cattle for the basic needs of its own small population, and there is little domesticated horse stock. It has very abundant populations of deer, tiger, bear, bison, beaver, otter, and also abounds in all manner of fish in its rivers, lakes, and bays on the Gulf of Mexico. The Spanish are but mere spectators to these

prodigious and very interesting products, of which the native Indians make a great commerce with the Anglo Americans.[52]

What Ramos Arizpe and other critics of the colonial Texas frontier failed to
notice was that the land itself contained obstacles to development. Efficient
communication between Texas and the rest of New Spain was often impeded
by both climate and topography. All the rivers ran perpendicularly to the line
of travel, and the Texas coast was considered unhealthful and treacherous. Periodic droughts and catastrophic floods often disrupted travel, ruined crops,
and endangered lives. In the absence of precious metals, the one natural resource that could have made the Spanish colonials interested in overcoming all
obstacles, there was little incentive to undertake the taming of Texas. Even the
most effusively positive descriptions of the province failed to overcome these
handicaps during the colonial period.

Bexareños did alter the natural environment in their settlement's vicinity,
although they did not have the means to fully exploit their natural world. To
the extent that their limited numbers and economic circumstances allowed,
they could and did harvest Texas's natural bounty. In promoting the growth of
extensive herds of domesticated livestock, cattle and horses in particular, they
started the long-term withdrawal of the American bison from the Texas landscape. In constructing sophisticated and extensive irrigation works, they mitigated some of the harsh effects of the region's semi-dry environment and
created a successful, if limited, agricultural economy. In the end, they thrived
in the Texas "wilderness" and made it their own.

3

✳

Char Miller

Where the Buffalo Roamed

Ranching, Agriculture, and the Urban Marketplace

Every winter, San Antonio goes country. In the weeks before the early February start of the annual Stock Show and Rodeo—an event that in 2001 drew more than one million spectators—the community is inundated with reminders of its historic ties to an agrarian landscape. Most compelling, perhaps because most thoroughly covered in the electronic and print media, are the twelve separate "Trail Rides": men and women mount up in Corpus Christi, Beeville, and Laredo, Bandera, Kerrville, and New Braunfels, in Johnson City, Austin, and Altair and then head out, clip-clopping down county roads, state highways, and interstate access lanes, retracing old lines of trade and commerce that once converged on the most important market city in south Texas. Wide-angle shots from television videocams beam back images of the riders' passage, and the local press frequently publishes daily postings of their journeys. Those journalists along for the ride eagerly compose elegies to a hard-scrabble existence. "For years I have been reading stories about rugged, hardy souls who mount up their trusty steeds and spend days on horseback," one eyewitness account began, plain folks who would suffer "saddle sores, tick bites and aching muscles from sleeping on the hard ground with only a blanket for warmth and a saddle for a pillow. Riding from sunup to sundown in rain, shine, sleet and snow, they endure rigors that only wranglers on old trail drives would know."[1]

The elegiac gush, composed before the warm glow of a laptop computer, is then trumped when the often-rookie reporter recounts his or her shock that the modern trailrider has no intention of replicating the travails that once confounded *vaqueros* and buckaroos alike: they sleep in comfy Winnebagoes, rise late in the morning, cover only a modest stretch of ground before breaking for a robust lunch; slung low over their hips are trusty cellphones and pagers. The Old Gray Mare, and her human passenger, ain't what they used to be.[2]

Neither is the grub. Kicking off the trail rides is the wildly popular in-town Cowboy Breakfast at which massive quantities of eggs, biscuits and gravy, breakfast tacos, juice, and coffee are served up in the predawn chill to more than 55,000 hungry urbanites; they roll up in their Suburbans, SUVs, and pickups, and jam together on the sprawling parking lot of San Antonio's Central Park Mall, hard by Interstate Loop-410. The crowd may be there to consume the culinary emblems of a bygone era, but it is hard to feel nostalgic when the food is served up in aluminum foil and slopped into paper baskets.[3]

Then there is the odd, if ritualized co-optation of western clothing most vividly displayed in the televised coverage of the Stock Show and Rodeo. During its two-week run, local newscasters nightly vie to outdo one another in their willingness to dress up in their freshly laundered, finest duds; shod in alligator-skin boots, wrapped in sequined shirts, and crowned in ten-gallon hats, they report "Live!" from the Freeman Coliseum, site of the annual exposition. Their sartorial splendor reflects the carnivalesque qualities that envelop what is branded as the "single largest event in South Texas." Want to stride down a 300-foot replica of a frontier main street? Then head over to "Bud City, Texas," where blacksmiths, saddlemakers, and leather artisans ply their wares. The swine barns, cow sheds, and sheep enclosures add an authentic stench to the air, and, after moseying over to the Hall of Fame, you will swear you have been transported to "the Old West." Throw in "20 heart-pounding, hoof-stomping PRCA performances, spotlighting the finest professional cowboys and cowgirls in the world," and, for good measure, line up an impressive list of country & western heartthrobs to wail the night away, and the extravaganza comes perilously close to parodying the very past it is designed to evoke.[4]

The Stock Show and Rodeo walks that fine line in good measure because, inaugurated in 1950 and set within a coliseum newly built to be its home, it was established at a critical juncture in San Antonio's economic history. During the Cold War, the city's financial fortunes were increasingly tied to federal largess that its five major military bases generated; in addition, the postwar rise in the nation's living standards, and the disposable income this created, only increased the amount of money visitors to the River City left behind in local cash registers. Each of these forms of spending accelerated in subsequent decades and have laid the foundations for growth over the last half of the twentieth century. How apt that ranching and agriculture, largely concentrated within two ecozones—the Gulf Coastal Plain to the south and the Edwards Plateau to the north and west—around which the region's development had revolved since the arrival of the Spanish in the early eighteenth century, now reinforce, through the Stock Show and Rodeo, the contribution tourism makes to the modern urban economy.[5]

The Gulf Coastal Plain

Rural work and folkways, and the physical environment within which they were enacted, have long supported San Antonio's development. The earliest of these contributions came from the south, from the San Antonio River valley which lies within the Gulf Coastal Plain. Frederick Law Olmsted recognized the relationship between the valley environment and the town's economic growth when in the mid-1850s he explored the region on horseback and marveled over its rich riverbottoms, fertile, low-rolling prairie dotted with mesquite and live oak; its abundant grass—what he called "mequit grass," most likely tall grama (*Bouteloua curtipendula*)—rippling before him in the warm breezes. The whole of the district, he observed, was covered with its fine growth: "It is extremely nutritious and palatable to cattle, horses, and sheep, and has the very great advantage of preserving its sweetness, to a certain degree, through the winter." Olmsted's mount, for one, which had shown "no disposition to eat" the more coarse and rank grasses of eastern Texas, browsed "eagerly" on the south Texas verdure, "as if it were an old acquaintance." This nutritional resource would give the San Antonio region its "great superiority, as a pasture ground, over those of the central and eastern parts of the state," and Olmsted predicted that this would "mark it as forever a pastoral country, whatever, in other respects, be its future."[6]

The fulfillment of his prediction was bound up with a social revolution, then everywhere visible along his route. Following the absorption of the Re-

public of Texas into the United States in 1845, and the conquest of land between San Antonio and the Rio Grande in the aftermath of the Mexican-American War, white residents and new immigrants to the state began to expropriate
the property and labor of those who once controlled this verdant landscape;
they did so, Olmsted acknowledged, "without shadow of claim." Yet such aggressive dispossessions—however lamentable—were, he thought, the way of
the world. So he mused as he poked along the banks of Calaveras Creek, just
to the southeast of San Antonio, where he came upon a cluster of Mexican-
owned farms and ranches; their "large herds in the finest condition" roamed on
what "seemed to us the richest grazing district for cattle or sheep we had yet
traversed." Its very lushness spelled its owners' doom, for they "are almost certain to disappear before the first American settlers who approach. A quarrel is
immediate, and the weaker is pushed off the log," a telling comment on the im-
balance of power throughout the region and the correspondingly rapid deterioration in postwar ethnic relations. But Olmsted also spotted the markings of
class conflict in the struggle to control these prairies, and the lives, livelihoods,
and livestock they sustained: "Throughout the South the same occurs—the
small whites are everywhere crowded upon and elbowed out before the large
planters."[7]

Whites muscled the now–Mexican American population off much—but
not all—of the prime grazing grounds along the San Antonio River valley,
through force, intimidation, or purchase. By 1865, a decade after Olmsted's so-
journ in south Texas, Spanish-surnamed ranchers accounted for less than 20
percent of all those so occupied in Bexar County, home to San Antonio; in
Atascosa County, directly south, they constituted less than 15 percent. Following the river as it flowed south and east to the Gulf of Mexico reveals an even
more dramatic transformation: Karnes, Goliad, and Refugio Counties "listed
no Mexican ranchers at all," according to historian Jack Jackson; by contrast,
in Wilson County, which had been carved out of Bexar, Mexican American
ranchers predominated. This exception proved the rule. By the end of the
American Civil War, whites in the valley had largely seized political authority,
social control, and economic power, much as Olmsted had projected.[8]

This dominance did not mean the disappearance of the Mexican people
from the region, or of the century-old ranching techniques they had developed
while working this semi-arid landscape. Cultural markers such as brands,
clothing, and terminology remained central to the livestock industry, as did the
concept of open-range stock operations, in which animals, after branding,
roamed freely. This is hardly a surprise, given the continued existence of Mex-

ican-owned lands, and, on Anglo-owned properties, the hiring of local talent to manage the range. Men such as Francisco Ruiz, Jackson observes, "sat high in the saddle . . . even when they began riding for other men, herding other men's cattle."[9]

For additional environmental evidence that Anglo-American ranching in the San Antonio region was rooted in native soil, one need look no farther than the sweet grass that so caught Olmsted's eye (and his horse's nose), and which he and a later generation of Texas promoters would tout as the key to the *future* of pasturage in south Texas. Its monocultural spread was a consequence of *past* patterns of human manipulation of the landscape. Anecdotal evidence suggests that Native Americans, to improve grazing terrain for the buffalo and other wildlife, set fire to portions of the Gulf Coastal Plain. Spanish and Mexican ranchers may have less frequently used fire to regenerate the grasses, but their cattle and sheep had the same effect of insuring the continued dominance of the short grasses (despite its name, tall grama is a relatively short grass). Their preeminence was reinforced through Spanish, later Mexican, legal codes regulating and permitting "the wild herds to flourish on the beckoning expanses of grazing land."[10]

Lured by the prospects of this landed wealth, late-arriving Anglos also built on another long-established pattern: the place of San Antonio as a regional hub. The Spanish had developed roads and trails between east Texas and the Rio Grande, along whose routes the Presidio de San Antonio de Béxar had been a vital interchange. Not all mid-nineteenth-century roads led to this city, whose population by 1860 had grown to 8,200; it lacked railroad connections until 1877, so that agricultural production in the hinterland heading to markets outside the regional usually was hauled on wagons straight to Gulf coastal ports such as Indianola. But it remained an essential organizing point for the transshipment of a wealth of goods and services. Merchants on both sides of the border made heavy use of the old trails leading to and from towns along the Rio Grande and into Mexico proper. Ferdinand von Roemer, a German geologist, witnessed the 1846 arrival of "a caravan of Mexican traders, a so-called 'Conducta,'" containing more than 100 pack mules, and on whose backs were loaded "Mexican blankets" and other consumer goods the traders hoped to exchange for cotton goods and tobacco. Roemer believed these caravans, which "come annually to San Antonio, and in great numbers," were what gave "the city its only importance," but about that he was wrong. Cattle trails that swung past the city on their way east to New Orleans and that the Spanish had blazed in the eighteenth century continued in use. Olmsted reported as well that an overland cattle trail west to California had been established in the 1840s, following a route from San Antonio to El Paso, over which also lumbered lengthy mule trains carrying provisions for the frontier garrisons that the U.S. Army had strung out on a line between those two cities. So important was transportation to the city that a full quarter of Bexar County's workforce was teamsters, wagon drivers, or cartmen. While the *San Antonio Express* and *Herald* may have brayed at those comic moments in town life in which its many burros and mules figured prominently—a pair "sang" nightly at the corner of Commerce and North Flores, much to residents' distress; another once had bellied up to a bar, courtesy of the "stimulated gentlemen" who had propelled it there—in their accounts of the "number of vagrant mules that wander the squares" lies a broader tale about the degree to which urban-centered, animal-powered transport pulled the regional economy.[11]

In death, animals played just as prominent a role in the town's life; their slaughter and distribution, and the jobs this work created, were a boon to San Antonio. The first public slaughterhouse and meat market in Texas had been established in the city in 1805, a result of Spanish imperial desires to extend political control over this frontier community and its hinterland, as well as to enhance the colonial revenue stream; five years later, new ordinances gave almost-exclusive slaughtering rights to the public abattoir, a move beneficial to beef contractors and government officials. Under the Republic of Texas, similar license fees were enacted (there was a head tax of twenty-five cents), and no animal could be butchered inside city limits except under the regulatory supervision of inspectors at the marketplace. This long-running attempt to centralize authority over meat production nurtured a small number of artisans who worked in the fledgling leather trades. In the late eighteenth century, Spanish soldiers had been outfitted with locally crafted leather shields, and throughout the colonial, Mexican, and Republic eras tanning and tallow-making, from which came the manufacture of shoes, soap, and candles, were important byproducts of the regional livestock business. But these endeavors remained on a small scale through much of the antebellum era, largely a result of the long distances that separated the community from other, larger markets to the south and east. Transportation problems and, until the 1850s or so, the threat of Indian raids compounded the difficulties associated with building a more specialized and sophisticated economy.[12]

All that would change in the wake of the Civil War. Between 1865 and 1900 the city experienced an economic boom and a corresponding population explosion. It registered a small increase during the war years, so that by 1870 it could boast around 12,200 inhabitants. Twenty years later more than 37,000 called it home, rising to more than 50,000 in 1900. At base, these alterations depended heavily on a remarkable transformation of the environment of the Gulf Coastal Plain. As with the northern plains, the southern lands' largest indigenous mammal, the buffalo, had been exterminated by the late 1870s. This was a partial consequence, historian William Cronon argues, of Philadelphia tanners who had by the beginning of that decade "perfected techniques for turning buffalo hides into supple and attractive leather"; a tremendous if short-lived market for these new goods powered the destruction of millions of buffalo. In the buffaloes' demise, San Antonio tanners played a part: they had learned to turn out stylish buffalo robes, an item for the leisure class's consumption that previous generations in the city could have neither made nor afforded. The buffalo's extinction signaled the rise in San Antonio's living standard and the increase in the numbers of its skilled workers.[13]

Even before the ensuing slaughter in Texas, however, the buffalo's place on the range had been challenged by new, massive herds of cattle that had been left to reproduce and roam across the coastal prairie during the Civil War; their owners either could not herd the cull to market or were themselves absent due to military service. Whatever the cause, the estimated 900,000 head of cattle that grazed along the Coastal Bend and San Antonio River valley before hostilities broke out in 1861 may have doubled in size by the time peace came in 1865. Their astonishing fertility, and the burgeoning mass market for beef that existed in cities of the Middle West and Northeast, was neatly tied together by the railroads that had penetrated the plains beginning in the late 1860s; the famed cattle drives from Texas to the stockyards and railheads in Kansas completed the link. The introduction of barbed wire in the 1870s—the effectiveness of which had had an early, successful demonstration on San Antonio's Alamo Plaza—signaled the end of open-range livestock operations. The southern plains became the nation's feedlot and once-distant San Antonio became more thoroughly integrated into the new American economy.[14]

The Edwards Plateau

Similarly profound ecological, economic, and social change occurred on the elevated terrain known as the Edwards Plateau that lies to San Antonio's north and west, and beneath whose folds the city is tucked. Native American peoples had long exploited its river valleys and creek beds, where they had hunted wildlife—mammals and reptiles—foraged for nuts and berries, harvested wild rice and other plant food, and fished. Archaeological evidence dug up in and around the headwaters of Olmos, Salado, Panther Springs, and Leon Creeks, tributaries of the San Antonio River, reveals temporary and "semi-permanent settlements" dating back to at least 9200 B.C.E. Those who inhabited these sites in the years before the Spanish arrival, known collectively as the Tonkawa, evidently conducted seasonal hunting expeditions up into the plateau, where bison and deer were plentiful, migrated along the arc of rivers that continued to flow during the dry, hot summer months from the Colorado to the north to the Medina on the west, and participated in trade networks that extended from present-day New Mexico to the Gulf Coast and eastern Texas.[15]

This range of movement, and the life it supported, came under intense pressure from two sources in the late seventeenth and early eighteenth centuries. The Spanish, pressing up from the south, brought with them new diseases that decimated indigenous populations; it was at the missions they subsequently established along the San Antonio River valley that many of the surviving Indians, often through compelled conversion, were transformed into agricultural laborers. Another force pushed the Tonkawa into Spanish arms: the Lipan Apache, an aggressive, horse-riding people, whom the Comanche had moved out of their more northerly territory, drifted south onto the Edwards Plateau, and dominated it by 1700. No match for these invaders' military prowess, and seeking protection the Spanish could provide, some of the Tonkawa and other displaced Indian peoples of the region chose to convert to Catholicism, as one Spanish prelate put it, "for fear of the Apache." Their calculation—"when weighing Spaniards against Apaches," observes archaeologist T. N. Campbell, "[most] seemed to have regarded the Spaniards as the lesser of two evils"—indicated a fundamental change in the region's human ecology. "By the end of the 17th century, the Indians of southern Texas were already beginning to face what most hunting and gathering peoples of the world have had to face," Campbell concludes: "population decline, territorial displacement, segregation and ideological pressure, loss of ethnic identity, and absorption by invading armies." That process was largely complete by the first decade of the eighteenth century, laying the groundwork for the next stage in the redefinition of the plateau's environment.[16]

The battering ram for this alteration was sheep. With their introduction in the mid-nineteenth century along the watercourses that cut down through the eastern edge of the plateau came a new human relationship with the land that in time would fully clear away indigenous peoples and eradicate much of the native flora and fauna. The development of a set of urban market forces reinforced and deepened these changes, changes that even the observant Frederick Law Olmsted did not fully grasp when he traversed the hilly terrain in the early 1850s.

Yet Olmsted saw much that indicated how complete some of these impending environmental shifts would be. Enamored of the low "montaines" that rolled away from San Antonio, he recognized that this rough landscape, with its limestone outcroppings and grasslands, rivers and streams, was perfect for sheep, goats, and other livestock. "The natural use of the country was, palpably, for grazing, and that, sheep grazing. We could hardly refrain from expecting, on each bleak hill, to startle a black-faced flock, and see a plaided, silent, long-legged shepherd appear on the scene." To realize this romantic vision would require an enormous effort on the part of a host of migrants who, like the German settlers Olmsted so admired, entered the Hill Country in the 1840s, and were in the forefront of destroying or expelling other claimants to its riches.[17]

Olmsted recounted innumerable bits of frontier lore that spoke to the forceful pacification of the countryside. "A good deal of large game is still found in these hills," he noted "though it is disappearing before the rapid settlement of the country." It was not settlement per se that eradicated wildlife but the deliberate hunting of them to extermination. One anecdote Olmsted related involved a "gentleman, who resided at Comanche Creek, [and who] undertook to make . . . a collection of skins of Texas wild animals"; he hired a hunter who in short order bagged 11,000 pounds of "wild meat." A family living along one of the banks of the Sister creeks, some forty miles to San Antonio's north, proudly fed Olmsted a rich dinner of turkey, one of eighty-five they had shot that winter alone; the dinner conversation revolved around stalking panthers living along the riverbottoms. Another gunner Olmsted encountered bragged of having killed sixty bears in two years. The northern traveler was equally transfixed when regaled about a legendary "great bear hunt" involving a local German sportsman of renown, who once had triumphed in hand-to-hand combat with a powerful black bear. The sportsman's greatest victory, however, occurred when he tracked a wounded female into its lair, only to find the cache of his life. This first bear, the hunter discovered after crawling down through a narrow cave mouth, already had died of its injuries, but others awaited; through deft use of revolver, knife, and fire, the stalwart hero killed four more, wiping out "the whole of the Bruin family," Olmsted breathlessly reported. "Imagine the cheers, when the *five bears* were carried by his neighbors, on poles into the settlement." In this gruesome parade, and the subsequent "three days' feast of bears'-meat and whisky," do we get a glimpse of the stakes involved in the collision of animal and human populations on the Edwards Plateau.[18]

The conflict between rival human societies was as intense, especially as the German and Anglo-American settlers consumed the Indians' traditional food resources. Adapting swiftly to the loss of hunting territory, and the buffalo, bear, and deer it once sustained, the Lipan Apache periodically raided and cut out the newly established herds of sheep, goats, and cattle. Deflecting some of these attacks was the presence of Army forts situated throughout the region along the new roads that thrust into the plateau. These outposts were the basis for this prediction: "a line of settlements will soon follow [the forts]," Olmsted wrote, "and the Indians will then be confined to the great desert plains, which can furnish them little game, and probably, no cultivated food. Starvation will compel submission or emigration, and this great district will become open to peaceable occupation." His expectation was not immediately met, as these encampments were shut down at the outbreak of the Civil War, and hostilities between Indians and settlers flared anew.[19]

Large sheep ranches were particularly exposed. At some remove from the tiny Hill Country settlements and the protection they might have afforded, and containing a valuable, and vulnerable, source of nutrition, they were easy targets. An assault on George W. Kendall's herd grazing on lands near Boerne in 1862 ended in the deaths of three shepherds, one of whom reportedly was "pierced by some seventeen arrows." The "dreadful spectacle," Kendall wrote in a letter to the *New Orleans Picayune,* of which he was part owner, "called up mingled feelings of deep pity for the unfortunate lad, boiling indignation against his brutal murderers, and deep-rooted disgust at the majority of our rulers who have never bestowed a second thought upon frontier protection." Unable to bring the shepherd back to life, or the distant Confederate government to heed, the rancher-journalist demanded a full-scale assault upon the indigenous peoples who inhabited the Edwards Plateau:

> The Indians must be worried and hunted down, killed to the last
> man, or driven so far beyond our borders that we shall hear of
> them no more. They should be sought in their hunting grounds,
> when killing their stock of Buffalo meat—should be allowed no
> rest or respite—should be granted no truce or treaty. The cruel
> war they are waging against us—and cowardly as well as cruel, for
> they attack none but the weak and defenseless—will last so long

as an Indian is left. This is a fact we must look in the face, and must act upon it, or else abandon the frontiers sooner or later.

Kendall did not exact his bloody revenge, but within a decade of Appomattox, the Lipan Apache, Comanche, and others were pushed off the plateau, often herded on to reservations in Oklahoma, opening the way for this arid high country to become a sprawling pasture land.[20]

The success of agriculture and ranching was not assured even with the extermination of competing animals and humans. Formidable environmental factors complicated the establishment of an agrarian economy on the Edwards. Kendall, long recognized as one of greatest promoters of the new economic order, endured many of these setbacks. A New Englander by birth, and an inveterate traveler, he had searched throughout Texas in the 1850s for prime grazing lands. Using San Antonio as his base, he wandered up a series of nearby river valleys and decided to establish a sheep operation on lands along the upper Guadalupe River, northwest of New Braunfels. The "pleasant and verdant valley was surrounded on all sides by rough, rocky and rugged mountains," he informed his French wife, and to give her a sense of its size described it as approximately "six times as large as all Paris"; most important was that it was "admirably adapted for raising both sheep and horses." The livestock and their human tenders did most of the adapting: in 1853 a blizzard killed many of his animals; some of the survivors later died of liver rot; then, in 1854, a prairie fire scorched the land, forcing Kendall to move his holdings farther west. Problems persisted. The following year another raging winter fire killed more than 400 of his sheep; the burned-over grasslands could not regenerate quickly enough to support the spring lambs, further decimating his herd. Not until 1856 was Kendall able to see results. Aided by more benign weather patterns, his flock stabilized and began to grow, the annual shear rapidly increased, and through diligent breeding he was able to enhance the quality of wool. By 1859 his confidence led him to wonder "whether a greater degree of good fortune ever attended the efforts of any one engaged in the business."[21]

He would come to regret that enthusiasm. The onset of the Civil War disrupted his access to eastern wool markets, he had difficulty selling the annual clip and therefore paying his herders, many of whom left for San Antonio in search of work; the abandoned flocks were easier prey for predators, animal and human. Added to these woes was incessant worries about water, a product of living in a semi-arid region. As Kendall wrote a correspondent in 1860: "[My] only fear is that our spring, which has now been running constantly for

8 years to my certain knowledge, will give out unless fed by copious rains, and then—what? Why, I must commence wandering about the country, like a Tartar, looking for water and grass." Like many who would follow him into the grazing business on the Edwards, Kendall relied heavily on a "hope for better things," that "we shall have rain enough 'to do us' before summer is over."[22]

The lack of water was a crucial factor in the movement of sheep to or from coastal ports. When that summer he contemplated trailing some imported bucks up from the Gulf to his Hill Country ranch, he blanched: "You might as well drive sheep across the Desert of Sahara in mid-summer as over the route between [New Braunfels] and Matagorda Bay just now. Why I was told the other day that water was 50 cents a bucket full at Lavaca, and I suppose it is as dear at Indianola!" That there had been no rain in three months, and that temperatures were soaring upwards "from 115 to 130 in the sun," only increased his anxieties about sustaining his flock on the road. "All of to-day I have been facing a perfect sirocco in an open wagon, the hot air ten times heated over the parched lower plains," a blistering heat that "would be insupportable on the Coast of Guinea."[23]

In his lament lay another concern, however unarticulated: the Texas sheep industry, poised in 1860 to press ever farther west onto an even more arid landscape, would also face almost insurmountable transportation problems. If Kendall—who once boasted that "the verb 'to fail' is not in my vocabulary"— almost buckled before a scorching 150-mile wagon ride, what hope was there for others who would confront exponentially longer routes to market?

An answer lay in an innovation in the dynamics of wool marketing that developed in San Antonio. Before the Civil War, Kendall, like many of his peers, had hauled his annual shear on wagons to Indianola, or Port Lavaca, for shipment to New York or New England. Lacking regular wheeled-transport, or access to the more rapid railroad, and devoid of warehouses in which to hold their wool off market, Texas ranchers were at a distinct economic disadvantage when they tried to sell their clip. "In New York there is no chance for us to get our rights," Kendall fumed. "What with forwarding charges, freights, commissions, guarantees, *and the cry against Texas wool* among the buyers of that city, we never obtain our own." Some of those disadvantages began to disappear in the late 1860s when Thomas Clayton Frost bought his first wagons and teams for freight service between San Antonio and the Gulf ports and contracted with other teamsters to haul in wool and other products from the Rio Grande Plain and the Edwards Plateau. Soon thereafter, he opened T. C. Frost Company on Main Plaza, which was stocked with "everything a man would need to finish

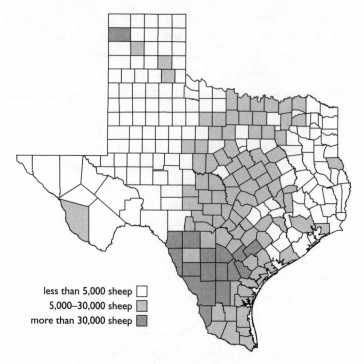

Fig. 3.1. Distribution of sheep in Texas by county, 1880 (*Source:* Paul H. Carlson, *Texas Woollybacks: The Range Sheep and Goat Industry* [College Station: Texas A&M University Press, 1982], 113.)

taming the land: axes, saws, rifles, pistols, ammunition, boots, work shoes, broad brimmed Stetson hats . . . work pants and jackets, rope, nails and neats-foot oil." These, plus a variety of harnesses, animal collars, saddles, bridles, and wagons, were one means by which he hoped to snare much of southcentral Texas's wool production. More effective still was the simple expedient of offering wool producers credit in his store in exchange for the right to market their shear. As business boomed, Frost and his family opened a 22,000-square-foot storage facility to keep the wool until market prices rose, and a bank that allowed them to better handle their clients' credit, strategies that stabilized Frost's customers' cash flow and enhanced his profit margins. Frost had become the dominant wool merchant in the city by 1887; within two years he thought his reach larger still: "I am all right this fall," he wrote in 1889, "clean sold out, at prices above all competitors and the largest amount of wool ever handled by one man in the state." His business acumen and swelling fame—as "a warehouseman and commission salesman," agricultural historian Paul H.

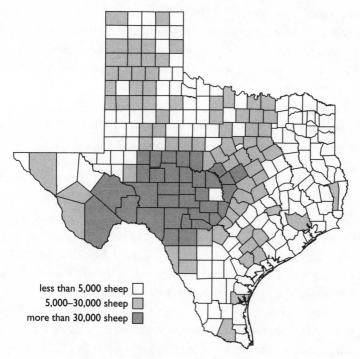

Fig. 3.2. Distribution of sheep in Texas by county, 1930 (*Source:* Paul H. Carlson, *Texas Woollybacks: The Range Sheep and Goat Industry* [College Station: Texas A&M University Press, 1982], 201.)

Carlson has noted, Frost "may have handled more wool than any other man in the country"—had much to do with making wool a staple in San Antonio's postwar economy.[24]

Even as he helped rearrange rural trade routes and economic fortunes, and linked both more directly to an urban hub, Frost and those who succeeded him in the transportation and marketing end of the business had to respond to an environmentally impelled shift in the location of the region's cattle and sheep. There had been warnings in the late 1860s about the impact of intensive grazing on the south Texas grasslands. A pseudonymous writer in the 1868 *Texas Almanac* bemoaned the thoughtless and rapid destruction of native grasses, a consequence of "our avarice that overstocks and exhausts our pasture grounds." Cattle had so thoroughly mowed down the once-lush grassland that rolled south along the San Antonio Valley that even before the Civil War ranchers were relocating their herds to the so-called Cross Timbers area in north-central Texas, a gentle "hilly region of tallgrass bluestem prairies, oak savannahs, and cedar breaks." They did not remain there for long; within twenty years, due to intense pasture depletion and the need to be closer to the Chicago markets, the herds were driven out on to the northern Great Plains. "Even very early in its development and expansion," geographer Terry Jordan concludes, the Texas ranching system, "with its huge free-ranging herds, lacked ecological sustainability."[25]

The same was true of sheep. While Kendall and others were forced to adapt to a series of ecological forces that complicated their early attempts to establish grazing on the Edwards Plateau, contemporaries were establishing much larger flocks on the more southerly Rio Grande Plain; of the 100,000 sheep in Texas denoted in the 1850 U.S. Census, half were located south and west of San Antonio. Within twenty years the Callaghan ranch near Encinal alone ran 100,000 head, with its 1881 clip totaling close to half a million pounds. By the early 1880s the Rio Grande Plain contained nearly 2.5 million sheep and goats (triple the number of cattle), and within four years the number bulged to nearly 4 million. The land could not sustain such spectacular numbers: "The practice of herding one sheep per acre proved too taxing for the buffalo grass and gamma grass," and poor range management, which led to such extensive overgrazing, turned "the once lush South Texas grassland into the veritable desert and scrub brush and barren waste that it remains today." Seeking greener terrain, many sheep owners headed north onto the Edwards Plateau, or farther west into the Trans-Pecos region of the state. The numbers tell the story: in 1900 there were but a quarter-million sheep remaining in the Rio Grande Plain; by then there was more than 1.5 million on the Edwards, turning it into the center of sheep grazing in Texas, finally realizing George Kendall's mid-nineteenth-century conviction of its superior range.[26]

Market Forces

For all his certitude, Kendall had not been above hedging his bets. Worried about getting fleeced in the still-risky sheep business, and concerned about the uncertain prospects of his hearing-impaired daughter, he started investing in San Antonio real estate in the 1850s, particularly in lots adjacent to Alamo Plaza. In time his investments paid off handsomely, but only after local merchants and entrepreneurs were able to take advantage of a new form of transportation, the railroad, and of the profound changes it engineered in the city's economy and spatial design, as well as in its hinterland's productivity.[27]

Well before the Galveston, Harrisburg, and San Antonio Railroad first pulled into town in February 1877, editorial writers waxed enthusiastic about its restorative powers: "Already does the shrill whistle of the locomotive reach our ear, and speaks . . . of an enterprise whose . . . spirit of progress has begun to arouse the old, dry bones of the Alamo City." After its arrival, newspaper boosters were even more convinced of the coming success: "San Antonio can now take a position in the great family of first-class cities of the American continent, and move grandly on to that greatness and prosperity that could never be reached without the aid of the iron horse." That process would be sped up when by 1883 the Galveston had linked up with the Southern Pacific to forge a transcontinental connection between San Antonio, New York, and San Francisco; a north-south line, the International and Great Northern, also had arrived by this time and had pressed into Mexico, establishing further the city's new role as an axis point between a set of more substantial markets. Within a few years the San Antonio and Aransas Pass Railroad had snaked south to the Gulf and north to the Hill Country. Although one newspaper conceded it was "impossible to foretell or approximate the great advantages" the city initially would "derive from her central position" on the first of these lines, the east-west Sunset Route, it did not hesitate to speculate that ramifications would be substantial: "it will undoubtedly open up for settlement and commerce a broad and fertile land, hitherto unknown to all except the uncultivated savage and the wild buffalo." Modernity would ride in on the rails.[28]

So would a ton of freight. Contemporary accounts reveal rapid increases in the shipment of select items: in 1879 2,200 bales of cotton left San Antonio, a figure that quadrupled in two years; the number of sheep shipped out grew tenfold between 1879 and 1881; the number of cattle doubled; exportation of wool leaped from 3.2 million pounds to a touch more than 5 million; and a community that imported no flour or lumber by rail in 1879 absorbed forty-three carloads of flour and more than 6.8 million pounds of wood two short years later. Spinoff commercial development—including new flour and grist mills, foundries and machine shops, as well as expanding numbers of tanneries, and marked increases in brick, tile, and cement production—reinforce the perception that the 1880s were a takeoff point in the city's economy. The changes seemed substantial enough that an otherwise wary contemporary observer of the local (and hitherto mercurial) economy was convinced that the "present prosperity of San Antonio" was not "transitory," reflecting instead "a rapid and steady growth based on actual business increase."[29]

The railroads also rearranged San Antonio's physical development. The siting of depots on the eastern and western edge of the central core (and the later construction of one to its south) pulled some of the economic activity away from the original market hubs of Main and Military Plazas; new stockyards, lumberyards, warehouses, and other storage facilities clustered around the transportation terminals. The increased number of visitors and commercial agents coming to San Antonio generated as well a related spurt of hotel and boardinghouse construction or renovation; many of the new or remodeled lodgings were sited along the streetcar lines that linked the railroad depots, from St. Paul Square on the east to Cattlemen's Square on the west. In between arose corridors of commerce. Most notably transformed was Houston Street: "in the fall of 1876, [it] was regarded as an out of the way avenue and entirely unnecessary to the trade of this city," remembered one journalist. "The buildings were few and far between . . . and mesquite brush grew in luxuriance even in the middle of the street. When it rained the street was almost impassable on account of the mud, and the alleged sidewalks were not much better." Twelve years later that scruffy tableau had vanished with the laying down of the "dou-

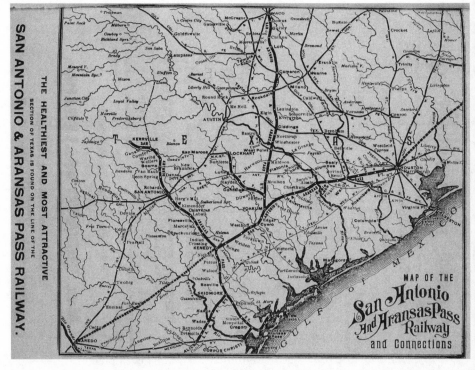

Fig. 3.3. San Antonio's late-nineteenth-century hinterland is defined by its railroad connections.

ble lines of tracks of street railway," for the "graveled road bed and paved sidewalks have replaced the thorny mesquite, and [today] the best business locations in this city are to be found on this now popular thoroughfare."[30]

As they created a new business district, mule-drawn trolleys also accelerated the separation between work and home then possible for people of means.
Indeed, the first line had been constructed north from downtown to San Pedro
Park and its much-heralded springs, one of the city's favorite pleasure grounds.
But catering to those seeking temporary refuge in this tranquil setting, however crucial their patronage, was not the sole reason this railway was laid down
over San Pedro Avenue, "a recently cut road over a hog-wallow prairie." The
streetcar, as its owner August Belknap expected, immediately influenced the
value of adjacent property: "no sooner had the line been completed than a
great transformation took place," the *San Antonio Light* reported. "Large lots,
which could be bought for $5 and $10, immediately jumped in price to from
$100 to $500. A rush was made by citizens to that locality, and very soon
dozens of residences were constructed on the Avenue." With its "fine residences, paved sidewalks, planted with beautiful trees, Telford road bed, fire hy-
drants and gas lamps," San Pedro Springs had fulfilled Belknap's ambitions and
its homeowners' aspirations when it was anointed "the fashionable quarter of
San Antonio."[31]

The materials that went into the construction of these well-appointed residences also reflected the changes the railroads brought to the larger urban
economy. The mid-nineteenth-century dependence on "the long trains of Mexican carts and prairie schooners" to haul all freight into San Antonio, and the
early clear-cutting of regional forests, largely limited the shipment of wood to
that which would be burned for fuel. One consequence was that San Antonio
remained "a one-story city, with quaint old adobe buildings 'huddled' together
near the common centre." The Galveston, Harrisburg, and San Antonio, and
the other rail lines, which more easily hauled such bulky items as lumber, and
at a vastly cheaper cost, enabled the Alamo City to grow up *and* out, an incal-
culable "donation to the cause of progress and civilization."[32]

The city's boosters hoped this new transport mechanism would enable
them to corral and civilize what the *San Antonio Express* boldly claimed as "Our
Tributary Territory." The terrain was as expansive as the community's reach
was imperial: "If you will glance at the map of Texas you will see a triangle
south of San Antonio to the Mexican border, formed by the Southern Pacific to
Eagle Pass and the San Antonio and Aransas Pass railways to Corpus Christi,
and pierced almost through its centre by the International and Great Northern

Railway to Laredo." Framed in this cross-hatching of tracks was an area comprising more than 36,000 square miles ("equal in extent to that of the states of New Hampshire, Vermont, Massachusetts and Rhode Island"), but this, the *Express* assured its readers, "is not all the territory directly tributary to the trade of this city." Incorporate the Hill Country counties to the north and west, and those to the immediate east and south, including Guadalupe, Gonzales, De-Witt, Goliad, and Refugio, and the city's sovereignty extended over some 58,000 square miles of rich and fertile lands.[33]

Land everywhere was being reorganized in response to the railroads' arrival. "Many of the thriving cities and towns" to San Antonio's east "owe their existence solely to Galveston, Harrisburg and San Antonio Railroad," and the increase in their populations depended heavily on those "brought to Texas by the immigration department of this railroad." New workers meant new work: "Before this railway was completed the country between Houston and San Antonio was sparsely settled and large herds of wild cattle roamed in unrestricted freedom where now are found the most fertile fields of sugar, cotton, grain, and garden truck." The economic and social benefits that this more settled form of agriculture and community "has conferred on Texas," one contemporary exclaimed, "is beyond computation."[34]

Others were more calculating. Those who invested in the San Antonio and Aransas Pass (known as SAP) knew full well that as the line worked its way south to Floresville, then Beeville, on the way to the Gulf port of Corpus Christi, it was opening up "stock country" whose cattle, sheep, goats, and horses would ride the rails to market in San Antonio and beyond. They hoped to tap as well "the incipient cotton culture springing up east of the Nueces [River], and the vegetable growing in Nueces County." More desirable still was the access the railroad offered to the shipping lines that plied between Corpus Christi and national and international ports. But when in late October 1886 the "last pile was driven across the Corpus Christi reefs," and passenger and freight traffic commenced operations, an environmental complication nearly scuttled the SAP's raison d'être. Aransas Pass, through which the Morgan Lines of New York and other freighters entered Corpus Christi Bay, periodically shoaled over, leading these shippers to cut back their service. Stabilizing "a deep water entrance at Aransas Pass is certainly a most pressing [question] for Southwest Texas," the *San Antonio Express* asserted, and its resolution lay in securing federal funds to dredge and shore up the channel; beginning in 1879, and accelerating after the railroad arrived, nearly $550,000 was appropriated for this maintenance program through Congress's annual Harbor and Bridges

Acts. It was money well spent, as far as San Antonians were concerned, many of whom had been lured to the port city as tourists by cheap introductory ticket prices, and who there developed a hankering for shellfish; oysters quickly became much in demand in San Antonio's restaurants, an unanticipated consequence of the city's newfound opening to the sea.[35]

No such delicacies were imported from the Edwards Plateau when SAP reached its northern terminus in Kerrville in August 1887. But the company's managers hoped this short branch line—it covered a little over seventy miles—would help San Antonio recover its former dominance of Hill Country trade; a decade earlier, "extensions of the Austin and Northwestern and Texas Pacific lines had driven San Antonio wagons out of this region." Once built, the *Express* trumpeted, "the proposed line would insure the greatness of San Antonio, and give her control of the trading zone." Apparently, the branch line had the intended effect, redirecting traffic through the Kerrville depot, a redirection that transformed the small town and intensified the emerging economic order on the high ground that fanned out to its north and west.[36]

The once-isolated Hill Country village, which had been at least a two-day ride from San Antonio in an empty, two-horse wagon, rapidly became an exchange point for goods and services flowing between more western settlements and San Antonio. One who took great advantage of Kerrville's pivotal placement was Charles Schreiner, an already successful merchant, who invested $150,000 in the SAP to insure rail connections to San Antonio; with the construction of the depot, he proceeded to build a succession of ever-larger warehouses along the sidings. Like T. C. Frost of San Antonio, Schreiner filled his storage facilities by hiring "freighters" to collect wool from far-flung ranches, provided credit in his store in exchange for storing these growers' annual shear before shipping it to market, and, as a banker, arranged loans to expand sheep or goat operations. Should his customers fail to meet their obligations, he foreclosed, absorbing the property into his holdings, which ultimately grew to more than 500,000 acres. Not only did he supplant Frost as the leading wool-commission agent in the state, but through his substantial investments in transportation and land also reinforced the preeminent position of grazing on the plateau.[37]

As the products wrested from this tough terrain rolled down to the regional hub—in addition to wool and livestock, large quantities of oats and corn, timber and finished lumber, made the transit—the return run carried a surprise cargo, travelers interested in Hill Country sights. The demand caught the railroad off guard: its local agents had assumed that a single passenger car coupled to the rear of the daily freight would suffice. In 1890 full passenger service was scheduled, and thousands sought respite among the same narrow river valleys, low hills, and craggy landforms that had inspired Frederick Law Olmsted's antebellum fantasies about the region's pastoral prospects; touting the area's "many natural attractions," or championing its "health-restoring climate" (the Hill Country, one promoter promised, was "nature's greatest sanitorium"), boosted the railway's receipts. Others quickly and purposefully seized upon this bit of accidental tourism, as passengers who alighted in Boerne or Comfort or Kerrville discovered. In every town along SAP's route new hotels and boardinghouses sprouted up and reportedly were fully occupied throughout the summer months; livery stables were built to meet the heavy demand for carriages that could wheel guests farther out into the country; and the first "dude ranches" and summer camps were opened to provide adults and children with a taste for the strenuous life that would restore body and soul. A new aesthetic was taking root.[38]

The railroad was its progenitor and as such helped delineate for contemporaries the next chapter in the narration of human settlement in the West. The "echoes of these hills," wrote a historian of Comfort, Texas, once "the haunt of the stealthy Indian, are now awakened by . . . the whistle of the locomotive as it thunders along track of that grand enterprise of our people, the northwestern extension of the San Antonio and Aransas Pass Railroad." Cutting through the rocky terrain, SAP overwhelmed historic relations to the land that the Tonkawa, Lipan Apache, and Comanche had carved out, and rolled over the frontier culture European migrants had fashioned in the mid-nineteenth century. Those pasts were becoming a piece of Romantic lore, feeding the new age's sense of appropriation and conquest.[39]

Stephen Crane used San Antonio to make the same point. In January 1889 he arrived in the city that for "all manner of people, business men, consumptive men, curious men and wealthy men" seemed to symbolize "the poetry of life in Texas," a place that, according to a hoary refrain, consisted of "three old ruins and a row of Mexicans sitting in the sun." But the prosaic had already triumphed, the "astonished visitor" reported. San Antonio's "principal streets are lanes between rows of handsome business blocks," its "prevailing type of citizen is not seated in the sun; he is making his way with the speed and intentness of one who competes in a community that is commercially in earnest." For Crane these "edifices of stone and brick and iron are reared on ashes, upon the ambitions of a race." The new San Antonio had deliberately eradicated its missionary heritage: "the serene Anglo-Saxon . . . strings telegraph wires across their sky of hope; and over the energy, the efforts, the accomplishments of these pious fathers of the early church passes the wheel, the hoof, the heel." Although fragments of historic architecture and remnants of an older character had escaped "the whirl of modern life," they too would get "trampled into shapeless dust which lies always behind the march of this terrible century." Nothing so perfectly captured this than the "important uproar" of the "almighty trolley car." Watching them careen around the city, Crane shuddered: these "merciless animals . . . gorge themselves with relics. They make really coherent history look like an omelet."[40]

The history of frontier outposts in west Texas was just as scrambled, and here again San Antonio served for Crane as the locus of change, a point from which emanated new cultural forms and social behaviors. The clash between these and older models of action is at the center of his short story, "The Bride Comes to Yellow Sky" (1898), which opens with a disorienting rush: "The great Pullman was whirling onward with such dignity of motion that a glance from the window seemed simply to prove that the plains of Texas were pouring eastward." The big city's magnetic power was inescapable: as the train swiftly crossed "[v]ast flats of green grass, dulled-hued spaces of mesquit and cactus, little groups of frame houses, woods of light and tender trees, all were sweeping into the east, sweeping over the horizon, a precipice."[41]

The frontier was being domesticated: aboard this hurtling projectile was the sheriff of Yellow Sky, Jack Potter, and his unnamed bride; together they "reflected the glory of their marriage that morning in San Antonio; this was the environment of their new estate." Its cheerful state did not last long: as the train approached Yellow Sky, the sheriff, well used to restraining criminals, now found himself bound by his wedding suit's stiff cuffs and his newly embraced, if awkward, marital ties. Worried about how the town would accept his sudden and secret marriage, he hoped he and his wife could elude attention by slinking home along back streets. They failed when they came face to face with Scratchy Wilson, "about the last one of the old gang that used to hang out along the river." For hours the gunslinger had been shooting up the town on a drunken rampage, searching out Potter, his "ancient antagonist." However deadly his pair of large revolvers, Wilson was a parody of his ilk, wrapped in a "maroon-coloured flannel shirt, which had been purchased for purposes of decoration" and manufactured in New York City's sweatshops, and stomping through the dusty town in red-topped boots with "gilded imprints, of the kind beloved in winter by little sledding boys on the hillsides of New England." Disarmed when he realizes Potter isn't wearing his gun, stunned to learn the lawman is married, Scratchy "was like a creature allowed a glimpse of another world." At last, he said, "I s'pose it's all off now." Slipping his weapons back into their holsters, the "simple child of the earlier plains" shuffled off, his feet making "funnel-shaped tracks in the heavy sand," retreating into a past that had no future.[42]

Show Time

San Antonio was in danger of being locked in a similar conundrum, as Crane might have predicted. The very forces that had allowed it to expand its commercial interests and economic clout in the late nineteenth century, and that had boosted the productivity of its extensive agricultural and ranching hinterland, would soon complicate its ability to diversify. The inability or un-willingness of the city's business elite to invest in railroad expansion into the Rio Grande Valley, for example, allowed Houston, which eagerly pursued such investments, to capture much of the initial surge of the valley's agricultural production in the 1910s and 1920s. San Antonio's growth was also stymied by a new mechanism of trade: trucks made inroads on the railroads' fixed lines of transport, allowing smaller communities on the Edwards Plateau and the Gulf Coastal Plain to compete successfully for freight that used to run through San Antonio. Even the gaudy oil booms that so powered Dallas and Houston into national prominence largely passed the Alamo City by; petroleum pumped from under the ranches that spread along the San Antonio River Valley, and to its southwest, was mostly refined in Corpus Christi or the lower Rio Grande Valley. There were resources on which to draw, Green Peyton argued in *San Antonio: City in the Sun* (1946), but most revolved around livestock. That explained the city's growing ecnomic and social problems. Its "ranch people," he wrote, who constituted the community's social backbone and funda-ment," failed to act upon their civic obligations. Instead they "are obsessed by the fear of being noticed and disturbed in their tranquil enjoyment of their wealth and cattle. The squalid lives of the Mexicans across San Pedro Creek are no concern of theirs. They are not interested in San Antonio's venereal disease rate or its medieval political structure." Stolid in their conviction that the city remained the "Cow Capital" of the nation, they apparently did not recognize the danger embedded in this claim: the numbers of cattle (and sheep and goats) roaming the range were in slow decline over the first decades of the twentieth century, and the prices they fetched at market were even less stable. In their unreflective contentment, Green read a white flag: "The city that once supplied the southwest has let Houston and Dallas take over much of the business and finance of Texas." This left the Alamo City, he wrote in an unconscious evocation of Stephen Crane's earlier image of arrested urban development, "sitting like an old man basking in the sun."[43]

To awaken the city's somnolent economy, an emerging pro-growth coalition gambled it could construct a new west out of the materials of the old. In the mid-1940s, city and county commissioners, the Chamber of Commerce, bankers, construction executives, and newspaper boosters proposed to build a coliseum; it would house the community's first Livestock Exhibition and Rodeo, which they hoped would lure thousands of tourists to its grounds. If this "gigantic enterprise for the development of San Antonio" panned out, it might narrow the widening economic gap between the south Texas metropolis of more than 250,000 people and its larger and richer urban rivals to the north and east, enabling it to assume "its rightful place as the center of the livestock industry of the Great Southwest." Built on 170 acres of city-owned land, and funded with a $1.75-million bond that Bexar County residents approved in 1947, the 8,500 seat, silver-domed facility had its soft opening in October 1949.[44]

Four months later, the ten-day-long rodeo received a noisy sendoff with a cavalcade through city streets: wild cheers washed over the 4,000 participants, 1,500 of whom were mounted—but none louder than for the governor of Texas, Allan Shivers; an upscale Scratchy Wilson, he had donned "western regalia in keeping with the occasion," rode a borrowed white stallion named Jo-Jo, and sat tall in its "$14,000 gold and silver studded saddle." Yet the loudest acclaim was reserved for the coliseum itself. Its cavernous roof arced over such a sprawling dirt floor—nearly 32,000 square feet—that a journalist chuckled when pondering how the first cattle driven into the arena would respond: they "likely will be fooled they are in their natural habitat." This conceit of approximation set up the final appropriation of nature on which the western-themed tourist economy would depend: by artifice and engineering, the coliseum enclosed an interior space "as big as all outdoors."[45]

THREE

Social Ecology

4

Char Miller and
Heywood Sanders

Parks, Politics, and Patronage

When in the late 1990s Mario Salas was elected to the San Antonio City Council for District 2, which encompasses much of the historically black East Side, he announced his commitment to increase the number and size of city parks in the neighborhoods he represented. Arguing that there were "hardly any parks at all in the northeastern part of my district," and that none had been created since the late 1980s as this sector of the city experienced rapid population growth, he pressed for the establishment of five parks totaling eighty acres. The largest, to be sited in the Lakeside area, bordering Rosillio Creek, would cover more than thirty acres and would include a large pond; several smaller parks under ten acres were located within or adjacent to new subdivisions; one was a donation from a developer. These new parks, and future developments he expected to pursue within the nearby Salado Creek floodplain, all of which would include trails and other recreational amenities, would offer a bit of much-needed open space to these outlying residents who lived far from the city's major parks facilities.[1]

Providing environmental relief and aesthetic enjoyment for his constituents was only part of Salas's concern, as was revealed in his stated desire that "neighborhood associations in proximity to each park come up with an appropriate name" for the new spaces. In a city in which such associations have become powerful factors in election campaigns—they have proved effective mechanisms for getting out the vote, and many members of the city council in the 1990s first had tested their political ambitions in such community-based organizations—Salas understandably wanted to give them a voice so that they would give his reelection campaign a boost. "Whatever happens while I'm in office," he affirmed, "I want to go down as the one who brought parks to my district—a parks guru if you will." Identifying more green space as "probably the biggest need in District 2," he deftly fused the American cultural appreciation for outdoor recreation and parkland beauty, and the cohesive impact such land use has on community life, with the electoral benefits that can accrue from their creation.[2]

In Salas's particularistic interest lies a larger story about the purpose and distribution of parks within twentieth-century San Antonio. Although civic promotion has long been tied to the Alamo City's fabled history and exotic character—crucial elements in the local tourist economy—capital spending for open space also played a critical role in defining and advancing the community's image. San Antonio's political leadership, for instance, frequently has argued that the community's parks were an integral expression of the city itself. As Superintendent of Parks Stewart King put it in a speech in early 1950, the city's green spaces were largely responsible for its "distinctive charm." So important were they, he concluded, that they were "one of the main reasons O. Henry once said, and Will Rogers referred to it many times; 'There are only three interesting cities in the United States, San Francisco, New Orleans and San Antonio.'"[3]

The source of this piece of self-congratulation actually lay not in the early-twentieth-century musings of O. Henry, but in an observation that Frederick Law Olmsted had made during his travels through Texas in the mid-nineteenth century. Quibbles about provenance aside, this connection between parks and charm has made its way into virtually every public relations campaign San Antonio has mounted. This is because the parks' aesthetic values have been linked consistently with an economic good—the increase of tourism. No visitors' guidebook or tourist brochure from either the nineteenth or twentieth century is complete without reference to the fact that San Antonio was, as a 1908 guide declared, "often called the City of Parks on account of the many ornamental parks and plazas with which it is adorned." But their value is not simply ornamental, at least not according to a late-twentieth-century promotion: "Our parks are among the first things visitors see," it advised, "and they continue to make a memorable impression."[4]

Parks and public plazas have also served more immediate purposes. Many cities found that parks set outside of the central core could be valuable vehicles for promoting urban real estate and boosting neighborhood property values. Land speculators in Chicago sought state legislation in the 1870s to allow the formation of local park districts. Their goal was public investment, albeit through special districts, that would add to the desirability of their subdivisions and the greater sale of lots. "After the Civil War the fame of Haussman's park and boulevard system in Paris reached [Chicago] that was seeking new outlets for fashionable expenditure, and the reports of the rapid rise in land values in the vicinity of Central Park in New York excited the imagination of real estate operators."[5]

San Antonio real-estate developers sought to employ parks in a similar fashion, albeit with the cost borne by the city government. Their enthusiastic support of the first major twentieth-century bond issue, the *San Antonio Express* explained in 1919, was tied to their understanding of the role parks played in boosting the local quality of life: "A city without parks is like a house without windows." Their support was driven, too, by a desire to enhance the city's national status: "The members of the Real Estate Board realized the benefits to be derived and soon helped put the bond issue in order to place San Antonio where she belonged—in the front rank of American cities."[6]

Green space also offered a set of political advantages. Most of the elements of public capital investment were expensive and limited to particular needs and locales. The quest for flood control in San Antonio, for example, required all parts of the city to support and invest in a dam and detention basin that offered aid largely to the downtown.[7] New bridges over the river and creeks were dictated by topography rather than merely neighborhood desires. By contrast, parks were both divisible and distributable. They could be spread around to all areas of the city at relatively modest cost. But, perhaps most important, they could be granted or withheld for purely political reasons and therefore offered a means by which certain neighborhoods could be enhanced and their residents rewarded for their electoral support.

Yet the provision of parks was neither regular nor equitable. Briefly put, it appears that throughout most of its history the city has been indifferent to park development. This indifference has had a cumulative effect, one the city's Parks

Master Plan of 1964 laid out in some detail. Although the report acknowledged that there were a host of public areas in and around the downtown core, and that the system boasted some large facilities, notably Brackenridge Park, it also pointed out that by comparison to other Texas cities San Antonio had a strikingly small parks system. Its 4.6 park acres per thousand in 1964 placed it well below Dallas (18.5 per thousand), Fort Worth (13.6) and Austin (12.6). The city compared favorably within the state only to Houston, with but 3.7 acres per thousand. In terms of total acreage, however, San Antonio fared far worse. With only slightly over 2,900 acres of public park area, the Alamo City had less than one-quarter the acreage of Dallas, and less than Houston, with 3,800 acres.[8]

The city's relatively modest commitment to parks is even more obvious when set against the national standards it has long held up as a goal. San Antonio's total of 4.6 acres per thousand people was less than half of the national standard of 10 acres per thousand. Even within that total, only a portion of these lands had actually been developed for recreational use. Worse, the geographical distribution was spotty: "Several sections of the city have no parks at all," the 1964 city plan noted, and it was clear to its authors that the situation probably would not improve. "Choice and logical sites have been taken by private development, leaving undesirable or poorly oriented lands as the only available locations."[9]

There have been exceptions to this legacy of indifference, moments in the city's past when investment in park development was a high priority. This was especially true in the period between the late 1910s and early 1930s. But these exceptions underscore an important point. The creation of parks in San Antonio is a direct reflection of the character of local politics and fiscal preferences and of the city's racial and ethnic electoral mix, and is the outcome of a widely varying set of political regimes over the twentieth century. It turns out that the needs of local voters, not those of tourists, are the key to understanding this "City of Parks."

Parks in Time

The early history of park development in San Antonio seems rich. The city could, and frequently did, boast that it was home to one of the oldest municipally owned parks in the United States, San Pedro Park, second in age only to the venerable Boston Commons. By the late nineteenth century it could also lay claim to a sizable number of plazas and parks that dotted the downtown area. Then there was its crown jewel, Brackenridge Park, acquired in 1899, and containing at that time more than 250 acres studded with "fine oak, hackberry, pecan, cypress and other trees," through which "the beautiful San Antonio River serpentines its way." Together, these natural pleasure spots, with their "delightful shade" and "pretty lakes," soothed the harried urbanite. This was, it seemed, a city that appreciated its green, open space.[10]

It ought to appreciate it, for rarely was San Antonio responsible for the establishment of its early parklands. Most of the downtown open areas that were (and remain) central to its spatial design—including Alamo, Main, and Military Plazas—were lands that the Spanish, following the edicts of the Law of Indes, had set aside in the eighteenth century. San Pedro Springs Park was another gift of the far-sighted Spanish urban planners. Rather than build on these early gifts, however, the city's government actually decreased their number and size. In the post–Civil War era especially, a series of badly strapped city governments either sold off portions of the Spanish land grants to pay their bills or lost title to them through legal challenges. In the early twentieth century this process took another turn when City Hall was built on Military Plaza, largely eliminating it as an open space. All in all, San Antonio hardly had a sterling record of parks management.[11]

The city's record of maintenance in the late nineteenth century was no better. By 1897 San Pedro Springs had fallen into disrepair, the whole resembling a "country graveyard." It was overgrown with "rank weeds and filled with refuse of every kind," the San Antonio Express reported; its "fences and bridges are rotten and rickety and what little is left of the once beautiful and luxuriant shrubbery is bedraggled and forlorn looking." Unable to maintain its existing parks, the city could also not afford to purchase additional sites. Instead, the system grew through donations, the most significant of which, Brackenridge and Mahncke Parks, totaling nearly 350 acres, were the gift of one donor, George W. Brackenridge; these acquisitions more than doubled San Antonio's then-total park acreage. The system had grown in spite of the city.[12]

The antipathy of San Antonio's political and civic leaders to investment in public parks continued well into the twentieth century. From 1900 to 1910, a time that William H. Wilson has described as "the heyday of the City Beautiful movement," when "middle- and upper-middle class Americans attempt[ed] to refashion their cities into beautiful, functional entities," San Antonio mayors prided themselves on making do with less. In his annual message of 1904,

Mayor Marshall Hicks described the city's "appalling financial condition" and patted himself on the back for having reduced the city's debt over the previous year. He went on to describe the work on the city's parks: "Improvements of an artistic nature are being added as rapidly as the meager financial allowance will permit."[13]

The city's public investment fortunes were little changed by the end of the decade. In his 1910 report Mayor Bryan Callaghan II listed a host of street and bridge improvements—but nary a park—and concluded, "[A]ll this without any increase in the tax-rate, or the issuance of a single bond, in fact the tax-rate has been steadily decreased, while the public improvements have been kept up." The mayor went on to compare San Antonio's frugality to other Texas entities:

> No City in the State has as low a tax rate and every City that is under the new form of government, known as the "Commission Government," not only has a much higher rate of taxation, but have issued hundreds of thousands of dollars in bonds, in order to accomplish what we of San Antonio have done with low taxation and no bond issue.[14]

Civic frugality no doubt aided Callaghan's electoral success. But it came at a price. As other Texas cities began to invest in economic advance and civic improvement, San Antonio lagged behind. In 1913 Census Bureau figures on city debt placed San Antonio at $18.55 per capita, while Dallas stood at $42.88, Austin at $73.71, and Houston at $97.23. San Antonio's limited debt and investment reflected a reluctance to tax, a political machine that dealt in jobs and contracts rather than park land, and a community ethos that valued the private over the public. New parks were not esteemed as a grand betterment. They nonetheless had a particularistic value, as a means of enhancing outlying real-estate development in a city bereft of public investment. Thus in the late 1910s, there was a spate of park acquisition, with six new parks added to the urban landscape. The three largest sites—Roosevelt, Elmendorf, and Wood-lawn Lake—accounted for more than 90 percent of the new lands, but housing developers donated each one to the city as enhancements for their speculative developments. In the first twenty years of the twentieth century, then, the city managed to purchase a mere sixteen acres of parkland.[15]

This inactivity is striking, for in the next decade San Antonio would,

Table 4.1. San Antonio park acreage, by acquisition date

Period	Acreage	Total (percentage)
Before 1900	509.27	13.6%
1901–1909	0.00	0.0
1910–1919	120.38	3.2
1920–1929	1081.58	29.0
1930–1939	9.51	0.2
1940–1949	355.14	9.5
1950–1959	96.24	2.5
1960–1969	1563.23	41.8
Total	3735.35	100.0

Table 4.2. San Antonio park acreage, by acquisition date (neighborhood and community parks only)

Period	Acreage	Total (percentage)
Before 1900	44.57	12.2%
1901–1909	0.00	0.0
1910–1919	58.38	16.0
1920–1929	71.58	19.6
1930–1939	9.51	2.6
1940–1949	8.69	2.4
1950–1959	96.24	26.4
1960–1969	76.17	20.8
Total	365.14	100.0

through the selling of bonds, buy nearly 1,100 acres of land, more than doubling the size of its park system (see Tables 4.1 and 4.2). Why was the city only then able and willing to invest in park development, and to expand the system so rapidly, something it had been incapable of doing in the preceding decades?

The transformation was heavily dependent on a critical change in the structure of governance. In 1914 San Antonio had adopted the commission form of government and explicitly designated one of the five members as "parks commissioner." Thus parks received a distinct and visible voice within the legislative body. The commission form was notorious for its tendency to functional logrolling and political trading among commissioners. In San Antonio's case, the result was to elevate the issue of park investment and to insure that parks (and their commissioner) received a share of the capital investment funds that the bond issues would provide.[16]

The reliance on bond funding was an essential element in building public support for new parks acquisitions. Rather than rely on donations or on its general fund to increase the number of urban parks and recreational spaces, the city government decided to float a series of bonds, the initial offering of which was voted on in 1919, and which authorized the spending of $200,000 for parks. The electorate supported the park bonds by a substantial four-to-one margin, and this victory was soon followed by a number of others: In 1923 the citizens voted to sell $100,000 worth of bonds for parks; in 1926 the figure rose to $150,000; two years later, separate measures for parks in general and for Exposition Park in particular totaled $650,000; and in 1930, in what would prove to be the last successful parks bond for three decades, the tab soared to $700,000. San Antonio had gone on a spending spree (see Table 4.3).

The city's political leadership cashed in on these electoral successes, as each victory built upon the other. When the 1919 bond passed, the mayor and his administration were emboldened to propose another; when it too passed, they proposed a third, and so on. And with each success the dollars requested to support the acquisition of parks grew proportionally. How extraordinary this set of initiatives was can be seen by comparing them to those that would

Table 4.3. San Antonio parks bond proposal, by year

Year	Parks Amount	Outcome
1919	$ 200,000	Passed
1923	100,000	Passed
1926	150,000	Passed
1928	650,000	Passed
1930	700,000	Passed
1935	65,000	Passed
1936	119,000	Failed
1945	325,000	Failed
1955	1,600,000	Failed
1961	500,000	Passed
1964	1,585,000	Passed
1970	6,492,000	Passed

follow. There was not another successful bond measure for parks until 1961, when one for $500,000 secured voters' approval; this was considerably less than the value of the 1930 bond, however, especially with inflation factored in. Moreover, the total city spending in the 1920s reached $1.8 million, a figure that dwarfed all parks spending until 1970, when a bond for approximately $6.5 million passed. By any standard, the 1920s were a remarkable moment in the city's fiscal and political commitment to park development.

The cumulative effect of those electoral victories cannot by itself explain the political success of these bond offerings. Part of the explanation as well lies in the rhetoric the city employed to sell the bonds. Always linked to a series of other "permanent public improvements," as their supporters liked to call them, they could be trumpeted as integral to "community progress and prosperity." By voting for these bonds, the voters were assured, "San Antonio shall keep her place in the procession; shall go on building up a bigger, better, busier city."[17]

They were told, too, in language that would have made George Babbitt blush, that such progress was critical. Their votes would determine whether San Antonio would descend to the status of "an overgrown village" or remain a "go-ahead city." San Antonio "should not stand still," the Express-News editorialized. "To stand still is to stagnate. To stagnate is to decay." To judge from the large majorities some of these bonds secured, few wanted the River City to meet that dreaded fate.[18]

Voters were not simply persuaded by the rhetoric appeal of progressive Babbittry, important though that language was in shaping the public's reaction to the bond measures. Its response was influenced, too, by another form of appeal, one tailored to a peculiar quirk in the nature of San Antonio politics in the 1920s. As the promotional language of the 1919 election indicated, the park bonds were particularly aimed at the city's working class. Parks are "the poor man's estate," one of the press releases touted, and as such they are "vital to [the] health and well being of the laboring people."[19]

This appeal to the advantages green grass held for workers' physical welfare was paired with a detailed discussion of who would ultimately pay for these parks and other improvements. Parks, the campaign rhetoric declared, would not impair the workers' financial health. "The small property owner is let off easy," one newspaper that supported the bond issues noted. "His pro rate tax is small. His returns from general improvements are large." Who then was left to pay? "The big property holder bears the brunt" of these new taxes, "but there has been no complaint on that score, and there will be none. The men who have large holdings know that the bond issue was the proper thing." The business and commercial elite would fund the people's playgrounds, if only indirectly.[20]

Politics, Race, and Distribution

How significant this appeal to class politics was in the selling of bonds emerges in an analysis of the geographical placement of the city's new parks and in the demographic characteristics of the bonds' most fervent supporters. The boom in the city's parkland acquisition and development in the 1920s took on a very clear spatial dimension. New parks were quite concentrated in one area of the city—the black East Side. One was developed there in 1919, and another three in the following decade; an additional East Side park was acquired in 1931. By contrast, only one major park development came on the city's North Side, largely populated by middle- and upper-income whites; that park, Olmos Basin, primarily served flood-control and stormwater-retention purposes, in which recreation and play were quite secondary gains; in any event, it remained largely undeveloped until after the Second World War. The city's West Side had received a large number of new parks in the late 1910s— one West Side census tract was the recipient of two parks in 1917, and a third park in 1918—but developers had donated most of these lands to the city to encourage the growth of white, middle-class suburban tracts. The city only developed one park in a West Side working-class district during the period of the greatest investment in park expansion, and that park was not designated for Hispanics, who constituted the vast majority of the West Side population, but for blacks only.[21]

This geographic and racial pattern suggests that park acquisition was not aimed at a broad distribution of these benefits. The process of city government decisionmaking instead resulted in a remarkable concentration of spending and public facilities, a concentration that is particularly intriguing when the distributive character of park development during these years is analyzed in demographic terms.

The first reliable small-area statistics for San Antonio come from the 1960 census. A review of descriptive evidence indicates that these figures provide a reasonable basis for defining demographic characteristics rather early in the century. We have compared those tracts that received new parks during this period with all other tracts in the city's pre-1940 boundaries to provide some sense of distributive equity.

In terms of most measures, those neighborhoods where parks were developed look very much like the balance of the city. For example, the 1960 median family income of park tracts was $4,590. Nonpark tracts had a slightly lower income—$4,049. A second measure, the percentage of housing units rented (rather than owned), indicates that home ownership was more common in new park tracts. The park tracts averaged 38.9 percent rental, while all other tracts averaged just over 50 percent. This relationship is in keeping with the development trends of the 1920s, for the city clearly sought to maximize its park acquisition investment by purchasing cheaper land at the edge of urban development.

Precisely on which edge of San Antonio, then laid out in a six-mile square, these parks were sited emerges in an analysis of a key demographic indicator— the city's African American population percentage. Tracts that saw park acquisition from 1919 to 1931 averaged 20.9 percent black. The nonpark tracts averaged less than half that—8.9 percent black. This sharp racial difference indicates that park development was highly concentrated in and around the city's predominantly African American residential areas, largely on the East Side. At a time when racial segregation and differentiation were the norm, the political process provided an unusual level of public benefit to the city's black population.

Votes and Benefits

The 1928 bond vote, for instance, reveals an aspect of African American electoral power. All the $4.8 million in bonds proposed were endorsed by the voters, generally by margins of about four to one. But, as the San Antonio Light noted, "the strongest vote for the bonds was in precinct 54, a negro district on East Commerce Street that went 157 for the bond to 1 against." The predictability of this kind of support would prove all the more important when, as in 1930, the city vote was quite close. That year the bond measure ran into sharp opposition from largely white, antitax forces, and as a consequence this particular election drew the largest number of voters in city history. When the vote was counted—and officially recounted—the tally stood at almost a dead heat across the city, with 17,595 for and 17,335 against. The suburban, North Side white neighborhoods were solidly arrayed against the measure; the antibond forces carried 52 of the 94 precincts in which votes were cast. But in the predominantly African American precinct 54, the vote stood at 238 for to 93 against. Although this was less lopsided than the 1928 vote, it is nonetheless clear that the votes of the black community played a critical role in passing this, and other, bond issues.[22]

Those African American votes were no less visible in the incumbent commissioners' reelection efforts. In the 1927 city election Mayor John W. Tobin was re-elected with more than 80 percent of the citywide vote. But in East Side precinct 54 he garnered 94 percent of the vote, and in neighboring precinct 55 that proportion exceeded 97 percent, margins that had remained fairly consistent for much of the decade, making these votes vital to the continued success of the commission form of government. As such, when the commissioners and their media proponents extolled the virtues of parks for the laboring classes, they had a particular (and very loyal) constituency in mind.[23]

The reciprocal relationship between African American voters and machine politicians was no secret to contemporary San Antonians. "For many years, every San Antonio election was swung by the Negro vote controlled by the late Charlie Bellinger, the mahogany-colored impresario of gambling and politics," journalist Ralph Maitland observed in 1939. "Negro voting and Bellinger's rule were tolerated by a corrupt city machine only because a large Negro vote, swung in the right direction, gave absolute assurance that the machine candidates would be elected." Bellinger was more than tolerated. He was an essential player in San Antonio politics from the mid-1920s until his death in 1937, so much so that Maitland could argue that Bellinger was "the man who told the boys how to run the city." This was an exaggeration, but it illuminates the perception of Bellinger's power and place in the city's political arena.[24]

It may have been precisely Bellinger's political effectiveness that so unnerved Ralph J. Bunche who, in his encyclopedic volume, *The Political Status of the Negro in the Age of FDR*, lashed out at Bellinger, calling him a "great menace and harm to Negro progress." Bunche suggested that whatever benefits that blacks received in San Antonio had been "incidental," and not at all due to Bellinger's political activity but to the "traditionally friendly" attitude of the city's whites to its African American population. Friendship had little to do with the scale of public investment on the East Side, however. Again, journalist Maitland captured the import of Bellinger's political organization: "Through the power of his organized votes, he forced city officials to give special attention to the Negro quarter," and the effect of that attention was plain: "Today that section of town is comparatively well paved; has adequate light, water, and sewer service; and enjoys numerous public schools, parks and playgrounds, fire and police stations, a public library and a public auditorium." A testament to Bellinger's acumen came in 1937 when he was imprisoned for tax evasion.

His legal troubles prompted then-mayor of San Antonio C. K. Quin, and the city's district attorney, Phil Shook, to travel to Washington, D.C., to seek and secure a federal pardon for the East Side powerbroker. Even the Roosevelt administration understood Bellinger's significance in south Texas politics.[25]

Although African American votes helped determine public spending priorities during the 1920s and 1930s and left a lasting legacy in terms of the siting of numerous neighborhood parks on the East Side, the public products of ensuing years were markedly different in form and location. The East Side received no new parks after 1932 until the acquisition of the three-acre Dignowity Park in 1951, and it was the last park there for nearly another twenty years. That inactivity, and the sharp decline in minority electoral power it represented, can be explained by a sea change in city politics that also occurred in 1951. That year San Antonio's governmental structure was revised from a commission form of governance to a city council–city manager. The rise in the mid-fifties of the Good Government League (GGL) to political dominance of this new system, when linked with the GGL's successfully altering of the city charter so that all members of the council were elected at-large, meant that the white North Side, with its preponderance of the electorate, now controlled City Hall. An indication of this transformation was that there were no new parks constructed in an East Side neighborhood until 1970, with the opening of the J Street Park, followed by Martin Luther King Park in 1973. Yet as these sites' development was largely funded with federal dollars from the Department of Housing and Urban Development, their location revealed the federal government's priorities and commitments more than local ones.

Parks and Politics

The history of park development in San Antonio reflects a number of broad themes, many of which are repeated in other cities of Texas and the Sunbelt. Despite the image of public amenity and green space often presented to the city's visitors, San Antonio took only the most modest public initiative in developing parks and open space until the 1920s. The city's public spending was limited and constrained, although the community benefited from the generosity of a few of its well-heeled citizens. The 1920s brought a dramatic change in both politics and public investment. The rise of a city-county "ring," the political entrepreneurship of Mayor John W. Tobin and his successor, C. M. Chambers, and the pivotal role that Charles Bellinger played in swinging elections, resulted in an unprecedented level of bond proposals and repeated victories at the polls. The physical outcomes of those electoral successes were new parks, streets, flood-control systems, the improvement of the San Antonio River, and a host of other public facilities. Ironically, it took a local politics that professional politicians dominated, a dominance predicated on the votes of the city's working classes and minorities, to generate neighborhood parks and other public improvements. In the 1920s and early 1930s, parks made for good politics.

It is significant that parks fared decidedly less well in the aftermath of yet another change in governmental form to a city manager plan in 1951. Four years later, for example, a parks bond issue went down to overwhelming defeat. In 1961 a quite modest issue succeeded. But it was not until the mid-1960s that a parks bond issue exceeding the value of the 1930 bond was successful. And when the major park improvement bond proposal finally surfaced in 1964, the Good Government League, "its hegemony so complete it merited the label of 'machine' in its own right," set its size and contents. The GGL's agenda did not include developing neighborhood parks within minority communities, but instead focused spending on the central business district, there to be developed a new convention center, and extensive facilities to accommodate a projected world's fair, known as Hemisfair '68. These, and additional elements of downtown urban renewal projects, absorbed a disproportionate amount of the city's capital spending from 1955 to 1977, accounting for more than $120 million, or about 37 percent. Spending on parks, by contrast, totaled approximately $40 million, about 12 percent of the budget; these figures for parks are deceptive, however, for much of these funds were spent on central core-related projects, such as the ongoing, extensive, and expensive refurbishing of the city's famed River Walk (see Table 4.4).[26]

The GGL approach to park development came with an equally significant change in political rhetoric. The proposed civic center and Hemisfair '68, for instance, were seen as lures for a much wider audience than that of the local residents who had been the focus of the commissioners' political agenda in the 1920s. The Civic Center facilities, the business elite and their political representatives in the GGL felt certain, would build bridges to South and Central America, making San Antonio an international crossroads, an internationalism that would lure tourists from far and wide. From the architectural dreams of its developers—grand buildings to suggest the city's budding monumentality—to the central, downtown siting of the Hemisfair, a new political and social vision had taken hold.[27]

The black community of San Antonio was well aware of these changes in

Table 4.4. San Antonio capital spending, by major purpose, 1955–1977

Purpose	Total amount[a]	Total[b]
Convention center	$ 22.23	6.67%
Urban redevelopment	99.88	29.92
Fire stations	3.39	1.02
Libraries	2.24	0.67
Parks	40.68	12.19
Streets and highways	59.56	17.84
Storm drainage	54.94	16.46
Other (including airport)	50.94	15.26
Total	$333.86	100.00

[a]In millions
[b]Percentage

the city's investment strategy and in the political agenda they reflected. The transition from neighborhood-based politics to that of the metropolis and the central business district could not help but be detrimental to black interests, the local chapter of the NAACP concluded. "The City Council of San Antonio has failed to give assurances," it declared, that "the income producing benefits that are to be derived from the bond issue, if passed, will be shared indiscriminately by all citizens." Moreover, its leadership was deeply concerned that these public facilities would be segregated along racial lines, and therefore strongly opposed the 1964 bond measure. As chapter president Harry Burns argued, integration in San Antonio was "superficial," and the NAACP's opposition to these bonds "was the only one we could take because of the [segregationist] position of the council." Although its fears about overt segregation at Hemisfair went unrealized, those worries speak to the racially exclusive character of politics in the GGL era, as well as to the recognition that the subsequent massive infusion of funds into the central core represented a different conception of community improvement and benefit, one that deliberately diminished the electoral influence of the city's minority populations.[28]

This decline was manifest most clearly when the citizens of San Antonio went to the polls to vote on the 1964 bond measure. It carried in the largely Anglo north and northcentral suburban districts and was heavily supported in the Hispanic West and South Sides precincts. The returns from the East Side, on the other hand, tell a different story. Black-dominated precincts, which in the end supported the bond measures, were nonetheless the most negative in the city, a telling comment on the shifting political tides that swirled around park development in San Antonio.[29]

The tide turned once again when in the early 1970s a federal court order forced the city to revise its charter and institute district-based city council elections. This broke the GGL's hold on power. The new voting patterns insured that Hispanics and African Americans secured seats on the new council, where they gained a greater voice in how city and federal funds were distributed. Only with this dramatic alteration in political structure would it be possible for an East Side politician later to think of himself as a "parks guru" and to act as if neighborhood parks were essential environmental amenities *and* vital political assets.

5

✳

David R. Johnson,
Derral Cheatwood, and
Benjamin Bradshaw

The Landscape of Death

Homicide as a Health Problem

Although it is the rarest crime, homicide simultaneously fascinates and repels contemporary Americans. Public interest ranges from rapt attention to "cop shows" where death always plays a prominent role to widespread handwringing over the "epidemic" of homicide over the last thirty years. The finality of homicide lies at the heart of our ambivalence. Violent death is irreparable, and the costs of even a single mundane domestic homicide reverberate both within and well beyond a victim's immediate family. Whatever roles the victims played in life— parent, relative, neighbor, wage earner, citizen— dies with them. Homicide thus affects the basis of the family and civil society, and when it becomes too widespread in particular communities like inner-city slums it blights not just the safety but the future of those neighborhoods.

Because it has so many costs, and has been a major public concern since at least the 1960s, a wide range of researchers have applied a variety of theories to the problem of homicide in the hope that their work will lead to policies that will reduce, if not eliminate, this crime. The effort to

treat homicide as a special type of health epidemic is one of the more prominent of these approaches.[1] Although health paradigms may in the end prove
more fruitful as insightful metaphors than as fundamental explanations for
homicide, the application of the epidemic framework raises the interesting
question whether a comparison with other diseases within a localized environment might also contribute to our understanding of patterns of homicide.

With that idea in mind, we have been exploring comparative historical patterns of homicide and disease in San Antonio. Specifically, we are examining
the relationships that may exist between public interventions in the infectious
disease environment and changes in the patterns of specific infectious diseases,
and homicide. Our approach relies very considerably on a historical compo-
nent because we believe that the relatively brief time periods encompassed by
the vast majority of homicide and public-health studies raise serious questions
about the general applicability of those studies. Their shorter time frames may
miss the importance of significant changes in the nature of the environments
in which disease and crime exist.

Historical Processes and Homicide

Historians working on homicide have conveniently, if coincidentally, approached this topic from the perspective of the long-term effects of public intervention. Borrowing liberally from the sociologist Norbert Elias, they argue
that a broad, long-term civilizing process promoted by an increasingly effective
centralized state and by the effects of urbanization and industrialization have
essentially created greater personal discipline and lower homicide rates over
time. According to this paradigm, individuals and groups who have been relatively excluded from this disciplining process have retained higher rates of violent and homicidal behavior.[2]

Despite the unfortunate use of the term *civilizing,* and the troubling implications it suggests for the applicability of such theories to society (are high-of-
fender populations "uncivilized"?), the core of this concept seems sound if we
understand "civilization" as an ongoing process being negotiated by all parties
involved, rather than as some platonic ideal currently reached by those formu-
lating the theories. In this regard, it is better to understand the basic concept of
"civilizing" as one of "investment" or "enfranchisement." Both of these terms
capture some essential features of this outlook.

To enfranchise is more than merely allowing one to vote; it is also to become a member of the body politic, suggesting that the person or population so enfranchised is an integral part of the working society. From the perspective of the larger society, extending membership to an individual or a group should have some benefit, perhaps in the form of altered behavior, for that society. If one is a good citizen and works hard within society's rules, then the individual or population can expect a proportionate return from that society for their contributions and good citizenship. In short, when any population, minority or otherwise, feels that it is genuinely a part of the community and its members believe that their investments in citizenship will pay off for them, they will act in ways that are socially adaptive, that add up to "civility" and create a civil state in the classic sense. Likewise, when they do not believe they are a genuine part of the body politic, they need not feel they have an obligation to that state. And, if as individuals they see no possibility of a realistic economic payoff from proper, law-abiding conduct, they will not necessarily follow that line of behavior. Finally, differences in the structure and character of a local state, and in its urbanization and economic development, differentially affect opportunities for enfranchisement. Some forms of a local state, such as those governed by American political machines, offer only selective opportunities for enfranchisement. That selectivity can affect the actual as well as the perceived sense of connectedness to a larger body politic. Further complicating matters, a local state's role in promoting or ignoring economic development and urbanization can affect not only the general sense of enfranchisement but also both the physical and social environments within which social pathologies occur. Some social pathologies are more amenable to public interventions than others. All of this suggests that there are practical limitations to both Elias's theory and to the disease paradigm for homicide. It also suggests that the best way to understand fully patterns of homicide and disease, and policies that may affect these pathologies, is to consider the historical evolution of the social and physical environment in which they occur.

We have chosen to compare the history and incidence of infant diarrhea mortality and homicide for the period from 1935 to 1984 to examine how public interventions that take the form of enfranchisement enrich our conception of public-health problems. The social geography of these two pathologies are quite similar. They tend to be concentrated among certain types of urban populations, and in certain types of urban environments. Despite those similarities, however, our data indicate that each "disease" is differentially affected by public intervention. It seems to have very significant effects on the incidence of infant diarrhea mortality, but very little effect on long-term trends in homicide; there is some evidence that public interventions may have the perverse result of indirectly contributing to an increase in homicide.

The San Antonio Environment Prior to 1950

In the mid-1930s a political machine dominated San Antonio. It combined corruption and indifference to critical public issues with a devotion to perpetuating itself by manipulating the electoral process.[3] Although this situation hardly made San Antonio unique among American cities at the time, the machine's control of the local state apparatus had important differential effects on the city's ability to deal with some of the more devastating problems within its physical and social environment.

Long before the 1930s, San Antonio had become sharply divided along ethnic, racial, and class lines. Shortly after the Civil War the West Side emerged as a Mexican American ghetto. A predominately black neighborhood evolved on the city's East Side by World War I. Middle- and upper-class white San Antonians lived primarily on the North Side, while working-class whites concentrated south of downtown.[4]

The local economy, whose prosperity might have ameliorated these social divisions, had begun to stagnate even before the Depression. San Antonio had emerged as Texas's largest city by 1910 on the strength of an impressive growth spurt fueled by the arrival in the late nineteenth century of a series of railroads that transformed it into a major commercial center serving the agricultural hinterland of central and south Texas. World War I fostered a boomtown mentality that obscured a fundamental shift in the state's urban network, as both Dallas and Houston launched public-private partnerships in major city-building initiatives rooted in industrial and natural resource development. Although federal subsidies flowing through three major military bases helped sustain San Antonio's economy, its business and political leadership was too adverse to risk to emulate Dallas or Houston, causing the city's economy to stagnate in the face of intense interurban competition. By the late 1920s pecan shelling had become San Antonio's largest business, dramatically demonstrating the city's weak industrial base and its indifference to the challenges of competing with its major rivals.[5]

Plagued by a moribund economy and deeply divided socially, San Antonio was ill prepared to absorb the shock of the major population shift that began with and accelerated during the Mexican Revolution. Thousands of Mexicans, the vast majority abjectly poor, sought refuge in the city and in the process created a demographic revolution in the composition of San Antonio's population. By 1940 Anglos were no longer the largest ethnic group in the city, having declined from 60 percent in 1900 to only 47 percent. African Americans also lost ground, declining from 14 percent to 7 percent of the population in the same period. In the meantime, the Mexican presence increased from 25 percent to 46 percent.[6]

San Antonio's preexisting social geography channeled this vast new population into the West Side, where the recent arrivals mixed with established residents in a four-square-mile area containing some of the worst slum conditions in the nation. Thousands of people lived packed into corrals, small houses (in reality more like cubicles) built around a central courtyard. Public services were either completely inadequate or nonexistent. As many as thirty families often shared a single water faucet; pit toilets unconnected to a city sewer system provided for sanitary needs; gas and electricity service were alien to the area. Residents subsisted by a combination of unskilled work (especially in pecan shelling) and migratory labor. Annual family incomes, in a city that paid these workers between twenty-seven and fifty-eight cents a day, frequently were less than $250.[7]

The combination of overcrowded slum housing and grossly deficient public services created a festering breeding ground for disease. Health studies in 1926 and 1934 found predictably appalling death rates from a variety of causes, but especially from postneonatal diarrhea and tuberculosis; in fact, San Antonio's death rate from diarrhea for 1934 was the highest in the United States.[8] And there was no doubt that such a high mortality rate was almost but not quite entirely a problem confined to the West Side. The mortality rate among Mexican-origin children was 48 per 1,000; among the Anglo population the rate was only 7 per 1,000.[9]

San Antonio's African American population did not have a great deal to fear from diarrhea mortality or, for that matter, from any other environmentally related disease. At first glance, this is surprising because this minority shared much of the same social and economic status of Mexican Americans. Confined principally to their East Side neighborhood through social prejudice, and suffering from employment discrimination so typical of this era, the city's African Americans were not inherently better positioned to fend off the dire effects of a disease-ridden environment than were Mexican Americans. Yet diarrhea did not stalk the East Side.

The reason for this unexpected boon provides a case study of the interconnections between enfranchisement and public intervention that can create beneficial consequences regarding some types of social pathology. Simply put, in an era of bigotry, poll taxes, and the all-white primary, San Antonio's political machine relied for much of its success on the votes of African Americans. Indeed, it appears that African Americans held the balance of power in local politics.

Why that should be so had to do with the twin issues of voter participation and community cohesion. Although the Mexican American population had increased dramatically as refugees sought safety from the upheavals of the Mexican Revolution, they had not been able to capitalize at the polls on their numerical strength. Their poverty and the large proportion of migrant workers among them (upwards of a quarter of the entire population) no doubt contributed to their political disorganization, but the absence of leadership focusing on local issues also did not help. Middle-class Mexican Americans were a tiny group on the West Side, and in this era many of them devoted most of their political attention to the situation in Mexico. Deprived of either community or political organizations that could advocate for them, most Mexican Americans lacked the incentive to pay their poll taxes or to vote. The political machine did provide some patronage jobs for the West Side, but not enough to spur the development of a reliable following among these potential voters.[10]

Through the accidents of local politics, black San Antonians were far better organized than their Mexican American neighbors. Machine politicians, who recognized that they needed a reliable source of votes to offset a divided white vote to win elections, actively cultivated influential leaders on the East Side beginning in the early 1920s. Although several black ministers made significant contributions to the creation of a reliable East Side voting bloc, Charles Bellinger was the most important link between the community and the machine. Bellinger was a gambler, saloon owner, and real-estate dealer with connections in bootlegging and prostitution. During the 1920s he combined business and politics to become the dominant figure on the East Side.[11]

Bellinger's cooperation with the local machine partially enfranchised his fellow African Americans. In return for his loyally producing a reliable vote for its candidates at elections, the machine spent considerable sums on a variety of improvements for the East Side. Surveying the results of this bargain in the late 1930s, a reporter concluded that "the colored section of the town is well paved, well serviced with light, water and sewer connections and has up-to-date schools, station houses, fire houses, parks, a modern public library, playgrounds, and a handsome public auditorium."[12]

This litany missed one extremely important benefit that Bellinger's political bargain gave the East Side. It, unlike "Mexican Town," was not a sinkhole of pestilence because African Americans enjoyed the kinds of city services that created a healthier environment. The most direct environmental causes of infant diarrhea are poor water quality and poor sanitation. Improving the infrastructure on the East Side had a direct effect on water quality and sanitation, and, as a consequence, had a direct impact on infant diarrhea deaths in that area. Proper sewage disposal and an adequate water supply meant that human waste did not contaminate the East Side. For example, in 1935, when 126 infants of Mexican origin died of diarrhea, there were only two such deaths among black infants. Bellinger's bargain therefore provides a vivid demonstration of the benefits that can accrue to a population group through enfranchisement.

Unfortunately, that same bargain also demonstrated that partial enfranchisement that improved the physical environment, not surprisingly, was insufficient to promote "civilized" behavior. Homicide rates in both African and Mexican American neighborhoods were appallingly high, and in fact the black rate was much higher than the Mexican. White male San Antonians in 1940 had a homicide rate of 8.67; for Mexican Americans is was 30.75, and for blacks it was 57.65. Clearly, adequate public services could not by themselves create the kind of social environment that discouraged violence. If that had been the case, the East Side would have been as free of homicide as it was of diarrhea.

The reasons for this high rate among blacks remain debatable, while Mexican American homicide is even less well understood. For our purposes, the extant literature on both groups provides an interesting context to understand the complexities of enfranchisement in a specific urban environment. That literature treats high homicide rates among these minorities as either a function of their history or their culture (although the two may be indistinguishable for analytical purposes, given the complex interrelationships between historical development and changes in any cultural constructs). Southern blacks and Mexican immigrants shared a common socioeconomic background rooted in rural, peasant lifestyles. Many anthropological, demographic, and historical studies have demonstrated that rural homicide rates are consistently much higher than urban rates.[13] Indeed, these findings form much of the basis for theories concerning the civilizing effects of state power, urbanization, and industrialization on behavior.

While there is irrefutable evidence that San Antonio's minorities suffered from much more homicidal behavior than the Anglo majority, we cannot yet provide any definite explanation for those behaviors. Given that such a large proportion of San Antonio's Mexican American population had arrived only after 1910, we are tempted to speculate that cultural and historical patterns of behavior within this group had some effect on the homicide rate in the West Side. Since black San Antonians' share of the total population had declined significantly during the same time period, however, it is unlikely that inmigration could have been a source for sustaining their violent behavior. It may be that norms governing violent behavior had become part of the community prior to this era. Whatever the explanation, it is clear that neither minority group had achieved sufficient levels of enfranchisement to moderate its homicidal behavior.

Modifying San Antonio's Environment

Beginning in the mid-1930s a variety of public interventions slowly altered the city's pathological environment. Since these interventions were designed to improve the physical environment, the West Side would be the principal beneficiary of most of this activity. Black San Antonians, ironically, would enjoy fewer benefits from these improvements and, indeed, with the decline of their political power due to the decaying political machine, the East Side's physical condition would deteriorate. In general, these improvements would have considerable effect on infant diarrhea mortality rates, but none on homicide.

Although San Antonio's medical community had warned of the dangers from infectious diseases for years, the long struggle to improve the local environment did not begin seriously until Father Carmine Antonio Tranchese, a Jesuit priest working in the heart of the worst West Side slums, began to agitate for change in the early 1930s. With the help of Maury Maverick, who won election to Congress in 1936, Tranchese became the central figure in a political battle to bring federal public housing to San Antonio. The San Antonio Housing Authority, established in 1937, received authorization to build four projects (all segregated by race), two of which were meant for the West Side. With Tranchese on its board of directors, the San Antonio Housing Authority chose to locate those projects (Alazan and Apache Courts) in the heart of the city's worst slums. Both projects opened for occupancy in 1941.[14]

In the meantime, the local medical community continued its efforts to reform the city's board of health. Long notorious for its inefficiency, the board had been one of the machine's favorite agencies for political patronage. Because of its political usefulness, the machine fought off the reformers for years, and it was not until 1943, when the war effort created a better environment for change, that the city's physicians won a temporary victory. Under the terms of a new ordinance, medical professionals dominated the board for the next four years.[15]

Reforming the board of health and razing the worst of the slums did have some effect on the pathological environment that fostered disease. The introduction of proper sewage and water facilities in the Courts took a little time to have an impact on mortality from infant diarrhea, but once begun it was strikingly significant. In 1940–44, as both projects opened, the death rate for infant diarrhea was 33.2; in the period from 1945 to 1949 it dropped to 19.3, and fell again by 1954 to 11.1. Tuberculosis, another disease that thrived in slum areas, showed equally dramatic declines, with the death rate dropping almost 50 percent from 1935 to 1945.[16]

The 1940s would also be the last decade before the 1990s that recorded a decline in the homicide rate. Anglo and Mexican American rates dropped approximately 11 percent during this decade. San Antonio's black community did not, however, enjoy a respite from violent death. Its overall rate remained basically unchanged. Moreover, the data conceal a disturbing shift in homicide rates on the East Side. African Americans between the ages of fifteen and twenty-four were increasingly likely to be homicide victims while the rate for older blacks declined slightly. Interestingly, Mexican Americans in that younger age group did not replicate the African American trend. Thus the usual explanation for the national decline in homicide during the 1940s—that it was in some way related to the nation's intense and patriotic focus on the war effort—seems to apply only to Anglos and Mexican Americans in San Antonio.

At this point in our research it is difficult to explain this pattern, but two possibilities suggest themselves. First, because the Mexican American population was so much larger, it may be that the armed forces drafted proportionately greater numbers of young San Antonio Hispanic males into their ranks than they did African Americans. In effect, the war may have removed from the local environment a fairly large number of young adults whose age group traditionally contributes significantly to the incidence of homicide. Even if true, however, this possibility still cannot explain why the homicide rate for African American adolescents and young adults should increase. It may be that this trend reflected two other developments: first, continued black inmigration, and second, San Antonio's failure to enfranchise fully these newcomers, leading to their subsequent acculturation into the East Side's subculture of violence.

San Antonio's African American population expanded more rapidly during the 1940s than at any time since the Civil War, increasing by 10,310 (54%). Many of these were migrants who arrived in a black community that was still sufficiently powerful to force concessions from the local political establishment. Several community leaders organized a Negro Chamber of Commerce in 1939 and spearheaded a drive to integrate the workforce on federal projects. By 1940 this Chamber had succeeded in placing skilled blacks on the Alazan Courts project, and in helping establish the San Antonio Building Trades Association, a labor union for black skilled workers. A year later San Antonio became the first Texas city to establish training classes for African Americans seeking work at the burgeoning Kelly Air Force Base, the city's most important defense installation. Valmo Bellinger, who had inherited his father's political mantle, reinforced his community's ties to the machine by helping to defeat a reform proposal to restructure city government in 1941. Perhaps because of these organized efforts African American employment at Kelly rose to 6,000 people (nearly a third of the total workforce) by 1943. That turned out to be the high point of the black community's campaign for self-enfranchisement. Within a year, African American employment had dropped to 1,600 at Kelly and the Chamber of Commerce had disappeared, indicating that the attempt at integration in the mainstream San Antonio's civic culture had failed.[17]

Changes in the annual homicide rate for African Americans during the 1940s may reflect these shifting fortunes. Starting at fifty-five per 100,000 in 1935 the rate fell precipitously to twenty in 1940, skyrocketed to sixty by 1942, fell again to about forty in 1943, the year of highest employment at Kelly, and then rose again to stay at sixty or above until 1946. The rate in the postwar years fluctuated widely, finally falling to about twenty-five in the last two years of the decade.[18]

The fact that the East Side's overall homicide rate did not decline indicates that the fundamental dynamics of violent crime did not change. Those dynamics may be related to the fact that the black community justifiably regarded the criminal justice system, and the police in particular, as biased and adopted a self-policing attitude that relied overmuch on a sense of personal justice in dealing with conflict.[19] That view is confirmed in the final words of Emma "Straight Eight" Oliver. After thirty-three arrests, including three for murder, Oliver was experienced in the ways of the criminal justice system. Having served only minimal time for two prior murders, she was not terribly concerned about receiving a death sentence for her final homicide in 1948. While awaiting execution she continued to believe until the end that she would be reprieved, saying, "Surely you're not going to execute a Negro for killing another Negro. If it had been a white man, it would have been different."[20] Oliver's attitude perhaps indicates that it was African Americans' practical historical experience, more than cultural characteristics, which created separate homicide trends for the East Side. Her case suggests that political enfranchisement is a necessary but not sufficient condition for altering violent behavior patterns.

The 1950s Patterns

Trends in disease and homicide continued to diverge during the 1950s. By 1960 infant diarrhea would cease to be a major health problem, but homicide would be on the verge of becoming a spectacular social pathology with rates that would dwarf previous historical records. And this divergence occurred in a rapidly improving physical environment.

Changes in that environment were not, however, uniform or equally beneficial to all areas within San Antonio. World War II and the onset of the Cold War permanently altered the socioeconomic and political landscapes of the city. Federal military contracts and employment at the city's five bases now became the single most important segment of the local economy. The population increased nearly 80 percent during the 1940s, creating the need for thousands of new homes for those newcomers. Attempting to accommodate rapid change and high demand for urban amenities, the city now resumed its northward march. Henceforth, the white North Side would dominate San Antonio.

That dominance played a crucial role in significantly altering the political landscape and the terms of minority enfranchisement in the city. Anglo reformers, appealing to the North Side's voting power and distaste for old-fashioned patronage politics, finally succeeded in defeating the old political machine in 1951. They celebrated their victory by enacting a new city charter that created a city manager/council form of government. Since council races were now at-large contests, San Antonio's minority voters lost what leverage they had had over city policies. Not content with this victory, the business community organized its own political machine, ingeniously called the Good Government League, in 1954. The GGL would dominate city government for the next twenty years and would pursue a growth-oriented agenda that, for the most part, neglected inner-city neighborhoods.[21]

San Antonio's minorities were not completely excluded from the advantages of prosperity in the 1950s. Kelly Air Force Base began to hire Mexican American workers in large numbers, a trend that would eventually make the base the single largest employer of Hispanics in the United States. Secure federal civil service jobs in turn created the basis, finally, for the rise of an extensive middle class with the incomes to move out of the old West Side. The emergence of the G.I. Forum, which fought for the rights of Mexican American veterans, helped gain that group access to jobs and federal housing subsidies. Responding belatedly to this emerging market, local housing developers began constructing subdivisions along the borders of the old West Side and also increasingly near Kelly. The GGL helped improve the local environment when it gained control of the City Water Board in 1954. Jettisoning the board's long-standing policy that water users had to pay for their own connections to the water supply, the GGL sponsored a large bond issue that would pay to build a truly adequate citywide water system serving all areas for the first time.[22]

Constructing that system would take time. In the interim the needs of the city's slum neighborhoods remained a challenge to local government. Alazan and Apache Courts had merely dented the horrors of life on the West Side. Only 10 percent of the slums had been razed to make room for those projects, and the demand for better housing far outstripped the supply during the 1940s. Even in 1950 more than half of the city's Mexican American and nearly one-third of the African American population lived in housing that lacked indoor toilets. San Antonio had obviously not managed to eradicate its slum problem by 1950, leaving much to be done.[23]

Although the reformers who overthrew the machine, and their successors in the GGL, had little interest in dealing with slum problems per se, they created a climate in which those who did could operate more effectively. The city's board of health, no longer a political football, could work cooperatively with the medical community to continue the assault on communicable diseases. Among other things, the board introduced a visiting nurse service. Trained nurses worked with the mothers of newborns in their homes, instructing them in proper hygiene and other health-care matters that would affect infant mortality. In addition, the board worked assiduously to encourage the use of streptomycin for treatment of tuberculosis.

These measures, coupled with the construction of a citywide sewer and water system, had dramatic results. By 1960 tuberculosis was a cause of death primarily among the elderly rather than a major killer of young adults. Infant diarrhea mortality declined from a rate of 11 in 1950–54 to 5.2 in 1955–59. And the percentage of homes in minority neighborhoods with indoor toilets climbed from 48 percent to 84 percent for Mexican Americans and from 70 percent to 91 percent for African Americans.[24]

At first glance even the homicide data for the 1950s look promising. The total homicide rate declined by one-third during the decade, with all groups sharing in the good news (see table 5.1). Even the African American rate dropped by 30 percent. And the rate of homicides involving firearms reached a historic low. San Antonio seemed to mirror national trends, as it generally had during the previous decade. One might be tempted to say that even with de facto political disenfranchisement San Antonio's minorities were displaying less homicidal behavior because they were also sharing in the decade's economic prosperity.

The gratifying decline in homicides, however, masked the persistence of the geography of this crime as well as variations in rates among age groups. As it had since the 1930s, homicide remained overwhelmingly concentrated in the traditional inner-city neighborhoods on the West and East Sides. In 1956, for example, 65 percent of all assault as well as homicide incidents occurred in the worst slum sections of those neighborhoods.[25] Among the different age groups, the homicide rate for fifteen- to twenty-four-year-old Mexican Americans increased from approximately ten to almost fifty per 100,000, and while the rate for African Americans in that age group remained relatively stable, the rate for those aged twenty-five or over returned to its 1940 figure of about eighty.

Although it will require further research to verify, the explanation for the rise in homicides among younger Mexican Americans and older African Americans may be heroin. Prior to the mid-1950s, several Mexican American and a few black wholesalers supplied San Antonio's illegal drug needs. In 1955, however, a U.S. Senate Committee held public hearings in the city in which its members interrogated most of the known dealers. While the hearings did not occasion many arrests, they thoroughly disrupted the local drug market. The wholesalers dropped out of the business, and the local market became dependent on smaller operators who had trouble building their businesses to the same scale and stability as their predecessors. Volatility in a drug market, as national experience in the 1980s demonstrated, creates an environment in which violence thrives.[26] It may be that some of the increase in homicide among younger Mexican Americans in the 1950s was due to the competitive violence associated with recreating distribution networks. Older black San Antonians, on the other hand, would have been forced to rely on Mexican American dealers for their drugs in the late 1950s, and simply finding a secure connection would have been difficult given that the new West Side dealers were reluctant to work with them.[27] For this group, relative scarcity could have generated vi-

Table 5.1. Age-standardized homicide death rates by means of assault, for males by ethnicity, Bexar County, 1940–1980

	RATES				
	1940	1950	1960	1970	1980
Total male					
Firearms	10.23	10.91	8.24	18.83	22.12
Cutting/piercing	4.54	5.89	2.87	4.03	8.12
Other means	2.82	2.15	1.62	1.86	3.21
Total homicide	17.59	18.95	12.73	24.73	33.45
Hispanic male					
Firearms	16.56	15.49	13.52	31.40	36.07
Cutting/piercing	10.66	9.43	4.97	7.25	15.04
Other means	3.53	2.47	1.86	2.37	4.51
Total homicide	30.75	27.39	20.35	41.02	55.62
Black male					
Firearms	37.01	30.42	25.51	62.74	50.73
Cutting/piercing	13.21	22.57	12.14	13.93	12.96
Other means	7.43	4.76	3.01	3.30	4.38
Total homicide	57.65	57.75	40.66	79.97	68.07
Non-Hispanic male					
Firearms	5.33	4.62	3.53	6.23	7.86
Cutting/piercing	1.11	0.81	0.76	1.04	2.30
Other means	2.23	1.65	1.30	1.40	2.14
Total homicide	8.67	7.08	5.59	8.67	12.30

	DISTRIBUTION (PERCENT)				
	1940	1950	1960	1970	1980
Total male					
Firearms	58.14	57.58	64.70	76.15	66.12
Cutting/piercing	25.82	31.08	22.56	16.31	24.29
Other means	16.04	11.34	12.75	7.54	9.59
Total homicide	100.00	100.00	100.00	100.00	100.00
Hispanic male					
Firearms	53.85	56.56	66.45	76.55	64.86
Cutting/piercing	34.66	34.42	24.41	17.66	27.04
Other means	11.49	9.02	9.14	5.79	8.10
Total homicide	100.00	100.00	100.00	100.00	100.00
Black male					
Firearms	64.19	52.68	62.73	78.46	74.53
Cutting/piercing	22.92	39.08	29.86	17.41	19.04
Other means	12.89	8.24	7.41	4.13	6.43
Total homicide	100.00	100.00	100.00	100.00	100.00
Non-Hispanic male					
Firearms	61.47	65.24	63.15	71.15	63.91
Cutting/piercing	12.83	11.50	13.62	12.05	18.67
Other means	25.70	23.26	23.23	16.12	17.43
Total homicide	100.00	100.00	100.00	100.00	100.00

olent competition for the few sources of heroin available to them in a market undergoing restructuring.

The Homicide Epidemic, 1960–1984

San Antonio essentially had solved its health problems by 1960, but its experience with epidemic homicide was only about to begin. And despite major advances in the enfranchisement of minorities, the next quarter century would, oddly enough, be the most violent in the city's history.

Nearly complete political enfranchisement became a reality in these years primarily because of the federal government. The Good Government League responded to a local business agenda by focusing its efforts on promoting the growth and development of the North Side and, to a lesser extent, the downtown. Proudly asserting that it served the entire city, not merely interest groups or particular neighborhoods, the GGL employed token minority presence on the city council as a tactic to convince itself that it represented all San Antonians. Every council had one black and one Mexican American, each of whom was carefully selected for their devotion to the GGL's growth agenda. In practice, the GGL simply ignored the environmental and social needs of inner-city neighborhoods. Low voter registration and voting patterns in the inner city, the small number of black voters, the absence of any effective minority political organizations, and the continuing growth of the North Side with its greater rates of political participation combined to prevent the city's minorities from challenging the GGL's dominance.[28] Genuine political enfranchisement began in mid-1965, when the Catholic archdiocese's Christian Youth Organization received federal funding from Lyndon Johnson's War on Poverty to establish the San Antonio Neighborhood Youth Organization (SANYO). Under the direction of Father John Yanta, SANYO quickly developed into a major means for educating local minorities, especially on the West Side, in the processes of political empowerment. Yanta created a network of thirty neighborhood councils in the East, South, and West Sides, each of which drew its members from their local areas. Yanta then gathered these councils into the Greater San Antonio Federation of Neighborhood Councils, which in turn dominated the boards of the Economic Opportunity Development Corporation and the Model Cities program.[29]

Yanta had created an inner city, minority-dominated school for self-enfranchisement. SANYO's neighborhood councils became training grounds for local residents to educate themselves in the processes of government. Furthermore, SANYO's grip on federal assistance in San Antonio gave it the opportunity to make real decisions about its disposition citywide. For the first time in its history, the West Side in particular had the opportunity to address many of its most pressing problems. It used its power to create a Model Neighborhood Area on the West Side, and to fund a great many projects designed to enhance and expand school facilities and to improve the physical environment. Dozens of miles of sewer lines, new schools, and a massive flood-control project "did more to improve the quality of life among the West Side residents" than anything since the federally funded public housing projects of the 1930s.[30]

The Chicano civil rights movement in the late 1960s and early 1970s also spawned a number of local organizations that taught the value of political empowerment. Communities Organized for Public Service (COPS), the most prominent of these, appeared in 1974, just as SANYO lost its control over local federal projects because of political infighting. Although that loss demoted SANYO to the status of a relatively small antipoverty program, many individuals who had served in its neighborhood councils now helped COPS become San Antonio's preeminent minority political organization. Like SANYO, COPS focused throughout the 1970s on the physical improvement of the West Side. COPS' tactics, patterned on the ideas of Saul Alinsky, forced city leaders to pay attention to its demands. Agitating for access to federal monies, and well positioned to stimulate voter turnout, COPS compiled a series of remarkable successes in drainage and street-improvement projects.[31]

A political revolution in 1977 completed the public enfranchisement of minorities, again through the intervention of the federal government in local affairs. Wracked by internal dissension and under increasing external criticism, the GGL finally collapsed in 1974, but not before it had obtained city council approval of the largest annexation in the city's history. Although bringing thousands of new North Side residents into the city made eminent sense as public policy, local civil rights activists regarded this annexation as a deliberate attempt to dilute the growth of minority voting power and sued under the provisions of the 1975 Voting Rights Act. Under federal pressure either to deannex or change its governmental structure to ensure minority representation, San Antonio's electorate narrowly abandoned the at-large system for city council and replaced it with elections by district. City elections under this new arrangement in 1977 reveal the extent of the local revolution. For the first time since 1836 minorities controlled the council.[32]

Inner-city residents' needs now had unprecedented representation in local government. Support for those needs reflected that new power. Prior to 1977, in accordance with the GGL's conservative attitudes toward poverty issues, the city had funded only five social agencies. Over the next seven years the council added thirty-eight social service organizations, ten economic development associations, and one health agency to its roster of groups receiving city assistance. In addition, the city now had a Department of Human Resources to coordinate and administer a host of programs designed to deal with the social consequences of poverty. Federal funding, however, remained essential to San Antonio's efforts to deal with inner-city problems. Despite minority control of the council, local businessmen still exerted considerable power in politics (not least because they helped finance the campaigns of most candidates in every council election). These businessmen had little interest in committing too many city resources to social problems. Because of the need to balance competing philosophies and interest groups, the council adopted the tactic of voting to fund the administrative costs of antipoverty and neighborhood improvement projects; the bulk of the funding would always come from federal sources.[33]

Despite the necessity for such political bargains in the everyday operations of city government it was nonetheless true that San Antonio's minorities, especially Mexican Americans, now had routine access to power and to public resources. Physical improvements, not surprisingly, proliferated within the boundaries of the historical West and East Sides of town. The socioeconomic status of African and Mexican Americans improved considerably. Thanks to the defunct GGL's pro-growth agenda and the influx of federal military funding, a relatively prosperous economy offered minorities opportunities for upward mobility. Reflecting that mobility, many West and East Side residents moved increasingly into emerging neighborhoods in the burgeoning North Side.

Ironically, as minorities moved toward greater social, economic, and political enfranchisement than in any previous era, the city's homicide rate exploded. Violence among African and Mexican Americans essentially doubled their rates between 1960 and 1970, while even the Anglo rate increased by 60 percent. With the exception of blacks, these rates continued to climb through the 1970s, so that by 1980 San Antonio had achieved the unenviable record of suffering from the highest homicide rates in its history. If twenty-five years of spiraling rates is any indication, San Antonio was in the grip of a homicide epidemic.

Although our statistics by themselves cannot explain why the incidence of homicide spiked so sharply, the data point to some possibilities. First, and most obviously, a combination of youth and firearms produced this epidemic. African Americans provide the most dramatic illustration of this combination. Young blacks (aged 15–24) suffered a 400 percent increase in their age group's homicide rate in the 1960s. Their rate reached an astonishing and extremely threatening 160 per 100,000. An increase in the use of firearms clearly accounted for most of that amazing increase. Deaths from firearms climbed from a rate of 25.51 in 1960 to 62.70 in 1970 (accounting for nearly 80 percent of all black homicides). Although it could hardly be a source of comfort, San Antonio's experience with this epidemic mirrored national trends.[34] Changes in the death rate by firearms among blacks during the 1970s simply confirmed the close relationship between guns and homicides. The death rate for African American youth began to reverse itself during that decade, and the decline in the use of guns again explains most of that decline. In a population as small as that of blacks in San Antonio, however, the very high death rates meant the community was literally losing its future.

Homicides among Mexican Americans in that same age group trended upward at a slower pace, reflecting the fact that firearms use in these deaths increased far less—from 13.52 per 100,000 to 31.40—than among blacks. The data do reveal, however, that there were differences in the ways blacks and Mexican Americans killed. While homicides by means other than firearms remained essentially flat among African Americans, Mexican American homicides by cutting and piercing nearly doubled each decade from 1960 to 1980. Despite that difference, though, guns were the overwhelming weapon of choice in homicides for both groups. Because the connection between firearms and homicide is so clear, the fact that the Mexican American rate remained lower than that for blacks indicates that there was a greater tendency for East Side residents to resort to guns than was true among West Side inhabitants. There seems, in other words, to be differences in attitudes toward the use of firearms that may have contributed to the much higher homicide rates among African Americans.

The West Side community had a problem with immigrants and homicide that was unique. Prior to 1960, the homicide rate among Mexican-born residents had been significantly lower than for Mexican Americans (see table 5.2). That situation changed dramatically during the sixties. Homicides among Mexican Americans increased by 71 percent, but among immigrants it skyrocketed 400 percent (indeed matching the increase among young adult blacks). Then, while the overall rate for Hispanics continued upward in the

1970s, the increase among these immigrants plunged to a mere 16 percent increase.

Such an extraordinary fluctuation is hard to explain, but it may have been due to a continuation of the problems with instability in San Antonio's drug market. Heroin remained the drug of choice, and Mexico remained the most important supplier to the local market. Dealers used the city's international trucking trade with Mexico to transport heroin to Produce Row, San Antonio's fruit and vegetable market, during the 1960s. A number of wholesalers operated from or around Produce Row, distributing to several retail groups that sold to both Mexican and African Americans in the inner-city neighborhoods. It is probably no accident that Fred Carrasco, San Antonio's first notorious drug "king," rose to fame in the 1960s. Carrasco used family connections with trucking firms to build a career that began with small-time dealing and grew to international drug lord. Numerous battles with rival groups contributed to the local homicide rate, and since his was only one of many violent drug organizations operating in the city, it is reasonable to assume that violent deaths among their employees—who often were Mexican nationals serving as "mules"—help explain some of the amazing increase in homicide among native-born Mexicans.[35]

Table 5.2. Age standardized homicide death rates for Mexican American and Mexican immigrant males, Bexar County, 1939–1941 to 1979–1981

Central Year	Mexican American	Mexican Immigrant	Ratio	Total
1940	34.5	23.1	0.670	29.7
1950	26.4	13.4	0.508	24.6
1960	22.5	10.5	0.464	20.3
1970	38.6	52.6	1.361	39.4
1980	48.3	61.3	1.268	49.3
Percentage change				
1940–50	23.3	41.8	24.2	17.3
1950–60	14.7	22.1	8.7	17.4
1960<–70	71.4	402.9	193.4	94.0
1970<–80	25.0	16.5	6.8	25.3

Note: Rates per 100,000 persons; directly standardized on U.S. population.

Homicide as a Chronic Condition

In the 1980s San Antonio's homicide rate tended to reflect national trends, especially when cocaine arrived and reinforced the violent competition among rival drug groups like the Mexican Mafia and Cuban Blacks. Again reflecting national data, San Antonio's homicide rate began to fall in the early 1990s, perhaps indicating that the battles over control of the cocaine trade had begun to taper off through a combination of greater market stability and/or a decline in demand. The nuances of local trends in homicide after 1984, however, await further research.

Our research for the period from 1935 to 1984, however, provides some interesting tests of the effects of enfranchisement on violence as well as a commentary on the disease model for understanding homicide. In general, as our geographical analysis demonstrates, there is a very marked difference in the results of public policies that affected a disease environment and those that might, according to the theory of civility, have decreased the homicide rate. Even though one could argue that fifty years is insufficient to change homicidal behavior through public interventions, the amount of intervention that has occurred in San Antonio to enhance the physical environment and to extend enfranchisement to minorities at least poses some serious questions for both models.

The geography of homicide over time shows an extraordinary persistence in the locations of its victims' residences. While the maps clearly demonstrate a diffusion of homicide out of its historic centers in the inner city, a diffusion that needs to be examined in some detail, the epicenters of violent death remain the same for the entire time period. There are definite "hot spots" within the city, but contrary to an epidemic model, those locales stay "hot" for decades, demonstrating that homicide is an endemic, not epidemic, phenomenon. Ethnic and racial patterns are strikingly consistent. If we compare those locations to intracity and intragroup migration patterns over the same time period, we find that suburbanization, broadly speaking, is drawing San Antonio's middle-class Mexican and African Americans outward, depriving the old neighborhoods of their ability to retain populations whose enfranchisement would contribute to greater social stability and less violence. The old ethnic and racial neighborhoods, in other words, are not receiving the social benefits presumably associated with the discipline of full-time, well-paid work. In short, the "civilizing" effects of becoming enfranchised are transferred to the new, suburban neighborhoods, not the older, declining inner-city ones. As a consequence, as the Chicago school of sociology found four decades ago, certain areas of the city remain high-crime areas over long periods of time, certainly as measured by plotting the residences of homicide victims.[36] Significant improvements in the physical infrastructure of the city and the sociopolitical enfranchisement of previously excluded segments of the local population have not altered those hot spots for homicide.

Infant mortality from diarrhea much more clearly fits a model that suggests that intervention has had a pronounced benefit. When we look again at the patterns of mortality from diarrhea we see that there were two extremely deadly locations in the 1930s. By the late 1940s these areas have either been significantly reduced or all but removed from the map, and the distribution of infant diarrhea has shifted outward as minorities or new immigrants have moved into these interstitial areas.

Our examination of infant diarrhea and homicide has some important implications for theory and policy regarding homicide. By considering both in the same context over time, we were able to see that public interventions in the pathologies of neighborhoods have differential effects. The analysis demonstrates that the problem of homicide does not appear to be amenable to the benefits of changes in environmental conditions. In contrast, when the problem (infant diarrhea) and the solution (improved sanitation) are both physical, policy changes affecting the physical environment have a clear and direct effect. This suggests the need for caution in evaluating the effect of public intervention, and an understanding that with a problem such as homicide, with fewer clear empirical or theoretical ties to physical conditions, the solution is much more illusive.

Maps of these conditions in San Antonio over time clearly show that the interventions made in the 1930s and 1940s had a pronounced impact on infant diarrhea. A historical understanding of the geographic differences in the infrastructure improvements, coming first to San Antonio's predominately African American East Side, and then only later to the primarily Mexican American West and South Sides, just as clearly demonstrates the basic political nature of these health-related decisions. But since these significant physical improvements to the community have no impact on an endemic social problem like homicide, we cannot rely on the same sort of solutions or policy that we can use to fight disease. We would conclude that the disease metaphor is useful but is just that, a metaphor.

Thus what we see in a detailed historical examination of one city is not a simple picture of a demonstrated need being met with physical improvements to a community, and those improvements bring about a better quality of life and a decrease in social problems. This study provides historical, geographical, and statistical evidence of the greater complexity of the interplay of politics and public policy. More important, we demonstrate again that only by knowing the unique history of the specific city under study are we even able to draft some of the more intriguing hypotheses about the intersection between the local environment, public health, and homicide.

6

Stephanie J. Shaw and
Craig E. Colten

Battlefields

The
Military and the
Environment

Simply driving through the city of San Antonio, one realizes the omnipresence of the military. Vast tracts of open land within the interstate beltway lurk behind high fences. Khaki-green vehicles fill sprawling parking lots. Empty airfields stand idle. The physical presence of the military is obvious in every quarter of the city and is a clue to why the Department of Defense serves as a cornerstone of the city's social and economic foundation. "If there is anything that the city of San Antonio—the people, business, and mood—thrives on, for better or for worse, it is the military."[1] Certainly, the military contributed greatly to the growth and prosperity of San Antonio; however, some fear it came with a price. Included in the potential costs are soil erosion, increased flooding, air pollution, noise, stress on municipal sewage-treatment plants and community landfills, soil and groundwater pollution, and removal of native habitat.[2] During the 1990s the military stopped some of its most polluting and damaging activities and made efforts to remediate previous damage to surface soils and vegetation as well as soil and groundwater contamination. Despite these efforts, completed and ongoing environmental investigations and ongoing health surveys show that the military's impact in San Antonio (especially at Kelly Air Force Base) is real and costly and perhaps not yet fully recognized.[3]

Public awareness of environmental problems has directed attention toward industrial pollution in the last quarter century, and that attention has spilled over into the secluded enclaves owned by the military. Discovery of serious contamination at the Hanford, Washington, nuclear production facility and plutonium in the Rio Grande River near Los Alamos, New Mexico, have prompted greater scrutiny of government properties.[4] Furthermore, dramatic accounts of military environmental misdeeds have attracted public concern.[5] The Pentagon has acknowledged over 17,000 facilities where the military potentially contributed to environmental degradation. The range of sites is vast: from the severe contamination caused by land disposal of chemical warfare wastes at the Rocky Mountain Arsenal near Denver to less extensive impacts at private-sector munitions production facilities. Much of the damage stems from casual handling of chemical wastes during the period before federal laws specifically addressed hazardous wastes. Yet, a 1987 U.S. General Accounting Office study found numerous military installations still out of compliance with existing federal hazardous-waste laws. While the private sector was moving toward more effective management of its wastes, the military lagged behind. Problems at Air Force installations have been particularly pronounced due to their extensive use of solvents and toxic metal-plating solutions. McClellan (Sacramento) and Wright-Patterson (Dayton, Ohio) Air Force bases, much like Kelly in San Antonio, have contributed to environmental damages through their aircraft maintenance functions.[6] The number of aviation facilities and the density of maintenance and fueling operations in San Antonio distinguish the military's role from civilian industrial activities.

With cutbacks in defense spending and numerous base closures, public tolerance for damages has diminished. The increased concern over environmental contamination at federal facilities has prompted public pressure for cleanup.[7] The Defense Environmental Restoration Program has become the primary mechanism for assessing the extent of contamination at government facilities and for initiating restoration efforts. This chapter will examine the particular mix of military activities in San Antonio, their contribution to environmental degradation in the metropolitan area, and the steps underway to remedy the problem.

Historical Context

As a Spanish outpost, San Antonio housed several religious missions and was not yet a key military bastion, but with the establishment of a Texas government and, subsequently, a federal government, defense became the city's main function. The U.S. Army made San Antonio its home as soon as Texas received statehood, and in 1870 the United States purchased the land known as the quadrangle at Fort Sam Houston for use as a military post. The base served as headquarters for the Southern Department of the U.S. Army, consisting of Texas, Oklahoma, Colorado, New Mexico, and Arizona. Following the Civil War, the U.S. Army returned to the city, playing a large part in its regeneration. The citizens of San Antonio had actually voted against secession, and after the war they renewed their efforts to secure a U.S. military post and quartermaster depot for the city. Their success in this effort prompted local businessmen to construct infrastructure improvements including sidewalks, rail lines, and public utilities, as well as to charter San Antonio's first bank. All this activity occurred despite stagnant business conditions. The desired effect of making the city ready to support the military was achieved, and an unintended benefit was that the improvements drew cheap labor in the form of immigrants. Both the military spending and this influx of population contributed to San Antonio's economic prosperity in the 1870s and 1880s. In 1898, at the outset of the Spanish-American War, Fort Sam Houston was the military hub for the United States and grew to be an unrivaled military complex. San Antonio entered the new century with military expenditures accounting for a large portion of local capital.[8]

The modern military complex in San Antonio began evolving in the 1910s as the country entered World War I (see fig. 6.1). The old Fort Sam Houston, a relic of the nineteenth century, straddled Salado Creek a few miles northeast of the Alamo. It included a hospital and an early aerodrome on the parade ground. The first airplane arrived at San Antonio in 1910 and ushered in an era of Air Corps activity in the generally clear skies over the city. General William H. Carter cast the noisy and dangerous aircraft out of his parade ground after an accident, leaving the pilots searching for a home until they finally returned to Fort Sam Houston in 1915. By 1917 the newer and more powerful aircraft had outgrown facilities there, and the Army established Kelly Field. Within that same year, the government purchased land for construction of Brooks Field southeast of town. Nearly ten years later, in 1926, San Antonio enthusiastically purchased land for the construction of Randolph Field northeast of town near the community of Schertz. Most recently, the Air Force separated Lackland from Kelly in 1942 and made it the center for basic training of new recruits. In addition to these air service training facilities, the U.S. Army educated soldiers at Camp Stanley, Camp Wilson, and Camp Travis, with an officer training facility permanently established at Camp Bullis.[9]

San Antonio's leaders recognized that the economic prosperity enjoyed during the 1920s was influenced by the presence of the military and, in order to ensure its presence in the future, they donated properties for the development of Randolph Field and Lackland Field in 1926 and 1941, respectively. City leaders in the 1930s and 1940s embraced the notion of the military serv-

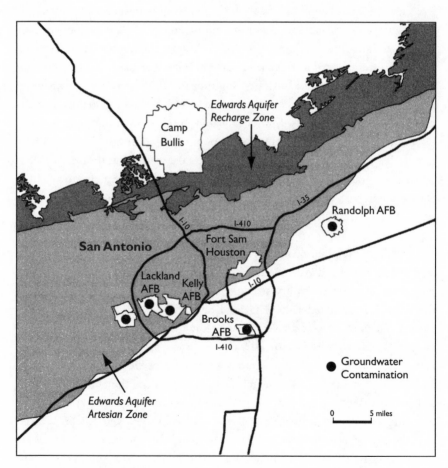

Fig. 6.1. Military bases in San Antonio and groundwater contamination

ing as the linchpin for the local economy. The existing military complex and a favorable flying climate influenced the military's decision to continue support-ing and to develop Air Force bases in San Antonio. This commitment served the city well during the Second World War when the city's "center of army avi-ation" drew a surge of population growth. Following World War II government spending accounted for one-third of all employment within the city of San An-tonio and its two main economies remain the military and tourism. Since San Antonio lacked the oilfields present in other Texas cities, city leaders "adopted the more conservative strategy of enhancing San Antonio's role as a center for defense, tourism, and regional services." Despite citizens' reluctance to vote for infrastructure improvement, bonds for street projects billed to serve Kelly Field won at the polls in 1964 and in 1970.[10] The military influence in late-twentieth-century San Antonio has not waned. San Antonio's growth in the 1970s and 1980s is attributed to military operations, government employment, trade, and tourism.

While all but Camp Bullis are located in urban areas today, each base was originally constructed on the outskirts of town or beyond, a common practice in siting military facilities due to their requirement for vast acreage. This ac-celerated the overall expansion of the urban territory and dispersed all poten-tially hazardous land uses. The Army constructed Fort Sam Houston at the edge of the existing developed area, so it took form within the overall urban area. As the military chose to build airfields, it sought out open areas beyond the built-up portion of San Antonio, the first of which occupied former farm-land south and west of the city. Military officials sought land that was suffi-ciently remote from urban populations to ensure safe operation of the somewhat risky aircraft. Kelly and Brooks both served as magnets for urban-ization and they lost their remote qualities by the 1920s. Creation of Randolph to the northeast reflected a desire by the Air Corps to secure a new field farther from the city center. Indeed, when the government acquired the property where it constructed Randolph Field, it displaced only a handful of ranchers. Rapid buildup of the bases during the late 1930s and the postwar urban ex-pansion placed Randolph well within San Antonio's urbanized territory. By the 1970s the interstate belt around San Antonio encircled all but Camp Bullis. Since 1970 urbanization has progressed northerly and not toward the military bases. The bases have lost their magnetic quality and, with demilitarization, this trend will continue.[11]

When the city engulfed the military bases that were once on the outskirts of town, land-use clashes sometimes ensued. Despite these clashes, "[t]he socioeconomic effects of these [military] facilities as a whole have been woven into that of the City of San Antonio resulting in some degree of natural dependency."[12] Currently, Kelly, Lackland, Randolph, and Brooks Air Force Bases occupy about 20,000 acres and Camp Bullis covers some 30,000 additional acres. The military bases account for such a large single land use that the Alamo Area Council of Governments (AACOG) mapped it along with industrial, commercial, and residential areas.[13] While similar in many respects to other industrial activities, the military bases are distinct due to the substantial tracts of land held by a single owner.

Despite land-use clashes, San Antonio's continued commitment to the military is reflected in citizen protests of the closure of Kelly.[14] With the purpose of "alleviat[ing] the impact of military base closure on the economies of local communities" Congress passed the Community Environmental Response Facilitation Act (CERFA). Kelly Air Force Base stands to lose over 20,000 government jobs over the course of its gradual transformation from military to civilian operation, although projections call for 28,010 more civilian jobs by 2017. In addition to provisions to soften the blow of base shutdowns, Congress sought to hasten the military's environmental cleanup program. In 1986 amendments to the Superfund Act called for federal facilities to comply in the same manner as private entities and established a special program to manage federal cleanups. This program, the Defense Environmental Restoration Program, addressed remediation efforts at both active and formerly used military facilities. In 1992 Congress finally passed the Federal Facility Compliance Act, which gave state agencies the ability to use enforcement tools against federal facilities that were not in compliance with environmental laws. This reinvigorated the federal effort to address military hazardous wastes.[15]

Military Activities and the Environment

The military's primary purpose has been to defend, and defense activities commonly took precedence over environmental concerns. In direct defiance of normal nuisance standards, for example, judges offered rulings on complaints that permitted the continuation of offensive military-related activities during World War II.[16] This permissive attitude toward environmental problems, coupled with the national security issues surrounding defense operations, allowed the military to manage its operations outside the normal, albeit weak, legal constraints of the time. As a result, the potential environmental impacts of military activity have been profound in some places. The Trinity site in New Mexico offers one extreme, while the countless bomb plants and training bases stand as lesser examples. In San Antonio the military's industrial activities are concentrated in several areas throughout the city, and the cumulative environmental impacts are significant if not threatening. The physical occupation of territory by bases has altered the natural land cover; training activities have produced wear and tear on surface vegetation and soils; fuel-management and maintenance operations have resulted in spills and the production of harmful wastes; and waste-management practices have contributed to water and soil contamination.[17] These impacts, though similar to civilian industrial impacts, are distinct because of the large tracts owned and managed by the military in San Antonio. In addition, the investigations and subsequent remediation activities began only in the 1990s, much later than at other urban industrial complexes.

Land Use

With over 50,000 acres devoted to military land uses, the Army and Air Force have made a pervasive contribution to the urban landscape. All of the military installations in San Antonio except Camp Bullis are located in an area that was part of the Backland Prairie Biome, characterized by black, waxy soils and bunch grasses including little bluestem, big bluestem, Indian grass, switchgrass, Texas winter-grass, and side-oats grama. The original vegetation was diverse and abundant due to the edge setting influenced by the Texas South Plains and the Edwards Plateau. The prairie originally supported wildlife such as buffalo, antelope, deer, peccary, and numerous birds but now supports only squirrels, sparrows, blackbirds, mockingbirds, robins, and other development-tolerant species. Nineteenth-century game hunting by base personnel contributed to the exhaustion of the bison, but displacement of larger mammals has occurred in concert with the overall growth of the urban area. Only deer and coyote still live within the perimeter of Camp Bullis. Little original vegetation remains within the base perimeters or in surrounding urban tracts; for example, the Air Force placed some 1,900 acres of nonnative Bermuda grass on Randolph Field in 1929, and vast tracts of turf occupy parade grounds and airfields. The military argues that "due to their long tenure and environmental management programs, [the bases] have become stable ecosystems even though affected by military activities." Current open-space use is restricted to ornamental lawns, golf courses, cemeteries, and firing ranges, with the only unused land along the undevelopable floodplain areas. In this respect the military has contributed to the maintenance of some of the city's open space, although public access is limited.[18]

Another important consideration regarding military land use in San Antonio is the relationship between these bases and a critical underground water formation. The Edwards Aquifer is the sole source of municipal water in San Antonio and many other surrounding cities, and threats to water quantity or quality would have dire consequences for the population. Since 1962 discharge has exceeded recharge, resulting in the possible future depletion of the aquifer. As large consumers of groundwater, all the bases contributed to its depletion. Randolph Field was consuming over 1,000,000 gallons a day by 1940 and surpassed 2,000,000 gallons daily during its peak training period in the 1940s. As of 1997 Kelly drew over 2,000,000 gallons a day from the aquifer. Despite concerns with depletion, the Edwards is not cut off from current precipitation like the Ogallala Aquifer and is not an example of water mining. Consequently, the people of San Antonio have been more concerned with potential groundwater contamination resulting from base operations than with depletion of the aquifer. Contaminated groundwater is virtually impossible to restore and remedial action is extremely costly, proving technically infeasible in some instances. There has been serious groundwater contamination at Kelly Air Force Base (to be discussed in detail later), although the polluting substances are not known to have reached the Edwards Aquifer at this time. Groundwater contamination has also occurred at Lackland, Brooks, and Randolph, but again not affecting the Edwards formation. In response to the damages, the Air Force has evaluated several failed groundwater remediation systems, underscoring the difficulty of cleaning up contaminated water.[19]

Training Activities

The military constantly oversees training activities to promote readiness for war. These activities primarily include weapon and tank field exercises as well as flight maneuvers. Although these training activities themselves can affect the environment by causing soil erosion and accidental hazardous material spills, the major impacts result from maintenance and waste disposal. Currently Camp Bullis is the only base providing large-scale troop training, but historically all of the bases supported those activities.

Physical destruction of the landscape is often caused by tank maneuver training, which the Army describes as "fast and violent." When simulating battle conditions on grassland, the tanks can rip the vegetation from the soil, pulverize ruts in the soils, and fracture limestone cover. Additionally, cover and concealment drills required troops to strip and collect local vegetation with which to camouflage their vehicles. Historically these drills paid no attention to soil erosion or vegetation damage. The only evidence of erosion resulting from these drills at San Antonio's bases is at Camp Bullis, where large gullies exist. To minimize such impacts, Camp Bullis now has tank trails designed to protect the remainder of the base from soil loss, and cover and concealment drills use synthetic plant materials rather than native vegetation.[20]

Until the 1970s the Army allowed overgrazing and practiced fire suppression at Camp Bullis, leading to the invasion of Ashe junipers and altering the vegetation communities at the facility. Impacts of military training activities coupled with overgrazing, fire suppression, and the simple clearing of vegetation resulted in the creation of the Army's natural resources protection program in the 1980s. This program continues to address and mitigate past damage through changes in current land use, replanting efforts, and controlled burns. The urban installations no longer support tank training exercises and historical maneuver areas currently support administrative or other activities, minimizing continued damage caused by these types of activities.[21]

Weapon firing has been and is currently conducted at all the installations. Historically, troops fired lead-containing ammunition on ranges and maintained guns using rifle-bore cleaner, dry-cleaning solvents, lubricants, corrosion inhibitors, and paint thinner. Potential impacts can result from accidental leaks and spills of stored dry-cleaning solvents and other chemicals, as well as from the deposition of lead into the soils at firing ranges. The impacts of these activities are exemplified at Lackland's Medina annex, where weapons maintenance and weapons firing caused lead contamination at a former firing range. Typically, weapons firing and maintenance resulted in small-scale contamination due to continued activities over long time periods.[22]

Flight training activities that may impact the environment include exhaust emissions, fuel dumping, and the storage of aviation fuels. Obviously, air emissions cause temporary air pollution, but fuel-storage leaks are more insidious. Impacts to soil and groundwater can originate from leaking underground tanks, spills, and from disposal of fuel wastes in landfills or incinerators. Examples of the impacts of maintenance, fuel management, and waste-disposal activities that supported flight training are discussed below.[23]

Fire-protection training, simulating the crash and burn of aircraft, has caused environmental contamination at several installations. Fire-protection training formerly involved the intentional burning and extinguishing of contaminated (unusable for aviation) fuel, used solvents, and used oils. These materials could, and did, readily enter soil and groundwater, as evidenced by contaminated shallow groundwater at two fire-protection areas each at Randolph, Brooks, and Lackland Air Force Bases and at least four areas at Kelly Air Force Base (see fig. 6.1 above). At Randolph, investigations of a six-acre site used from the 1950s until 1993 identified trichloroethylene (TCE) and benzene in the groundwater and investigations at a two-acre site used only in the late 1950s identified volatile organic compounds (VOCs) in the groundwater. The Air Force has identified similar contaminants beneath the fire-protection areas at Kelly and Lackland. At Brooks the TCE contaminant plume has migrated beneath several residences southwest of the base. These homeowners are concerned not only about their health, but about the value of their real estate. Although the city of San Antonio annexed the community in 1986 and provided municipal water, the community asserts that its residents may have been drinking contaminated well water prior to the annexation. Coincidentally, at the time the contamination was identified, the National Park Service was in the process of purchasing several of the homes for a demonstration of local historical farming techniques. These purchase plans were halted, and the homeowners were hit with a double blow.[24] Furthermore, such damages typically inhibit conversion of military property to private-sector uses due to fears of environmental liabilities.

Maintenance Activities and Fuel Management

In the late 1800s and early 1900s blacksmiths, wheelwrights, carpenters, plumbers, tinners, and painters operated maintenance shops on the bases. After 1926 and the passage of federal legislation that funded new maintenance structures, the scale and scope of maintenance activity escalated. New shops were much larger than their predecessors in order to accommodate large vehicles such as airplanes and tanks. Current maintenance activities fall into three categories: planes, tanks, and other motorized vehicles; fuel-storage systems; and buildings and other base infrastructure. Military technical and training manuals spell out procedures for all maintenance activities. In addition, the *Preventative Maintenance Monthly,* a comic book–like magazine designed for maintenance workers, provides some insight on historical practices in maintenance shops.[25]

The potential environmental impacts associated with airplane, tank, and vehicle maintenance revolved around the storage and use of solvents, lubricants, and other engine fluids. Articles in *Preventative Maintenance Monthly* discussed procedures for applying corrosion protection coatings, recycling oil, and recharging lead-acid batteries, as well as safety warnings about the associated materials. Advice included taking precaution with the carbon removing compound because "it bites" or could damage the user's skin. Safety tips included wearing gloves and goggles. By the 1970s the Army periodical encouraged oil recycling using two hydraulic lifts and hoses draining the oil to an underground storage tank. The military publications all point to the prolific use of dry-cleaning solvent as a degreaser and all-purpose cleaner, going so far as to say it is much safer than using paint thinner. Standard guidance called for recovery of solvents since the 1940s, and during the 1960s trade associations warned about pouring solvents on the ground. Some prescribed control practices seem to be measures to protect the environment but equally sought to minimize material loss.[26]

Three contamination sources derived from extensive fuel storage at San Antonio's military facilities. Disposal of contaminated fuels, leaks and spills, and disposal of fuel bottoms all have impacted soils and shallow groundwater. The Air Force designed aviation fuel-storage facilities primarily to keep contaminants out, and management of both aviation and ground vehicle fuels served to reduce losses from leaks and spills. As part of this management system, the War Department recommended inspections of sewers for gasoline or oil and required inspections of traps at motor-repair shops, filling stations, and aviation hangars. Although these management practices served to protect the environment as well as the fuel, the practice of disposing of contaminated fuel and fuel bottoms in fire-protection training areas or in landfills did just the opposite. When impurities present in the fuel settled to form fuel bottoms, this liquid sludge was then discarded by burning it during fire-protection training or by burying it in landfills. Potential environmental contamination resulted from the leaching of the gasoline, the added tetraethyl lead, or from other fuel additives. The extent of this fuel-related contamination is prolific, as shown by the number of areas impacted by dozens of leaking underground storage tanks present at all bases, fuel-sludge disposal areas documented at Brooks, Randolph, Lackland, and Kelly, and large-scale spills at Kelly.[27]

Base construction, expansion, and road maintenance not only continue to increase impervious cover but also generate sediments that enter local waterways. Historically, installations have stored large amounts of fuel oil and anthracite coal at installations for heating water and buildings. Pest control at the installations has included "[s]pray[ing] stands and can-washing facilities [at mess halls] with DDT at least once every 3 weeks." More recently, human health impacts of termite-control practices in base housing was the subject of a massive investigation during the 1980s. None of the national environmental reports discuss these impacts at the San Antonio bases.[28]

The Edwards Aquifer yields clean water that requires no treatment; consequently water purification facilities have been minimal. On the other hand, all the installations treated their own sewage in the early 1900s, and Camp Bullis continues to do so. Even after the installations began to utilize San Antonio's water-treatment plants, the military retained maintenance responsibilities for each installation's internal stormwater discharge. Most recently, bases have begun to maintain pretreatment facilities necessary for wastewater generated during environmental remediation projects.[29]

Waste Disposal Activities

Perhaps the most serious and insidious source of environmental impacts result from waste disposal practices. By mid-twentieth century, the Air Force was well aware of the importance of waste disposal:

> In view of the complexity of industrial waste problems, it is essential that waste disposal receive expert attention in the early stages of development of manufacturing or other processes and in the location, layout, and design of works for the employment of new or existing processes. Failure to give consideration to waste disposal in the early stages of project planning and design may have serious consequences.[30]

In 1951 Kelly Air Force Base conducted a major industrial waste survey to assess the volumes and methods of treatment. The survey identified oils, toxic metals from metal plating, and cyanide as the major problem wastes. The existing treatment system sought to separate oils and render the metals and cyanide nontoxic before their release to Leon Creek.[31]

"[C]lassically solid wastes have been disposed of in ways that appeared to be the cheapest and the least repulsive to the public."[32] This is certainly true of waste disposal on military installations. In addition to disposal in the "least repulsive" way, the military also was inclined to dispose of waste onsite (a common industry practice). The large tracts of land on which the facilities are located enabled onsite waste disposal, and because base personnel·sited land-fills in remote areas along stream beds, leachate has impacted soils and ground-water.[33]

In addition to landfills, the Air Force viewed "[i]ncineration [as] a good means of disposing of combustible material, such as waste oil, solvents, and solids," with "[o]pen burning areas . . . commonly employed for this purpose." This practice lasted until the early 1990s as evidenced by the use of these ma-terials in fire-protection training in 1993 at Randolph. The Air Force recog-nized the volatile, dangerous qualities of these waste products as early as the mid-1950s when manuals described purposeful diversion of such materials from sewer systems to incinerators to prevent explosions in the underground pipes.[34]

Environmental Impacts

In the 1980s the military admittedly felt the pressure to institute cleanup actions. Official recognition followed an eruption of public concern with envi-ronmental problems stemming from military operations. When the Love Canal incident gained national headlines in the late 1970s, investigators sought to confirm whether or not the military had transported wastes to the notorious dump. Although no proof surfaced, accusations of a federal role aroused fur-ther suspicions. Private parties sued the federal government to recover dam-ages caused by Air Force disposal practices.[35] Other incidents at Rocky Mountain Arsenal and various Department of Energy sites, such as Hanford, triggered further public discontent with government waste-management efforts. In response, the Department of Defense established the Installation Restoration Program to "identify and evaluate previous hazardous material/ waste handling and disposal practices and to take necessary steps to mitigate the potential adverse effect to human health and the environment at sites where affected media is identified."[36] Furthermore, the federal Superfund Act (Comprehensive Environmental Response, Compensation, and Liability Act or CERCLA, 1980) specifically states that federal facilities must comply with the same requirements as private ones. The significance of contamination at mili-tary sites is hidden by the fact that the federal facilities account only for a small percentage of the national total; however, the scope and complexity of the cleanup programs at these sites dwarf many private industrial remediation ef-forts. The federal remediation program has produced documented cases of impacts to the environment. As of 1993 the Federal Agency Hazardous Waste Compliance Docket listed 863 Department of Defense facilities, accounting for 44 percent of all federal installations. All six of San Antonio's facilities are on this list. The Fast Track Clean-up Program under the Base Realignment and Closure program (BRAC) lists seventy-five military bases, including Kelly Air Force Base, where remediation may require up to twenty years, with an additional ten years of monitoring.[37]

The concentration of military facilities in San Antonio above the Edwards Aquifer represents a potentially significant threat to the aquifer's health. Contamination could affect up to twenty cities, in addition to San Antonio, which depend on the aquifer for drinking water and irrigation. Any activity involving a hazardous material or wastes is threatening to groundwater because the hydrologic cycle is one of the primary pathways for migration of industrial wastes. The regional significance of the Edwards Aquifer cannot be underestimated, and the consequences of contaminating it would be grave.[38]

The combination of military operations and the presence of the "sole source" Edwards Aquifer in San Antonio presents an opportunity for disaster. Fortunately, the relationship between the location of the military bases and the recharge and artesian zones of the Edwards Aquifer appear to have protected the aquifer from contamination, and therefore have limited the subsequent cleanup and remediation efforts to shallow, unconfined aquifers (see fig. 6.1 above). All of the bases are located above the Edwards Aquifer, but only Camp Bullis is located within the boundaries of the recharge area where precipitation and streamflow replenish the aquifer. The remaining bases are located above the reservoir area of the aquifer, where water is stored but not replenished. This simple geographic difference is perhaps the only reason that military facilities have not caused verified groundwater contamination of the Edwards Aquifer.[39]

Serious contamination exists, however, in shallow aquifers at all but Fort Sam Houston and Camp Bullis. The groundwater assessment report for Randolph Air Force Base documents offsite migration of contaminated groundwater containing organics, fuel hydrocarbons, low-level radioactive wastes, trichloroethylene, automotive fuel, polynuclear aromatic hydrocarbons, and volatile organic compounds (VOCs). Contaminant sources include underground storage tanks, twenty-one acres of landfills, eight acres of fire-protection areas, and seven acres of fuel-sludge disposal areas. Although an offsite dry-cleaning facility immediately north of the base may have influenced the concentration of VOCs, the prolific use of dry-cleaning solvents for all types of cleaning and maintenance activities at the bases suggests otherwise. Similar contaminants, as well as low levels of pesticides, exist at Brooks Air Force Base. Major contaminant sources at Brooks include a 6,000-gallon pit of liquid sludge, a seventy-five-foot-diameter fuel-sludge burning area, and thirty acres of landfills. Offsite migration of a TCE plume from the burn area has reached residences southwest of the base.[40]

Originally, Lackland Air Force Base was a portion of Kelly Field known as "the Hill" and was used as a bivouac area and bombing range for aviation cadets. The Atomic Energy Commission (AEC) formerly owned Lackland's annex, which is located one mile west of the main base. The AEC used the property for weapons maintenance and storage, and fifteen of Lackland's twenty-five contaminated areas are located on the annex. The weapons maintenance and storage activities as well as historical activities of landfilling, fuel storage, disposal of low-level radioactive wastes, operation of explosive ordinance burn pits, dog-dipping solution leaching areas, open detonation grounds, and fire-protection areas have impacted the shallow unconfined aquifer used for irrigation of crops and livestock. As at Kelly, "a substantial thickness of clay and marl isolate the [Edwards] aquifer from surface contaminant sources."[41]

While significant environmental impacts exist at all of San Antonio's military installations, the known extent and concentration of contaminants in the shallow aquifer at Kelly Air Force Base is the most significant. Since the War Department founded Kelly Field in 1917, the installation's mission has been logistics and maintenance, requiring a large-scale industrial complex. In the late 1910s maintenance personnel repaired and built aircraft components. After World War I and the demobilization of the military forces, Kelly served as the consolidation point for similar operations in the region. Rapid expansion took place in the late 1930s, and by World War II thousands of aircraft were overhauled at Kelly. The volume of aircraft engines overhauled at the complex increased from 600 per month in the 1950s to approximately 1,400 per month by the 1960s and 1970s. The number of personnel and aircraft continued to ebb and flow with the status of war efforts, finally ending in post–Cold War downsizing in the military. Ultimately, the decision to return the base to private use will not end the maintenance activities but only shift them from federal to private responsibility.[42]

The Department of Defense selected Kelly for base realignment and closure in 1995 and has initiated intensive cleanup activities and corrective action measures under the Resource Conservation and Recovery Act. The long history of industrial activities at Kelly include fuel storage, machine shops, sludge burial, disposal of low-level radioactive waste, weapons storage, paint and solvent use, metal-plating, solid-waste landfill use, and the operation of blacksmith shops and foundries. All these activities contributed to serious contamination of the shallow discontinuous aquifer with dissolved chlorinated solvents as well as fuel plumes. The contamination sources at Kelly are so numerous that investigators coded the base surface into areas based on (1) whether contaminants were present, (2) whether those contaminants require remediation, and (3) the status of the remediation. In addition, investigators divided the groundwater beneath the base into zones of contamination due to the mixing of contaminant plumes.[43]

Under dry conditions, the contaminated shallow groundwater influences Leon Creek, which flows along the western edge of the base and crosses the base twice. In addition, at least one drinking-water well pumps from the shallow aquifer. Fortunately, 600 to 800 feet of clays and clay stone separate the shallow contaminated aquifer from the Edwards Aquifer. Although investigators identified contaminants in Leon Creek, they were below limits for recreation, drinking water, and aquatic life. There is risk associated with the presence contaminants in the shallow groundwater, but the *Management Action Plan* for Kelly states that it is low.[44]

Despite these reassurances, the massive remediation effort coupled with the Agency for Toxic Substances and Disease Registry's (ASTR) comprehensive health survey indicating increased rates of leukemia, low birth weight, birth defects, and liver, kidney, and lung cancers lend credibility to fears within Kelly's surrounding neighborhoods that the contamination present beneath the base and the surrounding area have affected their health and their property.[45] Perhaps the military has been insulated from large-scale public outcry because the contamination has not reached a resource vital to the entire region, but for nearby residents this localized contamination is a real threat. Over the years, these residents have clashed with the military over many environmental issues. In 1986 residents objected to the permitting of a hazardous-waste storage site near the eastern border of the base very near a community center and playground. In 1988 city workers discovered a jet-fuel spill southeast of the base during a public works construction project. The city halted the project and the neighborhood called for a health survey of nearby residents. In the mid-1990s residents north of the base began complaining of health effects they believed were due to fuel vapors from a tank farm near the edge of the base. In each of these instances, as well as in the cases of on-base contamination, the Air Force was slow to acknowledge the seriousness of contaminants in the soil or groundwater. Whether prudently holding back information to avoid panic or acting irresponsibly, the Air Force, by its actions, engendered distrust of the military within the community. This history, coupled with the rise of grassroots environmental justice groups, has led to a heated debate about the implications and motivations behind remediation activities (or lack thereof) in the primarily Hispanic residential areas surrounding Kelly. Residents have formed the Committee for Environmental Justice Action (CEJA), a subgroup of Southwest Public Workers Union (SPWU), and in April 1999 filed a civil rights complaint based on environmental racism.[46]

Conclusion

San Antonio's history is intertwined with nineteenth-century Texas military history and the early-twentieth-century Air Force development. Unlike the patriotic accounts of the Army and Air Force's accomplishments in defending the country, the military's environmental history in the city is more somber. Like other types of industrial facilities, military installations have dealt with the large-scale management and disposal of hazardous wastes for nearly a century. To protect human health and the environment, science and politics have changed management and disposal practices significantly, yet until recent years the military was somewhat insulated from enforcement of environmental regulations.

Within the ring of the interstate highway surrounding San Antonio's core are four major military complexes. These bases continue to employ a significant number of San Antonio's residents and contribute to the city's economy. The exceptional concentration of military facilities in an urban area, San Antonio's economic dependence on the facilities, the presence of serious contamination in shallow groundwater, and the presence of a vulnerable water supply make the potential for further damage very real. Fortunately, of the bases, only Kelly has contributed to serious environmental damage. Fueling and maintenance operations released contaminants to the base soils and they percolated to shallow aquifers. The bases in this part of the city are situated over the reservoir portion of the Edwards Aquifer and clay soils separate the military activity from the precious drinking-water source, thereby preventing calamity. Other operations, such as landfilling and training, have contributed to environmental harm, but to a lesser extent.

Other than a few very high-profile incidents, the moderate impacts of military bases have been largely invisible at a national scale. The rise in public awareness of environmental impacts at industrial facilities, coupled with a few extreme environmental impacts at military bases, prompted the development of programs within the military to address its past actions. In San Antonio, however, many locally significant events have had a sizable cumulative impact on the environment as well as on the relationship between San Antonio's civilian population and the military. This relationship is now strained both by actual and potential future damages. With the combined impacts of demilitarization and site contamination, those most affected, particularly neighbors of the bases, feel both economically abandoned and environmentally violated.

FOUR

Water Fights

7

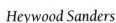

Heywood Sanders

Empty Taps, Missing Pipes

Water Policy and Politics

For the cities of the west, water has defined urban destiny. From Los Angeles's bold gamble in using its entire legal debt limit in 1913 to finance the construction of a 200-mile-long aqueduct to drain the snowmelt of the Sierra Nevadas, to Albuquerque's initiatives in securing water from the Colorado River in the 1950s, the quest for expanded water supply, and the funds needed to impound and move it, have defined Sunbelt urban politics and development.

But not in San Antonio. Where its urban counterparts, from Dallas and Houston to Phoenix and Las Vegas, were investing millions in the post–World War II era to develop expanded water supplies, San Antonio continued its reliance on the groundwater supply of the Edwards Aquifer. It was, admittedly, an abundant, high-quality water source. Yet it was clearly apparent that the aquifer had its limits and constraints. The newspaper headlines of the period tell a quite visible and dramatic tale. "S.A. Water Outlook Dim" reported the *San Antonio Light* in April 1948, noting that the city was pumping an unusually heavy volume of water for the spring. By that June the

City Water Board was posting a "Notice to Water Customers" describing the overburdened water system and resorting to an alternating-day scheme for lawn sprinkling. Three years later the news was no better. The *Light* reported that "Critical Shortages Faced with S.A.'s Longest Dry Spell," noting that the 114-day period from October 1950 to mid-January 1951 had seen only 0.42 inches of rain.

The rainfall situation proved no better into the 1950s. Water pumping increased and the *Light* ultimately reported in June 1956 that the city's underground water level had continued to drop, reaching a record low. San Antonio thus faced an obvious crisis of water supply and availability that extended for almost a decade, a crisis that ought to have provoked an aggressive search for more water. Yet the city did not succeed in acquiring a new water supply at the time, and only *appeared* to have succeeded at the end of 1998. San Antonio today remains fully dependent upon the Edwards Aquifer for its water supply, particularly after the city's voters turned down two successive proposals for a surface-water reservoir in 1991 and 1994.

Fig. 7.1. West Side slum, San Antonio, 1940 (*Source:* The UT Institute of Texan Cultures at San Antonio, No. 2322-C [The San Antonio Light Collection].)

Pressed by drought and water crisis, why did San Antonio not follow the lead and initiative of its Texas and Sunbelt counterparts in extending its water reach? The answer is far from simple. It is clear that the local booster imperative that drove other cities, and the political role of what sociologist Harvey Molotch has called the urban "growth machine," was just as evident in San Antonio as in its counterparts. The city's business leaders promoted a host of development efforts from the 1940s through more recent years, luring a university to the city in the late 1940s, promoting trade with Mexico and South America, and seeking to lure the nascent Air Force Academy.

The leaders of San Antonio's Chamber of Commerce even appointed a "secret" committee in 1947 to make a "complete study . . . in connection with the San Antonio water supply."[1] Although that group apparently concluded the underground water supply was "adequate," by early 1948 the reality of the drought had pressed the Chamber into further action. The group's general manager called for a further investigation, including the "possibility of having water diverted from the upper Guadalupe River to the Medina Lake Water Shed," and the Chamber executive committee once again appointed a committee to assess the proposal.[2]

If the reassuring findings of the "secret committee" served during the 1940s, the continuing drought made it evident that city had to do something about its water needs. In August 1951 the Chamber's leaders again met to grapple with the water issue. Civic leader Alex Thomas called on the Chamber leadership to "continue efforts inaugurated some years ago to assure a dependable water supply for San Antonio," calling for an investigation of using the "flood waters of the upper Guadalupe." The Chamber counsel responded by recalling the work of the earlier "secret committee," and noting its conclusion that "the present water supply was sufficient for domestic purposes in San Antonio now but not for future growth and industrial expansion." Yet another chamber leader called for a "strong committee . . . to work quietly to assure future water supply in sufficient quantities to take care of expansion of industries and population in the San Antonio area." Businessman E. C. Sullivan called upon the group to create "a strong committee . . . to work quietly to assure future water supply in sufficient quantities to take care of expansion of industries and population in the San Antonio area." The Chamber group's ultimate response was yet another "secret committee," this to "begin work immediately on investigation of means to assure proper conservation and control of surface and underground water resources."[3]

For San Antonio's business leadership, the recognition of water needs and some effort to understand and grapple with them was clear even in the early drought years. Yet what is striking is how modest the public action resulting from that recognition proved to be. Each new water committee was deemed "secret," presumably to keep the Chamber's activity and concern out of the public domain. Yet the evidence of dropping water levels and summer watering bans was clear to every San Antonian.

The city's business leadership was far from reticent or impotent in the larger political arena. Many of the same stalwarts of the Chamber had led an effort to replace the city's commission form of city government with a city manager, an effort that failed at the polls in 1950. The manager plan was resurrected by civic leaders again in 1951, and finally succeeded in winning public endorsement and approval. The first city council under the manager system was voted into office in November 1951.

Perhaps emboldened by the successful "reform" of the city's governmental system, the Chamber's water committee in November 1951 called on their colleagues to form a "permanent Water Supply Committee to work on a long-range program to insure proper and sufficient water supply for San Antonio." Still the charge to the group was that it work "without publicity in cooperation with the City Water Board and other agencies."[4]

The advent of council-manager government did not prove quite the panacea for San Antonio's ills touted by reform proponents. Even with a professional manager, the community remained hampered by poor public services and constrained city finances. One alternative fiscal approach, promoted by a group of local investment bankers in 1952, called for merging the city-owned gas and electric utility with the City Water Board to funnel the additional revenues from the two utilities into the city's general fund.[5] Despite the appeal of the seeming "free" revenues from the city utilities, even this plan proved unsuccessful.

San Antonio, its business leaders, and the City Water Board finally sought bond funds for an additional water supply in June 1956, as a $1.5-million part of a $20.885-million water bond program placed before the voters. Yet even with majority endorsement, the $1.5 million for surface water proved far too little, too late. The modest sum for surface water was planned for use in the Canyon Dam project, to secure for San Antonio a part of the flow from the Guadalupe River north of the city. When the city and the water board were finally able to afford to participate in the Canyon project in 1957 and 1958, its water rights were disputed by the dam's principal developer, the Guadalupe-

Blanco River Authority. The result was a legal wrangle that extended through the 1960s, and a persistent failure to acquire Canyon water.

Explaining Inaction: The Other Water "Crisis"

When the Chamber of Commerce first grappled with water needs in the 1940s, it was not at all concerned with the city's overall supply. It was instead faced with a crisis of public health and sanitation. The war years were a boom time for San Antonio, as the city's military installations were expanded and filled with war workers, troops, and their families. From 1940 to 1950 the population grew from 253,854 to 408,442, or some 61 percent. That population boom exposed weaknesses in the city's long-time infrastructure and public investment policies, and stretched the resources of the local water and sewer systems to the breaking point.

The first evidence of concern over water and sewerage within the business community came in 1943. The September 28 meeting of the Chamber directors included an "extended discussion" of the local health situation, which concluded with the sentiment that "San Antonio can help itself measurably with the army by taking the proper steps in this matter."[6] But by 1946, the city had apparently made relatively little headway in dealing with these. The immediate problem was an outbreak of polio cases in the spring of 1946. The chair of the Chamber's Health Committee noted that the fact that "the polio cases have occurred in May instead of in July and August as in the past is very disturbing and that it is a bad omen that there has been no appreciable reduction in the number of new cases reported from day to day." Dr. Royall Palmer of the Health Committee linked the polio outbreak to the city's sewage problems and concluded that the "solution, by providing thorough sewage disposal and elimination of pit privies and septic tanks, is a long time proposition."[7]

The Chamber discussion made it clear that their view of the problem did not involve ill health or the ravages of polio. Instead, its argument was "if [the] job is not done the City of San Antonio will suffer great damage."[8] But if the Chamber leaders were driven by a booster sentiment to preserve the city's image, the reality was undeniable. Chamber executive C. R. Crampton reported in June 1946 on "great progress" on cleanup efforts. Yet he also noted, "The sewage disposal plant is in deplorable condition," with its capacity of 25 million gallons per day exceeded by 10 to 20 million gallons, untreated sewage dumped into a local lake, and the state prohibiting the city from allowing the untreated sewage to pass into the Medina River south of the city.[9]

The overburdened sewage-disposal plant reflected the price of a long-standing underinvestment in city infrastructure. There was an even more serious problem with those homes and neighborhoods not even connected to sewers. Crampton reported "20,000 open pit privies in San Antonio, of which about 3,000 are in sewer districts." And the city's water supply situation was equally dismal, with several "outlying districts . . . not connected with any water system," and residents obliged to "purchase water and keep it in open barrels with consequent contamination."[10]

The sewage-treatment problem had a relatively simple solution—expansion of the city's overburdened plant. But one proposal for $3.3 million in bonds for plant improvement was voted down in May 1946, and a second, more expansive scheme for creation of a new metropolitan district to expand sewage treatment failed the following September. It was not until December 1947 that the voters approved bonds for sewage-plant expansion. Yet those bonds, delayed as they were, could only aid the neighborhoods of the city served by sewer pipes and connected to the plant. There was still, in the late 1940s, a large swathe of the city with no links to the sanitary sewer system, and the concern of the business leadership for public health showed signs of disappearing.

The Chamber of Commerce's May 1949 board meeting heard a report from the Public Health Committee that termed conditions in San Antonio "incomparably bad." This time the committee's conclusions reached beyond the overloaded sewer system:

> A major portion of the health hazards in San Antonio are crowded into the area occupied by our Latin-American citizens. Here poor housing, inadequate sanitary provisions, many unsewered residences and corrals [a local form of multifamily housing], crowding of large numbers of people into small tenements, ignorance and indifference in matters of public health—these and many other factors provide a situation which can be equaled in few American communities.[11]

Less than a year later, the Health Committee again called on the Chamber to deal with the city's public-health problems, this time recommending that the Chamber urge "immediate steps be taken to provide the water connections for the estimated 5,000 to 6,000 residences in the City of San Antonio which are not now connected to established water systems."[12] They were centered principally in the west and south sides of the urban area where its Hispanic population was located. With no water other than from wells or barrels, there were no indoor toilets and no sewer connections, just latrines, privies, and outhouses across a broad, developed stretch of the city, an area close to the downtown core and well inside the city limits. And although the problem had obviously existed for decades, it was only in 1950 and 1951 that the Chamber leadership was apparently able to recognize it and press the mayor and elected officials for some sort of public response.

The combination of civic embarrassment and political change brought some overt pressure on the city's public water utility, the Water Works Board of Trustees, to address the service needs of the inner city. Mayor Jack White wrote the board in March 1951, referring to "numerous complaints and pleas made to him by people in need of water service." The mayor argued that the board "should take a different view with reference to furnishing water to consumers in development areas, the lack of which service constitutes a health hazard." In response, the manager of the water works proposed using special bond funds to extend water mains to unserved areas, and to "double the allowance of free main for sanitation benefit."[13]

The mayor reported the movement by the water utility to the Chamber of Commerce the following day, noting that the City Council had "made an agreement with the City Water Board whereby approximately 40 miles of new water mains will be placed in sections not now having water connections."[14]

The same March 13 Chamber board meeting brought some more distressing news about the community's image. The Chamber general manager reported on an article in *Look* magazine, "relative to the Latin American problem in Texas" as "receiving much attention," although it did not describe "the great progress which has been made in recent years in the betterment of these conditions."[15]

The Chamber's leaders were quite properly concerned about the *Look* portrayal of San Antonio, for it provided a devastating indictment of city policies:

> San Antonio, more than half Mexican, has the highest T. B. rate in
> the nation. . . . In five years in San Antonio, infant diarrhea killed
> 920 babies—865 of them Latin. . . . An inside faucet is an item of
> envy. A single alley faucet shared by a dozen families is more
> likely to be the only facility. But few Latins know even that luxury
> in Las Colonias, the shacktown on the edge of San Antonio.

Shacks started springing up on these sunbaked flats ten years ago
when the city's slums just couldn't absorb the influx of population. In those days, the flats were outside the city limits. There
were no schools, no water, no roads and no police or fire protection. Also no city taxes. Recently, the city absorbed the area. As a
result, city taxes were slapped on Las Colonias residents, but
there are still few schools, almost no police or fire protection, and,
for roads, high-grade cow trails that turn into miniature lakes
when the rains come.

Water has been piped to only a small section of the area. Before a
Las Colonias shack owner can get connected to a water main,
every resident in his area must pay a fee. When one fails to pay,
nobody gets water. To a Mexican laborer earning an average wage
of about $800 a year for his family of six, a $35 fee seems like a
small fortune. So, few of the 10,000 people of Las Colonias have
running water.[16]

In light of this larger reality, the mayor's promise to provide forty miles of new
water mains appeared a bit late and too modest.

Just two weeks after the mayor's appearance before the Chamber's leaders,
San Antonio's water problems were on the business group's agenda, neatly labeled "Confidential." As the Chamber recognized, the lack of water service in
"several large areas" was a result of water board policies. Although the board
and Chamber agreed to "consolidate all water systems serving various areas in
the city and find a means to provide water facilities for everyone," there were a
number of impediments. First, it was not even clear where the water lines did
not go, forcing the Chamber to purchase a set of aerial maps so that the water
board and Health Department could determine the "exact areas without water
mains and the number of residences therein." Then there was the problem of
money. The bonds that had financed the public purchase of the water board
decades before contained restrictions on payments for extending water mains
that "present certain problems." The conclusion of the Chamber group was
that a plan to grapple with the lack of water service might well require purchase of the outstanding water board bonds, or "that a new bond issue be voted
to provide funds for extension of water mains."[17]

The Chamber leaders had thus come to recognize both the failures of the
city's historic infrastructure policies and the crucial role of public finance.

Their education may well have been aided by the observations of attorney W. L. Matthews, a leader of the effort to reform city government since the 1920s. Writing to Dr. Herbert Hill, Matthews argued for the use of a charge for sewer service as a mechanism for funding a citywide sewer-expansion program. But Matthews was particularly direct about the community's policies:

> Throughout the history of San Antonio the building of sewers has constantly lagged behind the increase in population and the extension of the areas to be served. Sewer lines have been constructed by the City out of bonds issued at intervals of ten to twelve years. These bond issues have never been sufficient in amount to catch up with the growth of the city, and therefore, we have not only had a deficit between periods of the bond issues, but even after the expenditure of substantial bond funds a deficit has always remained. Most of the lateral sewers have been built by subdividers of property or by contributions made by homeowners on a single street or community basis. In the main the sewers have not been maintained because of the lack of funds for this purpose, or to put it another way, because of the competition of other needs for the operating dollars available for city purposes.[18]

Matthews captured the dual realities of public services in San Antonio. The city had historically done only the most minimal provision of even critical infrastructure, leaving much of the burden to subdividers or homeowners. Where neighborhood residents could not afford to provide sewers—or streets, curbs, sidewalks, and water service—they were simply not built. Yet even as the Chamber's business leaders and political reformers like Matthews tried to remedy the long-standing public-health ills of the underserved zones of the city, they faced an enormous fiscal burden and no history of the political will to fund these services.

The juxtaposition of Chamber concerns was remarkable. At the same March 1951 board meeting where its manager reported on the lack of running water in as many as 6,000 residences, the business group also discussed the promotion of San Antonio as "America's Fastest Growing Major City," the successful wooing of three new conventions to the city, and the plans to lure the new Air Force Academy to the city. If San Antonio expected to meet the promise of its boosters, and attract tourists, new jobs, and new federal government installations, it would have grapple with a public-health situation that held the city up to national shame. Not all of the business leadership was reluctant to publicize the city's health and sanitation problems to secure necessary reform. The Chamber's Public Health Committee recommended in June 1951 that the Chamber press city officials to "pass an ordinance to correct in future construction certain conditions which have tended in the past to increase public health hazards." Lax city development policies had long been a boon to land developers and subdividers, and had assured that decent sanitation and public infrastructure went only to those with the resources to pay for them. And the ill-health and inequity built into the city for decades, and continuing in new developments like the "Las Colonias" described by *Look,* had been downplayed by a civic leadership intent upon growth and promotion:

> The Public Health Committee recognizes the difficulty of publicizing weaknesses or bad health conditions, but realizes also that through such publicity it is possible to get the public to realize actual conditions and to do something to correct them. Contrary to public opinion, health hazards exist not only in one section, but throughout all sections of the city.[19]

Even the impetus provided by *Look's* description of the city's "forgotten people" was not enough. In May 1953 Mayor White again pressed the City Water Board to expand service but was rebuffed: "The Board did not commit itself, but [Board member] Mr. Giesecke assured Mayor White that the Board would do everything possible to render service to residents of San Antonio who are not now receiving service."[20]

The problems of limited water service to the city's poorer neighborhoods would not be fully resolved until the water board's finances were restructured and a new source of revenues created. That eventually came in May 1956, with the passage of a $20.885-million water bond issue. Most of the those funds were committed to the extension and upgrading of the city's water service. It was only at that point that San Antonio could begin seriously to remedy its other water crisis, and then deal with the longer-term issue of water supply and surface water.

Institutional and Political Legacies

Although San Antonio's water service and supply was a public function, it was not carried out by the city. When San Antonio sought the funds to purchase the privately owned water works in the mid-1920s, both potential bond purchasers and civic leaders were extremely leery of the machine politicians who had long controlled the city government. The result was the crafting of a set of forty-year bonds that vested control over the water works in a self-perpetuating four-member board, with the mayor as an ex-officio member. The scheme was fully intended to insulate the water board from city politics, for elected officials had absolutely no say in the membership of the body: if a member resigned or, more likely, passed away, the board itself chose his successor; board minutes also reveal that mayors only rarely attended board meetings, which focused narrowly on the delivery of water service.

The ethos of the board centered on efficient, economical provision of water to San Antonians. Its rate structure thus favored city residents, charging suburban residents a higher monthly rate. Providing water economically meant that should the water board manage a surplus, it simply reduced its rates. Thus even as the city was booming, and as problems of increasing demand and poor rainfall pointed up problems with service and supply, water became steadily cheaper. Beginning in 1926 and until 1944, the board reduced rates on twelve occasions. From a minimum monthly charge of $1.20, the monthly rate fell to $0.76 by 1944—a decrease of about 40 percent.

Keeping water cheap aided major local businesses and bolstered the arguments of boosters that the city was a good place to locate a business. But it also meant that the water board lacked the resources to develop a major addition of surface water to supplement the Edwards Aquifer supplies. As the city grew outward, the board merely had to add some new wells, at modest cost. That meant there was no need for a system of aqueducts or pipelines, filtration or treatment plants, that characterized other Sunbelt cities. It also meant no need for an elaborate distribution system within the city, like the underground water tunnels built in New York. Wells were drilled close to consumers, and distribution lines were kept short and small.

The board's commitment to "one main objective—to furnish the water users with pure water, together with good service at the lowest possible cost" also had implications for who was served and where.[21] As the Chamber's Public Health Committee discovered and *Look* magazine documented, the water board did not view its "service" as public in the broadest sense. The utility was unwilling to extend water lines to areas unable or unwilling to pay for them, or to use a sufficient volume of water to justify the investment. Cheap water was a mantra that did not extend to the entire community.

Community concern over the lack of both water service and, consequently, sewers had become quite evident in the mid-1940s, as both the Chamber and elected officials began to question the inequity of the board's policies. Its rebuttal was blunt: as water board chair and local lawyer Conrad A. Goeth argued, the water system was purchased from revenues rather than from general taxation. For the revenue-based water works, every "extension made under this system should be governed by anticipated revenue . . . the Board adopted regulations relating to extensions and providing for investment on extensions from revenue, *only* when anticipated new revenue justified the extension."[22] That was why, in the face of demands for water service and extensions in the city's low-income neighborhoods, the board adamantly opposed subsidizing service, whether in the name of equity or public health.

The water board's resolute position against uneconomic extensions was paralleled by its refusal to extend service cheaply to new developments outside the city limits. In December 1947 Marshall Eskridge "came before the board in behalf of W. K. Ewing and Company, H. B. Zachry, Terrell Bartlett and other developers of areas outside the city limits, with a plea that the board grant refunds on mains constructed by developers outside the city limits on the basis that refunds are made to developers within the city limits."[23]

The petitioners were major forces in San Antonio: Zachry a builder active in the reform movement and the Chamber, Bartlett a civil engineer and developer. Yet the board's response was far from supportive of new outlying development. "Mr. Goeth explained to Mr. Eskridge that the primary function of the Water Board is to serve consumers within the limits of the city and to operate the plant for the benefit of the city and that the Board could not consistently consider such a change at this time."

The water board's commitment to low rates and limited service was increasingly taxed by the city's growth in the late 1940s. The population growth, and annexations of outlying areas beginning in 1944, obliged the board to extend lines to new developments and provide an increasing volume of water. By October 1949 General Manager W. D. Masterson was beginning to recommend a water rate increase "to meet the increased expenditures and cost operation."[24] In just a few months, the need for a rate increase became fully evident. A formal report to the board in February 1950 brought the argument from Masterson that

> since the board can not borrow it is important that we do not dip too deep into this reserve, so in order to finance improvements during these years of rapid growth it is evident some form of in-

crease in water charges should be made. . . . Taking all of this into
account it is very evident that we must make some upward adjust-
ment in water rates in order this year to reduce and eventually
stop the drain on reserves.[25]

The 1950 rate increase marked a significant change in the long-term policy of rate decreases and inexpensive water. Strikingly, it was propelled neither
by the reduced rainfall and threat of drought already evident in the area nor by
the Chamber's concern over the public-health problems in the neighborhoods
lacking water and sewers. Nor were the rate increase and additional revenues
to be dedicated to dealing with either of these larger problems. The board instead chose to boost rates to maintain its fiscal reserves as it was forced by the
city's growth to expand.

The water board had been created to insulate water service from politics.
For twenty-five years it had done so admirably, although perhaps too well. Yet
by 1951 it was clear that the board itself constituted a political problem. With
limited resources and no real plans, it had fallen behind on the demands of
urban growth. It had sustained a set of penurious policies that doomed poor
neighborhoods to high rates of disease and death and simultaneously angered
developers by refusing inexpensive extensions. In perhaps the ultimate measure of its insulation, it had largely ignored the pursuit of an alternative water
supply for the city.

Together with city officials, the water board eventually came to the conclusion that the only resolution of the city's water needs would come in re-
funding the original debt of the water works, freeing the utility to take on new
revenue debt. By late 1954 a citizens' group had drafted a scheme whereby the
voters would authorize a large water revenue bond issue, which would include
the re-funding of the original debt, funds for system extension and rehabilitation, and (more modestly) additional water supply.

The $20.885-million water bond program approved by an 84 percent ma-
jority in June 1956 finally provided the water board with the fiscal resources to
extend water service throughout the city and develop the system. But the water
board's long-standing policies of limiting spending and keeping rates down
would have a larger, longer-term, more expensive legacy.

The 1956 bond issue had been based on an analysis of the system by Black
and Veatch consulting engineers in 1955. Four years later, with a newly constituted water board considering the needs of the water system and a possible
rate increase, Black and Veatch had some more expensive news: "Replacements

of corroded and inadequate mains, and the replacement of services, have not been made as planned at the time of the last rate increase due to the shortage of funds for this purpose." The bill for bringing the water system up to modern standards was, in short, growing rapidly. "While it has been known for some time that some distribution system pipe in San Antonio was seriously affected by a corrosive action of certain soils which seems unequaled elsewhere, no comprehensive survey or measures of accumulated damage was available by which to program replacements or set up remedial methods on a large scale."[26] The engineering firm estimated that some 230 miles of water main would have to be replaced.

Many of the mains were too small, too. Building a system as cheaply as possible, the water board had installed some 450 miles of two-inch or smaller pipe in a system of some 1,200 miles. "Present practice over the country is to install no distribution pipe less than six inches in size, and 8 inch is preferred."[27] Black and Veatch concluded that some 120 miles of undersized pipe had to be replaced, with the eventual likelihood of replacing all of the two-inch pipe.

The commitment of the board to cheap water, and the inability to buy out of the 1925 bonds until after 1956, left the city with a serious backlog of spending needs simply to provide water service to the entire community and meet contemporary engineering standards. Only after meeting those requirements would the post-1956 board have the resources and political capacity to seriously pursue surface water.

Politics, Rates, and Political Reformation

The larger political environment within which the water board operated changed fundamentally in 1951. The passage of a charter change creating a city manager form of government, which began the process of altering city policies to support growth and development, also had the effect of injecting water supply, water service, and water rates into the broader political battle for control over city government and policy. For just as the water board had failed to provide for either effective growth or service equity, the city of San Antonio itself had long failed to sustain public investment in sewers and sewage treatment, storm drainage, and streets. The reformation of city government now made those problems the responsibility of the business leaders and reformers who had long argued that the city needed a modern, professional government. After 1951 they had to deliver on the promise of better services delivered more efficiently, as well as with the votes needed to pass bond issues for improved facilities.

The new "reform" city council that took office on January 1, 1952, faced an immediate need for more public dollars for public improvements. The water board and its regular monthly bills offered a tempting fiscal target. In October 1952 a group of local investment bankers floated a scheme to merge the city's gas and electric utility and the independent water board, with the aim of generating more revenues for the cash-starved city. The bankers' plan was designed to procure "sufficient revenue to provide adequate municipal services, which the citizens expect of the new Council."[28]

Yet the central problem that the investment bankers sought to resolve was the essential fragility of the city's new council-manager government.

> The enemies of council-manager will seize upon every opportunity to influence the mind and vote of the rank and file. It, therefore, behooves every friend of good government in San Antonio to give thorough study to the most feasible means of raising additional revenue, *short of hiking the ad valorem tax rate to the $2.50 legal limit* [emphasis added].[29]

For the bankers, and perhaps for a larger group of government reform supporters, the existence of the manager government was dependent upon keeping taxes down, despite the obvious service needs of the city. They were concerned about "hiking the ad valorem [property tax] rate from the present $2.00 levy to $2.50, which might or might not mean the end of council-manager government."[30] Siphoning revenues from the water system might enable the city to improve streets and sanitation without the political risk of boosting the presumably more politically dangerous property levy.

But there was an additional benefit derived from altering the structure of the water works. The bankers' report noted that 1925 bonds for the water system would be paid off in 1965 unless the board took on new revenue debt. In that case,

> the board would no longer exist and the management and control would pass to the City Council. For obvious reasons, such a situation would be politically unwise. Utility rates would become an issue at each city election and demagoguery in various other forms would be practiced. The prospect of controlling

$13,500,000 of net revenue (probably $20,000,000 by 1972) would cause persons seeking personal gain to run for public office. It is unthinkable that such a situation should be allowed to come about.[31]

The bankers' scheme came to naught. Yet it defined the most plausible means of grappling with the interrelated aspects of the city's water needs. By floating new revenue debt the board could address the sanitation problem and the quest for new supplies while maintaining its formal independence and keeping water out of fractious city politics. That seemingly simple step, however, would require a period of years and an eventual public vote.

The first step in changing the board's fiscal situation involved an increase in water rates. Despite the rate boost in 1950, the water system still found itself behind in expanding the system and keeping up with the demands created by the drought of the early 1950s. For a water system that depended upon a network of wells, the drought had an immediate impact. As the city drew on the Edwards Aquifer, its water level dropped, requiring the board to drill new, deeper wells. In December 1951 General Manager Masterson noted the need to "cover the expense of new wells and work on old wells to help overcome water shortage caused by depreciation or depletion of supply" and recommended a special transfer of some surplus funds.[32] It was obvious that the board would sooner or later face the need for a rate increase, but it did not act, and instead ordered Masterson to make a further study.

It was not the March 16, 1953, meeting that the water board was willing to consider a rate increase proposal, yet even then it deferred the effective date until May 1, 1953. The choice of the May 1 date was shaped by local politics, as a city runoff election was scheduled for April 21. By delaying the increase, the board eliminated water pricing as an issue that could affect the tenuous hold of the reformers on City Hall and bought itself two years before the public could express its displeasure at the polls.

The 26 percent rate increase generated a critical response from independent city councilmember Henry B. Gonzalez, who argued that it would be a burden on the city's low-income populace. Yet the larger reality of water board finance was that the delayed and deferred local water needs really required a 43 percent increase, not just the 26 percent. Once again, in the fall of 1954, the board found itself effectively without money. It passed a resolution on February 8, 1955, noting the "urgent need of additional financing for the purpose of making improvements and extensions to the existing system, as well as the

procurement of an additional supply of water," and contracted with the investment banking firm of Dewar, Robertson and Pancoast for assistance in refi-
nancing the old bonds.[33] But the board's seemingly simple answer to the city's
pressing water needs and its own fiscal limitations could not be implemented
by the water board itself. It required a dive into the depths of the city's con-
flictual politics.

The water board's capacity to issue new revenue debt was defined by the
terms of the 1925 bonds; any new debt would require that the old debt be re-
funded and replaced. That re-funding would require the acquiescence of the
city council and the Texas State Legislature, so in early March 1955 the water
board was obliged to present its scheme for re-funding old bonds and issuing
new debt to San Antonio's elected officials.

The city council at that time was in the midst of open political warfare. The
first city council elected under the new council-manager plan had hired a professional city manager, C. A. Harrell, who had sought to modernize the city's
administrative system and improve the city's persistently weak finances. His
solution was a massive annexation of some eighty square miles of outlying territory that doubled the city's area and boosted available tax revenues. But a
number of major property owners now faced with increased property taxes organized to gain control of City Hall in 1953, promptly removing Harrell. Budget changes by a new city manager, Ralph H. Winton, led to a battle with Mayor
Jack White, and Winton in turn was fired in August 1954.[34]

Winton's firing proved sufficiently political to motivate a group of San Antonians to begin a recall petition to force the mayor and council from office.
White's reaction was to begin a process of resignation by council members,
with the balance of the council appointing their successors. The result, termed
"CHAOS AT CITY HALL" in one banner headline, led a group of local business
and civic leaders to form a new local political party in December 1954, which
they dubbed the "Good Government League." And the new League, bolstered
by substantial campaign funds and a new level of political organization, organized to contest for control of City Hall in April 1955.

The water board's bond initiative and the question of control of the water
system became fodder for the ongoing political battle. The board's debt plan
called both for re-funding the old, 1925 bond and for issuing new debt for expansion and improvements. Any new debt, however, would serve to prolong
the existence of the independent, self-perpetuating board beyond 1965. That
the water board's plan called for no public review of the new debt led Henry
Gonzalez to charge that the "backroom boys are at it again . . . [with] some ten-

uous and mysterious proposition about some projected legislation that would permit further perpetuation of a board which two years ago didn't even have the courtesy to consult with the governing body of the city before proposing a rate increase."[35] The city council also balked at the water board's re-funding proposal, calling on Bexar County legislators at the state capital to stop the board's power grab; the council also endorsed a proposal for an independent study of the water board's re-funding proposal, eventually demanding that the city manager conduct an audit of the board and its finances.

For newspaper editorial writers, the contest over water control exemplified the failures of the council majority:

> "Peoples' Ticket" candidates and cohorts in the city council showed their hand on the water bond deal, and what a hand full of political jokers it is! . . . Hard put to find a campaign issue against the Good Government League, its opponents are obviously puffing frantically to blow up the water-bond plan as a political football. And it's one likely to explode in their faces. . . . Taxpayers and water consumers in San Antonio had better consider quick and hard what could, and probably would, happen if the patronage politicians ever got a hold on their water system. It is not a pretty prospect.[36]

The editorial arguments, however, did little to deter the opposition of the council majority. On March 24, 1955, the city council passed an ordinance calling for the city manager to audit the books of the water board with particular reference to the board's bond holdings, contracts, and spending on professional fees. Faced with the demand for a vast array of information on its internal business, the board deferred, with

> the consensus of the Board that the Manager be requested to draft a letter to City Manager to the effect that, since it is obviously impossible to complete an audit before election, and since it is uncertain whether a new council would desire an audit, the Board declines to open the books until after the election on April 5, 1955.[37]

Its intent was clear. By stalling the audit, it hoped to weather the storm until after its allies on the Good Government League (GGL) could alter the character of the council. The GGL, in fact, won eight of nine council seats that April, with the commitment to press ahead with a program of public improvements and investments. Although the new officials would not take office until May 1, they were pressed by civic leaders and newspapers to embrace the water board's plan quickly during the state legislature's biennial session, with the call that the GGL victory was "a mandate from the people for the council-elect to undertake completion of that plan."[38]

The ultimate compromise worked out by the two councils called for a plan that endorsed the re-funding and new debt scheme, while calling for a public vote on the bonds and greater city council control over any new debt. With the compromise in place, the city's representatives at the state legislature were in a position to press ahead with the necessary legislation. But the apparent agreement by no means covered all of the outstanding water governance and finance issues. There was the question of who would control the water system. The editorial writers of the *San Antonio News* called for giving "the elected representatives of the people in the city government a voice in the selection of new board members" and making the system more responsive to public opinion.[39] Yet even beyond governance were the old problems of rates and service.

The elimination of the old 1925 bonds would free the water system to invest a great deal of money in improving and expanding the water works. That would still require more money, in the form of a rate increase. The water board had long known of the need to boost rates, and the proposed expansion and improvement of the water system made it obvious that "revenues available from the present water revenue rates will be inadequate to permit accomplishment of the recommended program."[40] The board's proposed rate increase of about 30 percent would provide for both the re-funding and improvements. But once again, any discussion of a rate boost occurred in a political context shaped by the GGL's agenda and its view of critical city improvements.

One central issue for the new council involved payments to the city in lieu of property taxes. The water board had long furnished free water to the city. However, the same fiscal constraints noted earlier in the decade were still present, and the water system offered a tempting source of revenues to a strapped City Hall. Meeting in secret at the end of September 1955, the board and the city council agreed on a plan of annual cash payments, escalating over five years to about $200,000. But with the water board still strapped for cash, the payment arrangement meant that the water rates would have to be raised even further, something like a 35 percent boost. This proposed water-rate increase stirred the traditional divisions within the city and on the city council. Independent council member Gonzalez, the lone outsider on the GGL-controlled body, rose in opposition: "The people of San Antonio must not pay out of a gold nozzle for water they must have. If the council seeks the interest of a few bondholders and loses the interest of the people of the city they are pressing on the brow of the poor a crown of thorns."[41]

His words could not stop the movement to re-fund the water board's outstanding debt, but they pointed up a larger political problem. The GGL's council slate had been elected with the promise of defending the council-manager plan and the "vital interests of San Antonio's growth, progress and decent repute."[42] The first major goal of the council was the passage of a bond issue in late November to fund a broad set of needed city improvements. Evidence of continuing conflict was to be avoided in presenting the united civic front needed to pass the bonds; with the $15-million bond package tied to the promise of no increase in city taxes, it was vital to soft-pedal the issue of higher water rates. Council thus deferred any consideration of the water-rate increase until after the November 25 vote, promising that the water bond proposal would go to the voters in January.

The November 25, 1955, city bond vote marked a test for the GGL's political organization and a portent of the electoral chances for the water bond proposal. The results were encouraging but mixed. The voters approved $9.2 million of the $15-million package, defeating bonds for a police building, parks, and libraries. The GGL had clearly won the embrace of the city's Anglo, middle-class voters, turning out a substantial new vote. Yet the success of the water bond program was far from assured. Indeed, one local political observer noted that for the water bonds, "[t]his time the election can't be tied to a 'no tax increase' pledge. It will virtually coincide with a water rate increase."[43] The GGL council needed to bolster popular support for the water debt proposal beyond that garnered for the city's own bonds, while reducing the public reaction to a water-rate increase and the potential blame placed on the city council and the League. If San Antonio was to solve its water crises—from aging pipes to lack of water service and sanitation to a new supply to sustain the city through drought—it would have to do so in a fully political environment.

Forced to deal with an unpredictable electorate, and the increasingly uncomfortable issue of a water-rate increase, a change in the organization of the water board had clear appeal. The old, appointed board could suffer the blame for decades of low rates and poor management, allowing the council to claim that they were sweeping out the old. And so by mid-December the GGL-dominated council proposed that the voters choose not merely whether to issue new water debt, but also who should control San Antonio's water, all the while sidestepping the question of the water-rate boost.

Yet if the council sought to solve a political problem by taking over the water system itself, it did not reckon with those local business leaders who remained fearful of the influence of "politics" in the management of water. Local investment banker Elmer Dittmar immediately led a group determined to keep the board in charge of the city's water works, and free from interference and control by elected officials. Having sought to boost its credibility and the political appeal of the water bond proposal, the city council set off yet another firestorm. The inevitable result was yet another delay in the date for water bond election, and a further deferral of the rate increase proposal. Faced with an overt public debate over control of water as well as pricing, the city council next sought some sort of compromise that would moderate the 38 percent rate increase and enhance the image of the GGL as effective watchdogs of the public purse. The council selected a local accountant, Roy Pope, to evaluate the work of the water board's consultant and propose some sort of fiscal compromise.

Pope's analysis and proposal, presented to the city on January 7, 1956, offered the possibility of limiting the rate boost. He argued that the city's water program could be managed with a 16.66 percent increase if the board altered its policy of reimbursing developers for 100 percent of the cost of extending new water lines. By switching to a 25 percent reimbursement, and eliminating the annual cash payment to the city from the board, the debt could be managed with a relatively modest rate increase—one presumably more politically acceptable and palatable.[44]

Pope's plan did not resolve the ongoing debate between the city body and water board or assure support for the bonds at the polls. So the bond election was once again deferred until sometime after January 31, and the rate increase pushed back to the water board.[45] By mid-February the water board was finally ready to propose a slightly higher rate increase than Pope's, 18.4 percent, while putting the developers' refund at 50 percent rather than 25. The board's scheme accommodated the interests of the politically powerful subdivision developers, while keeping the boost to a palatable level. The rate resolution cleared the way to move ahead with the long-planned bond vote.

It did not resolve the issue of who would run the water system in the future because the water board remained opposed to shifting the water system to city control and seemed willing to defer the vote on control and new bonds. By the end of March 1955 the city council appeared ready to call for a vote at the end of May. But, once again, the council was reluctant to press without a clear sense of public reaction. Finally, armed with the results of a poll of public opinion, the city council set the election date for June 12 and called for a report by city manager Steve Matthews on the possibilities of city operation of the water system.[46]

The protracted debate over the fate of the water board demonstrated a clear fault line in San Antonio's political landscape. For many, politics was something to be feared and avoided. Through most of the first half of the twentieth century, San Antonio's electoral politics had been dominated by a coalition of African American and Mexican American organizations, with a set of policies often oriented to public spending and tax increases. The success of "reform" forces in implementing the council-manager plan and electing the new GGL city council did not necessarily imply a persistent change in the city's politics. In Elmer Dittmar's words:

> San Antonio's City Government, in its present form, is not yet stabilized. Should the Council Manager group lose the next election or the 1959 election, the machine element would then have charge of the Water System in addition to the other City Departments. No City Department is as vulnerable to graft as is a Water System.[47]

Others viewed the work of the water board, and its pattern of low rates and low spending, as an impediment to the community's growth and development. The *San Antonio Light's* political observer, "Don Politico," noted that the water board "was taken so completely out of politics that it completely ignored the urgent needs of the city—from a standpoint of health, from a standpoint of industry and from a standpoint of growth."[48] The Don then went on to note that the "Save the Water Board" committee included a large number of residents of the incorporated suburban cities of Olmos Park and Terrell Hills among its members—thirteen of thirty-six total; in a community long divided between a largely Anglo North Side and a largely Hispanic West and South Sides, "the whole area of the city south of Commerce Street boasts not a single member."[49] The implication was that an independent water board meant a board continually unresponsive to the needs of water-short minority neighborhoods.

The vote on control of the water system and debt re-funding plan occurred on June 12, 1956. By an overwhelming margin of 5 to 1 they backed the $20.88 million in water bonds that finally could free the city from the 1925 bond indenture. But on the issue of control, the water board and its allies' promotion for independence from politics proved successful. Bombarded by a "last minute water board propaganda barrage" orchestrated by public relations man Ellis Shapiro, who represented both the water board and the Good Government League, to "keep rates [the] lowest in Texas," a 57 percent majority backed maintaining the water board.[50]

The June 1956 vote began the process of reshaping water policy and politics for San Antonio. The re-funding arrangement enabled the water board to take on a substantial expansion and improvement program, with $10 million for expanding the distribution system and another $4.8 million for new pumping stations. That spending would be the first installment on providing an up-to-date water system for the city. But solving the two crises of lack of water service and a new surface-water supply received only a modest sum. Service for areas without water garnered $764,000 of the $20-million bond program, while the $1.5 million for the Canyon Dam was intended only to support legal fees and further engineering studies. The full cost of surface water from Canyon was estimated at some $44 million.

It would take almost a year for the re-funding plan to be put into effect and for a new water board to be appointed to manage the improvement effort. With the new board taking office on May 21, 1957, the *Express* could headline "At Last! Water Progress," noting that the city had finally ended "a quarter century of neglect, frustration, and poor planning," concluding that major "credit for this achievement accrues to the incumbent Good Government League–sponsored City Council headed by Mayor Ed Kuykendall," and that "the civic victory achieved here last week ranks in importance with the establishment of council-manager government five years ago. And the one led to the other."[51]

The conclusion of the *San Antonio Express* in crediting the GGL with triumph over the water board was a rather neat rewriting of the city's history. Faced with an overt conflict over the image of the board, the need for voter approval, and the issue of higher rates, the city council had deferred, avoided, and temporized, finally adopting the minimal improvement program proposed by the old water board. Over and over, the council and the GGL had demonstrated a preference for avoiding political conflict over difficult issues, and limiting both tax and rate increases as a means of assuring continued political control. Thus were local policy and the larger need for an improved water system submerged in the interest of maintaining the GGL's political control.

Having started with low water rates and proved itself incapable of building a consensus around higher rates or larger needs, the League and its city council sustained the preferences of the city's business leadership that cheap was better. Even as the new water board was taking office in May 1957, the leadership of the Chamber of Commerce passed a resolution of support for the board while calling upon its members to "aggressively pursue the search for additional sources of water," while at the same time asking that "the operations of the present City Water Board be studied as quickly as possible . . . with the view of effecting economies that could result in savings under present existing rates that would make additional funds available for capital expenditures."[52] Yet little more than two years later, the general manager of the water board would present the city's pressing water-supply problems to the Chamber—the need for additional water "no later than 1965"—with the argument that "the utility will require a rate increase in the very near future in order to maintain a program whereby it can supply needed water to present users and keep pace with the extension of the system to serve the expanding growth of the community and its suburbs."[53]

The Failed Search for Surface Water

On the day San Antonio newspapers reported the victory of the water bonds, they also reported "Water Level at Record Low."[54] The level of the city's Edwards Aquifer test well stood at 619.56 feet, a historic low and a considerable drop from the approximately 680 feet recorded in 1946. The impact of the ongoing drought formed a fitting coda to the bond victory. As San Antonio had long struggled with the intertwined crises of water and politics, it had singularly failed to acquire a water supply to supplement the Edwards underground aquifer.

There had been no lack of attempts to get water. Beginning in 1949, even the conservative water board had considered the need for more water and begun a number of studies of additional sources. At a meeting in May 1949 the water board heard a proposal from local attorney Lester Whipple to develop "a supply of water in the Medina Lake for future use of emergency purposes" and authorized one of its members to meet with the state board of engineers to secure an up-to-date study of the area's underground water supply.[55]

By mid-1951 the city's water level had dropped sufficiently to cause concern over the community's supply. With an ongoing survey by the U.S. Geological Survey of the Edwards Aquifer, General Manager W. D. Masterson

> explained to the Board that the constant lowering of the water
> level had produced a situation so serious that he thought it neces-

sary to call it to the Board's attention. He explained that although he thought that reasonable water service could be maintained throughout the summer from present sources, he thought it very necessary that some plan be worked out for securing an additional supply of ground water or some surface supply to augment ground water supply to meet the constantly increasing demand: even though the watershed from which San Antonio's supply is derived should receive normal rainfall it might not be enough to meet the demand.[56]

The search for more water was thus born out of the emergency of the drought rather than through any long-range planning or concern over the community's development. Yet even with the pressure of dropping well levels and summer watering restrictions, the board faced its own peculiar institutional constraints—the restrictive terms the 1925 bond indenture imposed: "During the discussion reference was made to the inability of the Water Board to borrow to finance a project that would probably require the expenditure of several million dollars and that if bonds were issued for any water supply project, such bonds would necessarily have to be issued by the City."[57]

Although the city was an unlikely source of new water-supply financing in mid-1951, the issue of water supply could no longer be deferred. By November General Manager Masterson addressed the board with "reference to the problem of meeting the contemplated demand for water next summer" and argued that the "idea of buying an interest in the proposed Canyon Dam project should I think be followed up but at the present writing the completion of that project seems to be very indefinite."[58] For the first time, the board was made aware of the potential of the Canyon Dam proposed on the Guadalupe River. There were another possibilities as well, including the purchase of Medina Lake and its water rights, and a dam on the San Antonio River near the eastern edge of Bexar County, which would recapture the city's used water.

By early 1952 the water board had a clear sense of urgency and a general plan for additional water sources, and the agency began to pursue water options from Canyon Lake and Medina Lake. Yet even as the board members debated potential new water supplies, they pressed the point that new water would be expensive and that the fiscal burden should fall on the city, not the water board. Board member Martin Giesecke argued that the project "would involve the outlay of considerable money by the City in purchasing its water rights as it would be expected to pay its pro rata share of the cost of the construction of the dam, in addition to the cost of the feeder main from the project, a purification plant and the installation of larger feeder mains in the City's distribution system."[59]

An organization so long committed to low rates and limited capital spending, the board found that its search for more water was hobbled by its meager fiscal resources. The fiscal problem would eventually be solved by a series of often-delayed rate increases, and by the passage of the $20-million water revenue bond package in June 1956. Yet by the time a new water board was in place, with some modest fiscal resources to commit to getting more water, the window for success had effectively closed.

By late 1953, as the water board moved ahead with a host of engineering studies and consultant reports on surface water, there were only two plausible surface-water resources for the city. Closest to San Antonio, where state law obliged the city to begin its search, the Medina River offered the most reasonable location for a dam and reservoir. What came to be known as the "Applewhite Project" had the advantage of a nearby location. But it was a poor resource for water, owing "to the erratic nature of the rainfall, high evaporation rates and lack of suitable sites for construction of economical dams, development of a supplemental supply within the San Antonio River Basin was found to be inadequate in quantity and economically unfeasible."[60]

The water board nonetheless filed for rights to the Medina/Applewhite water, routinely extending its application over the years. Finally, in 1991, the city endorsed moving ahead and funding the Applewhite Dam project as the city's first source of surface water. But an initiative campaign succeeded in forcing the issue onto the city ballot, and a bare majority of San Antonio turned the Applewhite project down, employing almost exactly the same arguments the water board itself had made in 1955. After the creation of a new citizens' water committee, the city once again put the Applewhite project on the ballot in 1994. And once again, a majority of San Antonio voters said no to the surface-water project.

The water project that had made sense to the water board in 1953 (and subsequently) was the Canyon Dam on the Guadalupe. With a much greater storage capacity and flow, and the promise of a substantial share of the construction cost from the federal government through the Army Corps of Engineers, Canyon was seen as the city's best potential added water supply. Yet even as the water board was moving ahead on claiming a portion of the Canyon water, it faced a combined political and legal problem. The state legislation passed in 1953 contained a formal prohibition against diverting *any* water out of the Guadalupe and San Marcos River Basins. That law "left only one course open to the water board: that of instituting a suit for a declaratory judgment in order to test the constitutionality of the preventive provision."[61]

The result was an odyssey of lawsuits, appeals, and bureaucratic judgments that would extend for years. In August 1953 the manager of the water board informed the group that the Canyon efforts were "being continued but that this was developing into a difficult procedure."[62] That would prove to be a magnificent understatement. When at its February 11, 1964, meeting the water board set up a five-year capital improvements program, it finally "reallocated" the $1.5-million fund for surface water created by the 1956 bond issue to its regular improvement program, for there was no longer surface water to spend the money on.

Today, the Canyon Dam and Lake built by the Corps of Engineers serves flood-control and recreation purposes, providing an opportunity for local boaters and a steady supply of water for tens of thousands of tourists who "tube" down the Guadalupe. But not a drop of its water comes to San Antonio.

Conclusion

In the 1940s and 1950s San Antonio had not one water problem, but several—inadequate service and sanitary failure, institutional structure, fiscal policy, and local political conflict. The community dealt with those several intertwined problems with some success. The "20,000 open pit privies" described by C. R. Crampton in 1946 had been reduced to some "5,000 or so" by September 1957.[63] The water board continued to employ a revolving fund to expand water to unserved areas of the city well into the 1960s. The old City Water Board, long the subject of editorial scorn, was finally replaced and restructured in 1957 with the retirement of the 1925 bonds. That gave the board and the city the capacity to issue even greater revenue debt and to better keep up with the expansion of the city. And so when in October 1962 banker Tom Frost Jr. came before the board representing the Chamber of Commerce, seeking 14,300 feet of water line to serve an industrial development area on the city's East Side, the board did not hesitate in approving the extension.[64]

These were accomplishments to be sure, although they did little more than finally, after some years, place San Antonio where Dallas, Houston, Albuquerque, and Phoenix had been decades previously. It was the city's penultimate water problem—the problem of dollars and politics—that proved the most difficult and intractable. The City Water Board had been established as an insular, self-perpetuating body to keep the water works out of politics, for San

Antonio's business elite long believed that "politics" was bad for the community and manifestly for them. In a community with a tripartite racial and ethnic division, and a long history of electorally powerful Mexican and African American political organizations, "politics" meant that the Anglo business class often lost and paid.

Yet in keeping water out of "politics" for decades, the city's leadership created a system that discriminated on the basis of wealth, that built a water system to standards long out of date, so decentralized that a surface-water source would have proven enormously expensive to distribute within the city limits, and that did little more than assure that such water as was available was cheap.

The kinds of policies pursued by the water board were far from unique. The city's sewers stopped where the water lines did, as often too did the street paving. Even today, the only parts of the older city that have sidewalks, curbs, and gutters are those better neighborhoods where residents or developers could afford to pay for them. And the city, in seeking to solve a persistent problem of deaths and damages from flooding, managed to build a dam and river channel to protect the downtown core, thereby creating the renowned River Walk, while ignoring no less serious and life-taking flooding in the Hispanic West Side.

The public service inequities that had long characterized and, in the case of the *Look* magazine coverage, embarrassed the city could have been easily reduced and remedied. Water lines could be extended to the entire community, regardless of ethnicity or income, through a simple policy change and some modest public investment. Yet even as San Antonio's business and civic elite sought to reform the city's governance, they appeared consistently unwilling to pay the price of boosting property taxes or water rates to a level commensurate with needed public spending. The lesson of the November 1955 bond issue—that it was appropriate to ask the voters only for what could be afforded without a tax increase—was sustained throughout the era of GGL dominance.

The political import of water rates, clearly visible in the 1950s, remained part of the Good Government League's electoral calculus, and so it remained for several more decades: any serious public discussion or pursuit of alternative or additional water sources remained effectively taboo until 1991. Meanwhile, the city pursued a set of development policies that allowed the water board to grow from 945 miles of water line in 1948, to 1,495 miles in 1958 and 1,916 in 1968, eventually to 3,742 miles by 1997, while avoiding any vote on water board debt and keeping water rates the lowest in Texas.

8

✳

Laura A. Wimberley

Establishing "Sole Source" Protection

The Edwards Aquifer and the Safe Drinking Water Act

In the late 1960s a growing environmental awareness within the American public targeted the visibly polluted waters throughout the nation. Burning rivers and lakes clogged with wastes grabbed the most attention, but a few people suspected that groundwater supplies also faced contamination and posed health risks. The realization that approximately half of all Americans relied on groundwater for potable drinking water made protection of unseen supplies appear more critical to legislators and the public. In some parts of the West, the percentage of groundwater in the supplies consumed exceeded the fiftieth percentile; for instance, in Texas, groundwater provides over 60 percent of the drinking water. Continued national and regional economic development added impetus to groundwater protection. One governmental response to water pollution, the Gonzalez Amendment to the Safe Drinking Water Act of 1974 (SDWA), addressed human consumption of unseen waters. Taking advantage of both the opportunity to address a local issue within a national one and the temperament of the U.S. Congress during the first months of Gerald Ford's presidency, Texas Congressman Henry B. Gonzalez's amendment responded to perceived weakness in state and local pollution controls for the Edwards Aquifer, the source of much of the drinking water for central Texas and his home city, San Antonio (see fig. 8.1). The amendment established protection for "sole source" aquifers or those that provide at least 50 percent of a population's drinking water. Designated aquifers receive federal protection from contamination through the oversight of the Environmental Protection Agency (EPA). By 1999 thirty aquifers west of the Mississippi River carried the EPA "sole source" designation (a total of seventy aquifers held the designation nationally by 1999). In this continuing program, the EPA guards these aquifers by limiting federal assistance to development projects above them that might contaminate the water supply. Additionally, the program allows federal agencies to fund modifications for projects over these aquifers to insure water quality protection. This national program owes its existence to a superficially local conflict—a bitter argument over urban growth and the protection of the city water supply in San Antonio. San Antonio and the Edwards Aquifer led the way for the nation, and the Gonzalez Amendment's "sole source" designation for the Edwards brought the threat of a federal presence to the region and infused local activists with a sense of power.[1]

The "sole source" rider to the Safe Drinking Water Act of 1974 added

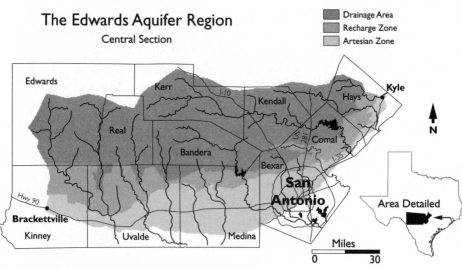

Fig. 8.1. The Edwards Aquifer's drainage, recharge, and artesian zones (*Source:* Adapted from Eckhardt, 1994.)

groundwater protection to a bill focused on the quality of public water systems. Prior to the 1960s, protecting land and water from contamination fell under the purview of state police powers; the Safe Drinking Water Act of 1974 revolutionized water protection by moving power from local and state agencies to federal oversight by providing funding for sewage and water-supply system upgrades. Federal funding became a valuable and effective tool for implementing compliance with new federal standards. In 1975 the Edwards Aquifer, specifically targeted by Gonzalez, was named the first "sole source" aquifer by the EPA. The Gonzalez Amendment helped slow recharge zone development, but it did not restrict economic growth or development in the area. Nonetheless, the "sole source" protection led to increased public and government awareness of the importance of groundwater throughout the West. Gonzalez created the EPA program to address the specific problems of San Antonio, but he did not limit the impact to that city's aquifer. As a result, the program became a viable alternative for groundwater protection throughout the United States. This program provides a tool for balancing the popular urge for suburban sprawl and the public necessity of pure drinking water. In this instance, local affairs led to a widespread federal program of "sole source aquifer" protection.[2]

The Edwards Aquifer, a "water-bearing layer of cavernous, fractured and cracked limestone," stretches 180 miles across six counties in southcentral Texas much like a lopsided grin along the edge of the Texas Hill Country (the Edwards Plateau and Balcones Escarpment) and contains some of the purest water in the United States. The northeastern end terminates just north of the state capital, Austin. Water flows from southwest to northeast in the formation. Divided in half by geology, the lower and most productive section curves southwest from Austin through the cities of San Marcos, New Braunfels, and San Antonio before stretching westward into rural counties. The aquifer generally has three parts: a recharge zone where water from rivers and streams enters the aquifer over exposed limestone, a drainage zone that feeds the surface streams that eventually flow across and into the aquifer, and an artesian zone where water is confined under pressure between layers of clay and denser limestone and discharges from the aquifer through springs and, more prevalently, flowing artesian or pump-driven wells.[3]

In spite of the aquifer's smiling shape, this particular groundwater formation, like many others, ceased to bring constant delight to its users when its limitations became apparent. Central Texans utilize the Edwards for municipal and domestic supplies, pump-irrigated agriculture, and spring-fed recreation.

By 1970 the aquifer served as the exclusive water source for San Antonio, five military installations, and sixteen smaller cities and towns. Unlike more contained aquifers such as the Ogallala, the Edwards recharges easily when precipitation occurs. However, quantity shortages arose after World War II when the region began to withdraw water through springs and wells at a constant rate that did not always remain in sync with the recharge rate. The importance of the Edwards became apparent to average central Texans in the 1950s when a prolonged drought exposed the area's vulnerability and proved that, while not endangered by mining as much as other aquifers, the Edwards was not without its own limits. By the end of the 1960s the question of water quality also shaped the debates over the aquifer's use; the same quick recharging ability that makes the aquifer so often productive also makes it vulnerable to pollution from septic tanks, sewage systems, and surface runoff. In San Antonio's case, quality and quantity issues became entwined and have yet to untangle.

For decades San Antonians have remained stubbornly committed to using only the inexpensively accessed and high-quality Edwards for their supply. Because the city repeatedly delayed the acquisition of alternative surface-water supplies, Representative Gonzalez worked with local interest groups to gain protection for the Edwards Aquifer. The region's population relied upon several local agencies to protect the quality of their drinking water. Most believed that local leaders knew best how to handle the city's growth and blindly trusted government officials to safeguard their water supply. At the state level Texas had been trying to control water pollution since the early twentieth century and instigated drinking water standards in 1945. In 1967 the state combined several water-pollution control agencies to create the Texas Water Quality Board (TWQB). The highest level of authority over the quality of the Edwards, the board coordinated state and local regulations, investigated potential polluters, and brought court action against violators. In 1970 the board provided nominal development guidelines for the recharge area to counter the aquifer's susceptibility to runoff pollution.[4]

However, a lack of personnel and the TWQB's poor record of regulatory enforcement revealed the board's weakness. In the early 1970s the legislature voted to cut the director's salary because he seemed uninterested in enforcing environmental protection policies. Other entities also claimed jurisdiction over aquifer areas. In 1959 the Texas Legislature created a smaller regional body, the Edwards Underground Water District (EUWD). Funded at the local level and comprised of local citizens, the EUWD hoped to safeguard, conserve, and recharge the aquifer, but the district had little enforcement authority over groundwater users or landowners. At the local level, city governments and water suppliers sought to control their access to the aquifer. As landowners, most pumpers could utilize as much of the aquifer as they desired without regulation from anyone. In San Antonio citizens relied upon the municipally owned City Water Board (CWB) to minimally cleanse the water with chlorine and bring it to their taps. San Antonians expected the city council to keep the CWB in check and thereby insure their water purity and supply at a low cost.[5]

Development and population sprawl over the recharge zone brought all levels of government into a situation of both conflict and cooperation. San Antonio continued to annex lands and extend services to them through the CWB, while the EUWD and TWQB maintained their control over the property as part of the counties they served. While developers had to seek construction permits from each entity, environmentalists and social activists complained that growth to the north/northwest put development on a collision course with the city's water supply.

Although the nation had moved toward water quality protection in the 1960s, citizens of San Antonio and other southcentral Texas towns did not actively participate until the proposed construction of several large developments above the recharge zone, including the University of Texas at San Antonio campus and a federally funded planned community in the early 1970s. The controversial housing development, "San Antonio Ranch New Town" (Ranch Town), designated over 9,300 acres of the Hill Country for development and raised public awareness of the aquifer to a higher level, resulting in pressure for greater protection of the city's source of drinking water. Ranch Town, part of a new federal Department of Housing and Urban Development (HUD) program to encourage the mixing of economic classes, stimulated a rash of lawsuits by local agencies and environmental groups to stop development over the recharge zone.[6]

Citizens' groups, such as the local incipient Aquifer Protection Association and Citizens for a Better Environment (working with the League of Women Voters as the Edwards Aquifer Protection Alliance in 1972), rallied against the threat in an attempt to prevent contamination of the area's sole source of water. The League of Women Voters (LWV) with its allies investigated legal means of stopping the development of Ranch Town. The LWV wanted the developers to accept responsibility for treating the water if the aquifer ever became polluted. The alliance stressed the potential pollution of the aquifer at the recharge location chosen, not blanket opposition to the building of federally guaranteed new towns.[7]

Reinforcing the significant catalytic power of San Antonio Ranch Town, the development earned the position as the "first federally assisted new community" challenged in the courts in April 1973. During the trial expert witnesses concluded that the development did pose "a significant threat to water quality in the Edwards Aquifer," but Judge Adrian A. Spears found in favor of Ranch Town because the developers had not violated the letter of the law. Spears expressed concern for the aquifer repeatedly throughout the proceedings and ordered the developers to pay some of the court costs for the plaintiffs after stating, a bit prematurely, that they "lost the case, they lost the battle, but they won the war to protect and save the Edwards Aquifer." He argued that the plaintiffs had performed a public service by suing and creating publicity about the dangers to the Edwards, noting that "if this trial had done nothing more than to alarm the public about water, then it has served its purpose."[8]

In July 1974 the EPA announced that local efforts to protect the Edwards from urban pollution appeared adequate. The federal courts also ruled that Ranch Town's proposed construction standards would prevent harm to the aquifer. The TWQB and EUWD promptly incorporated those provisions in local regulations. However, the EUWD announced that study of the aquifer would continue because the district took "nothing for granted." The 5th U.S. Circuit Court of Appeals upheld San Antonio Ranch New Town's federal grant ($18-million private bond from HUD) in October 1974, saying that developers had taken sufficient measures to protect the aquifer. Local interests and the outcome of the case on appeal undoubtedly fed Gonzalez's interest in amending the Safe Drinking Water Act to protect the Edwards.[9]

Some local government entities, such as the Alamo Area Council of Governments (AACOG), insisted that current measures could not protect the aquifer. The AACOG suggested that the TWQB change its regulations to control the density of developments. Citizens' groups and the Texas attorney general seconded the call for stricter controls over the aquifer. Aquifer protectionists suggested that the problem required extra handling because "we're not just dealing with any water. We're dealing with drinking water."[10]

As San Antonians argued over the Ranch Town development, other Americans also focused on drinking water quality. Congress responded to a sharp increase in the number of drinking water–related illnesses by holding a series of hearings on drinking water purity in 1971. The investigations dovetailed with previous efforts to address water quality through the 1966 Clean Water Act and the revision of the Clean Water Act in 1972; under both acts the federal government pledged funds to pay up to 75 percent for construction of new sanitation systems to remove chemicals and viruses as well as bacteria and solids. Oversight of water quality began to swing away from local and state health departments or other agencies dedicated to environmental concerns (twenty-four states had environmental agencies by 1973, but many received federal funds for operations). Between 1971 and 1973 both the House and Senate held hearings and issued reports about safe drinking water standards, but Congress failed to pass any major legislation. The only new federal standards during that period addressed discharging pollutants into navigable waters by 1985.[11]

Congress once again took up drinking water standards in 1974. The proposed Safe Drinking Water Act of 1974 addressed problems of water contamination from inadequate treatment systems and polluted sources as well as the inadequacies of inspections and water provider training. The committee report accompanying the legislation pointed out that while a little progress had been made to protect groundwater sources, the restrictive definition of "pollutant" in previous legislation would most likely prevent the EPA "from adequately protecting underground drinking water sources." Simultaneously the committee bolstered the case for national standards by citing the transboundary nature of both ground- and surface-water sources and the hydrologic cycle. However, controversy about the appropriateness and extent of federal involvement in the area of drinking water safety swirled through the congressional discussions. Those seeking federal involvement argued that only national resources could adequately assess and address the health and technical problems involved; those opposed feared duplication of efforts and loss of state power.[12]

The bill came up for debate on the House floor on November 19, 1974. First proposed in 1971 and authorized primarily by Rep. Paul G. Rogers (D-Fla.), the Safe Drinking Water Act of 1974 culminated efforts to address public health and safety issues. The legislation received a boost from alarming reports of sixty-six different cancer agents in several metropolitan water supplies that prompted public pressure for passage. Gonzalez offered the "sole source" protection amendment to the committee chairman, stressing that San Antonio's situation surely had counterparts elsewhere in the nation. He stated that danger of contamination already existed because of San Antonio's rapid growth over the recharge area and that state laws did not sufficiently protect the aquifer from "unconscionable predators" seeking federal funds but oblivious to the danger to the community's water supply. Even though some House conservatives feared overriding state laws and giving the EPA too much power, opposition faltered and the Safe Drinking Water Act with the Gonzalez Amendment easily passed in the House by a 296–84 vote.[13]

While the "sole source aquifer" protections did not affect private, local, or state-funded projects, the Gonzalez Amendment gave the EPA the authority to review projects receiving federal financial assistance to determine any contamination risks. If the EPA found potential pollution, it could deny federal funding or allow the use of federal funds to change project plans in order to protect the aquifer. The San Antonio media heralded Gonzalez, calling the amendment a "swift victory" that provided "strong federal environmental protection" for the Edwards and placed "stiff controls on any development over the Edwards."[14]

Local reaction to Gonzalez's action also included vehement opposition from business organizations and local government agencies. The North San Antonio Chamber of Commerce claimed the amendment would "adversely affect the growth and prosperity of our community" without adding any protection not already available through Texas and local law. The TWQB requested that Texas senators and the governor oppose the amendment and TWQB director Hugh Yantis Jr. argued that it simply represented an attempt to block Ranch Town's development. Yantis raised the specter of the EPA cutting off farm subsidies and loans for certain landowners, and local home builders appeared before the San Antonio City Council to argue that the aquifer was already "adequately protected."[15]

Gonzalez quickly denied that the amendment would hurt San Antonio's growth toward the north and claimed that if developments did not endanger the aquifer, growth could continue. However, projects that posed a threat would not "get one leaf off the federal money tree." Gonzalez admitted that the amendment might not stop all groundwater pollution. Yet he did not understand how anyone could oppose the amendment, claiming that opposition appeared to emanate from people having "either a direct or related interest in exploitation of that area," specifically the Ranch Town backers.[16]

Nevertheless, the San Antonio City Council drafted a resolution urging the Senate to delay action on the legislation until local hearings could be held and asserting that state and local authorities were "best equipped" to protect the Edwards. Gonzalez responded by charging that commercial interests had taken over local politics and that the council had greater interest in protecting developers' investments than the city's water supply. He further explained that the council had acted irresponsibly, inexplicably, "if not downright criminally," by becoming upset over his efforts to protect the city's water when the council continually delayed obtaining alternative surface sources. In parting he said, "I tell them, 'Go ahead if you want to pollute, but don't use federal money, use your own private funds.'" Editorials supported Gonzalez, citing the lack of comprehensive protective standards or clear plans for coping with contamination at the local and state level and the distant, and still dubious, acquisition of surface supplies.[17]

The Senate included the Gonzalez Amendment in the Safe Drinking Water Act it approved on December 3, 1974. Pundits speculated that agreement between the House and Senate came earlier than expected to guard against an anticipated pocket veto by President Gerald Ford; the Senate passed the measure by voice vote and prepared itself to override any veto. Ford's potential veto stemmed from opposition to new controls on well injections by oil companies and from concerns about limiting federal money and power in state matters. As San Antonians awaited action by Ford, the city's mayor, Charles Becker, echoed congressional opponents by charging that the Gonzalez Amendment brought "federal intrusion into state and local affairs." He called for the formation of a locally unified group to adequately protect against pollution of the aquifer. Others spoke in support of Gonzalez, expressing trust in him rather than in local politicians or developers and hailing him as a true patriot working for the good of the people. The San Antonio River Authority urged Ford to sign the bill and reassured Gonzalez, telling him "you do not stand alone."[18]

While voicing concerns over greater federal involvement at local levels, President Ford considered the Safe Drinking Water Act of 1974 an assurance of public health and signed the act on December 17. One local broadcaster accused Gonzalez of pre-empting the rights of Texas and decried giving the EPA administrator so much power over local affairs. He despaired that the amendment might be "used and abused by overzealous ecologists" and put the area's future economy at risk. He suggested that local leaders "offset our sole dependence on the aquifer" by strengthening laws to protect the Edwards and acquiring clean surface-water supplies. Others argued that the EPA would be unable to support the legislation due to a lack of staff and finances for enforcement.[19]

Despite the previous council's opposition to the Gonzalez Amendment, a newly elected San Antonio City Council led by new mayor Lila Cockrell unanimously approved a resolution that designated the aquifer as San Antonio's "sole source" of water in anticipation of an EPA hearing on the matter. Once again, some very real conflicts of interest arose within the various departments of city government: while the council and mayor encouraged "sole source" designation, the City Water Board did not, and in fact expressed the opinion that the EPA should not be involved until after pollution had been detected. The CWB felt that the aquifer had adequate protection and argued that worrying about possible pollution was "like taking medicine before you get sick." Although CWB General Manager Robert Van Dyke admitted that the aquifer stood as the "sole source," he and the CWB feared more government controls on the agency's actions. Mayor Cockrell refuted the CWB position by arguing that the city needed outside help to coordinate antipollution efforts outside its jurisdiction.[20]

A formal petition for designation came from the Sierra Club, the League of Women Voters, and the San Antonio Citizens for a Better Environment in January 1975. The EPA sought comments and data from interested parties and tried to calm local fears by stressing that designation as a "sole source" would only eliminate federally funded projects that might pollute the Edwards.[21]

The local populace responded to the possible designation both positively and negatively. Those who spoke against the designation generally stressed local control and/or the adequate controls of municipal, county, and state officials. Others stressed the need to develop to the north of the city for continued prosperity, the continued employment of construction workers, or the protection of private property rights. As might be expected, the Chambers of Commerce and developers seconded all such arguments. The other side weighed in by stressing that local authorities had failed to protect the aquifer adequately. Some pointed out the incongruity of people who desired federal funds to develop over the aquifer, but complained about the "bad, bad federal government" imposing regulation to prevent the pollution of the water supply.[22]

The purity of the water became a supporting point for both sides of the argument. Those who disliked the Gonzalez Amendment argued that the aquifer's purity showed that locals had adequately protected the formation, while those in support of "sole source" designation argued for more protection to keep water purity at a high level. The EUWD contended that the EPA did not need to designate the aquifer as a "sole source" and EUWD General Manager Col. McDonald D. Weinert advised the EPA that the EUWD and TWQB, in conjunction with county authorities, had sufficiently protected the aquifer and would continue to do so through monitoring of streams and wells and strict construction standards. Generally, the district stressed the use of local authority to solve a local problem.[23]

More than three hundred people attended the morning session of the "sole source" hearing, and forty addressed the panel during the day. The hearing continued for eight hours and about two hundred people stayed throughout. Everyone appeared to agree that the aquifer alone served as the source of the area's water, but they disagreed over whether or not state and local regulations protected the Edwards sufficiently.[24]

Gonzalez sent a prepared statement to the hearing urging the public and the EPA to recognize the unique and precious nature of the aquifer and to guard it jealously. He expressed his hope that regulations would emerge that protected the public's right to clean water without "unnecessarily restricting" private property rights. Gonzalez also promulgated the idea that only a buyout of the zone would absolutely protect the area and suggested that local governments act to purchase some of the remaining "natural" areas. Texas Assistant Attorney General Phillip Maxwell also testified in favor of "sole source" designation. He claimed that surface development over drainage areas also presented a contamination threat and that EPA should ban septic tanks, landfills, and feed lots from the recharge and drainage zones.[25]

Opposing the designation, Ranch Town attorneys claimed that a designation would be premature and duplicate the EPA's role in reviewing environmental impact statements for federal projects. The North San Antonio Chamber of Commerce emphasized that most of the economic development had occurred in the northern part of the city since 1970 and that residents would not welcome yet another instance of federal control in their economy. The City Water Board told the panel that the designation would provide no protection. The Uvalde County Farm Bureau president labeled the measure "political blackmail" because farmers and ranchers feared that federal controls would make it impossible to sell their land at a later date. Comal County representatives, whose towns relied on springs fed by the aquifer north of San Antonio, also voiced opposition to EPA control; they argued that local people could and would handle the development of strict regulations to protect the aquifer without the presence of the federal government. Another San Antonio area congressman, Bob Krueger, publicly announced that he supported greater restrictions on development, but that he believed the Edwards quality should remain a local responsibility.[26]

Unfortunately for proponents of local control, the enforcement of previous aquifer protection orders by the TWQB appeared slipshod at best. Although the rules appeared stringent, the agency sent a minimal number of inspectors out at random times and only regularly checked septic tanks. For this reason, the developers' contention that local control and current regulations adequately protected the Edwards appeared a fable. If the EPA took over inspection of developments, developers would face more stringent requirements including effectively collecting runoff, building stronger sewer systems, and a possible ban on septic tanks.[27]

Even as the EPA prepared to designate the Edwards as a "sole source" aquifer, the CWB overcame its historic hesitancy and embarked on a new quest for surface-water supplies. The CWB contracted but later rescinded an agreement to take water from Canyon Lake to fulfill about 10 percent of the city's needs beginning in 1980. In so doing, the board hoped to make federal enforcement of the Gonzalez Amendment "a moot question" by undercutting the "sole source" argument. The EPA did not agree, stating that the agency required a secondary source of equal magnitude of the original source. Many observers felt the CWB's interpretation of obtaining surface water and thereby short-circuiting the role of the EPA simply gave encouragement to potential polluters. Gonzalez supported the Canyon Lake agreement, but pointed out that the lake could only make a small contribution to the city's long-term needs, and reaffirmed his support for "sole source" designation.[28]

The EPA designated the southern San Antonio segment of the Edwards as a "sole source" aquifer in December 1975. In the designation the EPA decided to review "major" projects on a 1,600-square-mile area of the recharge zone and to consider exceptional cases in the drainage area of the aquifer. The immediately effective rules preceded similar guidelines for other areas in the United States which the EPA had only begun to consider. Under the new rules any citizen could petition the EPA to require an environmental impact statement from projects receiving even small amounts of federal funding. The EPA also explained that the legislation did not stipulate that a lack of state or local controls had to exist in order for the agency to designate an aquifer as a "sole source." Projects such as highway or road construction, public wells or water transmission lines, wastewater treatment, storm-water disposal, animal-waste management, or block grant–funded developments represent the type of projects most often reviewed since 1975; as often as possible the review is done in coordination with other state and federal agencies.[29]

Born in the crucible of San Antonio's politics and debates surrounding city growth, "sole source" protection inched its way across the United States in the years after the Edwards designation. Most designations occurred after the EPA received greater authority and created more general guidelines and Congress revamped the SDWA at regular intervals. As of August 2000, the EPA's Office of Water reported evaluation of hundreds of projects by regional offices but noted that although some modifications had occurred after reviews formal denial of federal funding has yet to occur under the program. EPA Region 6 (Texas, Louisiana, and Oklahoma) weighs thirty to seventy projects per year for the five protected aquifers under its jurisdiction (including both segments of the Edwards). Acknowledging the limited scope that the designation can have, the agency clearly states that the "sole source" designation "is not intended to be used to inhibit or stop development of landfills, publicly-owned treatment works or public facilities financed by non-Federal funds" and cannot be the only method for protecting an aquifer from contamination. The agency notes for the public that "many valuable and sensitive aquifers have not been designated because nobody has petitioned EPA for such status or because they did not qualify for designation due to drinking water consumption patterns."[30]

Nonetheless, "sole source" protection provides a mechanism to prevent the federal government from unintentionally doing harm to the public. The control of federal funding above these sensitive and crucial groundwater sources, such as the Edwards, does not preclude development over them, but does limit federal contributions to an often oblivious public intent on spoiling its own nest. The "sole source" designation failed to stop Ranch Town, and the subdivision, unlike many other new towns that failed in the national real-estate recession of the 1970s, became a part of the metroplex. Developments such as Ranch Town, apartment complexes, shopping centers, and strip malls now lie over portions of the Edwards recharge zone. Like many western cities, San Antonio succumbed to the lure of suburban sprawl. The Gonzalez Amendment only slowed the process, but perhaps the lack of ready federal funds inhibited the growth just enough to prevent the destruction of the city's "sole source" of water. In the wider picture, it has had the same results for other urban populations in the West. The Gonzalez Amendment's power rests in providing concerned citizens with both a means of turning attention to the often unseen water supplies and creation of a sense of potential protection of the water on which they rely. "Sole source" designation rallied people around the Edwards aquifer, spurred discussion about the aquifer, and continues to shape how San Antonians think about the Edwards in a pattern repeated elsewhere since. A local conflict—a struggle to keep one large development off of the Edwards recharge zone—brought a greater understanding of the delicate nature of groundwater to many and a safeguard for more than half the American population's drinking water. Most citizens remain happily unaware and blindly trusting that somehow their water remains pure and never consider what their actions may mean for their own "sole source."

9

John M. Donahue and
Jon Q. Sanders

Sitting Down at the Table

Mediation and Resolution of Water Conflicts

City councilman Bob Ross was frustrated. After the recommendations of two mayoral committees, and the expenditure of hundreds of thousands of dollars promoting the construction of a surface-water reservoir, the citizens of San Antonio had voted down the proposal twice, the second time by an even wider margin. After five years of debate, not only was there no consensus on a plan to manage San Antonio's water needs, but the two sides in the conflict seemed to be even further apart. Ross had been in opposition to the building of the surface reservoir (called Applewhite), but not to a water-management plan. He concluded that a different approach to the conflict was necessary. Within a week after the defeat of the Applewhite referendum, Ross wrote a letter to the editor of the *San Antonio Express-News*. In part, it read, "Now that the Applewhite question has been laid to rest, this will give us an opportunity to concentrate on solutions to overcome the problems that are facing us."[1] Ross proposed the creation of a panel of experts who would review the existing plans and make recommendations "based on science, hydrology and geology, not on political considerations." He continued, "The process that I am proposing is similar to an arbitration process. All sides agree on the composition of the panel. Since the panel would propose various options and the price tag for those options, the final decision would be made by the elected representatives of the people."

Some days later Rafael Aldalve, a local lawyer with experience in arbitration, contacted Ross and suggested a plan. They agreed to propose to Mayor Bill Thornton and the city council that a professional mediator be hired and given a staff apart from the city council or the San Antonio Water System (SAWS). In March of 1996 the city council agreed to allocate $300,000 for the mediation effort. John Folk-Williams, a professional mediator based in Santa Fe, New Mexico, was hired since he had considerable experience in water-conflict mediation efforts. Folk-Williams joined Aldalve and together they contracted a support staff and began to lay the foundations of what would become the Mayor's Citizens Committee on Water Policy (MCCWP).

Overview

Parties in conflict over the management of natural resources have often resorted to litigation and mediation, or a combination of the two, to resolve the disputes.[2] While court records document litigated disputes, less is known about the process of mediation in environmental resource disputes. In a now-classic treatment of negotiation, Roger Fisher and William Ury note that interests among parties in conflict include not only the substantive issue(s) in question, but also procedural and psychological interests.[3] This chapter will review this triad of interests as they were played out in the water-mediation effort in San Antonio, Texas, from July 1996 to January 1997 and discuss the conditions under which the mediation took place and isolate those elements that contributed to or detracted from its success.

Methodology

The authors collected and reviewed the minutes of the 36 committee meetings between July 13, 1996, and January 15, 1997. They also studied the technical reports presented in the course of the mediation. In addition, the researchers interviewed the two mediators, seven members of the MCCWP, a geologist who advised the committee, and Bob Ross, a former city councilman who helped initiate the process. Finally, they attended a meeting of the San Antonio Water System where a follow-up committee, called the Citizen's Working Group (CWG), made recommendations to the Board of Trustees of the SAWS "regarding the goals, methods, and direction of water planning for the San Antonio area."[4] This group took its lead from the former Mayor's Citizens Committee and had overlapping membership.

History of Water Conflicts in San Antonio

The semi-arid region that characterizes the area between the limestone hills of central Texas and the Gulf Coast is blessed with a rechargeable, underground aquifer—the Edwards Aquifer—whose waters percolate to the surface at springs in the central (Bexar County) and eastern expanses of the aquifer (Hays and Comal Counties) which, in turn, have been sites of urban population growth.[5] With advances in pumping technology in the early twentieth century, large tracts of irrigated farmland were opened up on the western expanses of the aquifer in Medina, Uvalde, and Kinney Counties.[6] Human adaptation to the geology of the region has created a socioeconomic landscape that concentrates the agricultural/ranching economic sector in the west, the more industrial and metropolitan sector in the center, and a major recreational/service sector to the east around the springs in Comal and Hays Counties (see fig. 8.1 in chapter 8).

To the north of the aquifer in each of the six counties lies an area of recharge where runoff from rainfall flows into the aquifer through porous limestone and sinkholes and percolates downward in the aquifer. Because the aquifer varies in altitude, its flow is from west to east, emerging at various springs along the way.

Estimates place the capacity of the aquifer between 25 and 55 million acre-feet of water,[7] which is more than all the surface water in the state of Texas.[8] The region's annual pumping is about 450,000 acre-feet or 1.0 to 2.4 percent of capacity, according to the 1988 estimate. On average Medina and Uvalde Counties account for 38 percent of overall pumping primarily for crop irrigation and livestock raising. Comal and Hays Counties account for 8 percent of aquifer pumping,[9] and the water then flows south in the Comal and Guadalupe Rivers to petrochemical plants downstream, where industrial effluent is discharged into the rivers. The major pumper of Edwards Aquifer water (54 percent) is the city of San Antonio and the farming communities in Bexar County.

Several species of the aquatic life found in the springs at San Marcos and Comal (New Braunfels), the San Marcos salamanders (*Eurycea nana*), the fountain darter (*Etheostoma fonticola*), Texas wildrice (*Zizania texana*), and the

Comal Springs salamanders (*Eurycea sp.*), are all on the federal Endangered or Threatened Species List and protected by the U.S. Fish and Wildlife Service. The springs at Comal went dry during the drought of record in 1956. Fears of a similar drought, combined with increased pumping from the aquifer, led the Sierra Club and the Guadalupe-Blanco River Authority (GBRA) in 1991 to go to federal court. They argued for pumping limits across the region so as to maintain spring flows and protect the endangered species.[10] This court case was only the most recent attempt to resolve water conflicts through litigation. In 1973 La Quinta Motor Inn's CEO, Sam Barshop, had proposed the construction of the Southwest's largest mall over the aquifer recharge zone. The core opposition group, Citizens for a Better Environment, joined forces with a newly created community-action group among working-class Mexican Americans on the west and south sides of San Antonio, Citizens Organized for Public Service (COPS). COPS, affiliated with Saul Alinsky's Industrial Areas Foundation in Chicago, and Citizens for a Better Environment, forced a public vote on a moratorium on development over the aquifer. The public voted in favor of the moratorium and the developers sued. The vote was overturned by the Texas Supreme Court, which ruled that the Texas state constitution disallowed overturning a city council zoning decision by referendum.[11]

A new group, the Aquifer Protection Association (APA), then collected 20,000 signatures calling for the county commissioners court and the city council to purchase for public trust 15,000 to 20,000 acres over the recharge zone. The developer-controlled city council rejected the idea. However, in 1974 U.S. Congressman Henry B. Gonzalez was able to amend the Safe Drinking Water Act, which prohibited federal assistance to any project that might pollute urban groundwater supplies.[12]

By the late 1970s it became clear to many that if the northward growth of the city over the recharge zone were to continue, an alternative to the Edwards Aquifer as the city's sole water supply had to be found. They found a ready advocate of alternative water sources in the newly elected mayor, Henry Cisneros. He strongly promoted a city council vote on July 19, 1979, to approve a three-part water-management plan that included conservation, recycling, and the construction of a surface-water reservoir, called Applewhite. Council directed the water board to seek the necessary permits and environmental impact assessments. Opposition to the Applewhite reservoir did not fully organize until nearly ten years later when permits had been secured and environmental analyses completed. Faced with increasing opposition, a council majority voted in a second vote on July 21, 1988, to continue the project. Opponents to Applewhite included those who had earlier argued for a moratorium on development over the aquifer. They feared that the construction of the Applewhite reservoir as an alternative source of water to the aquifer would eventually lead to increased development over the recharge zone. Others, so-called water activists, saw the reservoir as a scheme to fleece the ratepayers and provide construction firms and land developers with a windfall at the taxpayers' expense.[13] They argued for a clear management plan for the aquifer which, if implemented, could satisfy the region's water needs without expensive alternate sources.

On May 5, 1991, the voters approved by a vote of 63,258 for and 59,833 against an ordinance directing the city to cease construction on the Applewhite Reservoir. On May 10 a majority of the council concurred and voted to cease construction on the reservoir. On May 19 a lawsuit was filed by the Lone Star Chapter of the Sierra Club and the GBRA before Senior U.S. Judge Lucius Bunton in Midland to force the U.S. Fish and Wildlife Service (USFWS) to protect the endangered species in Comal Springs even if that meant limiting pumping from the aquifer in the other counties. The plaintiffs claimed that the USFWS was violating the Endangered Species Act by failing to implement a plan to preserve flows at the aquifer-fed springs in New Braunfels.

In response to threatened court action, the Texas State Legislature in 1993 considered three aquifer-management bills that were eventually brought together in a compromise bill. The compromise called for replacing the Edwards Underground Water District with the Edwards Aquifer Authority (EAA), or the Authority, with seven representatives elected from Bexar County and two each from the eastern and western counties. The Authority would issue water-rights permits based on historical usage and alter pumping rights up or down depending upon water levels at certain test wells. The Authority would issue a comprehensive water-management plan for the region, including the development of alternative water supplies. The operations of the Authority would be funded principally by aquifer users through management fees, but also by a small portion from downstream users. Irrigators could sell only 50 percent of their allocations. The Authority would install meters on irrigation wells and be responsible for monitoring and protecting water quality.[14] The legislation called for an initial cap on pumping of 450,000 acre-feet with successive reductions to 400,000 acre-feet by 2008 and to whatever was necessary to protect springflow by 2012. The legislature left the Authority some discretion to raise these caps.

In November 1993 Mayor Nelson Wolff of San Antonio named a twenty-six-member citizen committee to study city water needs through the year 2050 and, since the city would, in his opinion, face pumping limits, to suggest new sources of water, including the Applewhite reservoir.[15] The 2050 Water Committee members represented a range of city powerbrokers. Notably absent were the opponents to the Applewhite reservoir and vocal supporters of aquifer recharge and spring augmentation. The 2050 Committee was charged with developing a water master plan for the city but lacked the legal mandate to take into account regional issues that impinged upon city water policy.[16] On May 19 the 2050 Water Committee presented its report to the city council and endorsed construction of the Applewhite reservoir. The council majority who approved the 2050 Water Plan called for a second Applewhite referendum to be held on August 13, 1994. Yet opponents on and off the council quickly noted that there were alternatives to Applewhite. They argued that better aquifer management would be more cost-effective than building an expensive surface-water system. More than 100,000 voters turned out on August 13 and voted down the Applewhite referendum 55 percent to 45 percent, which was a greater majority than in the first referendum in 1991 (51 percent against and 49 percent for). Such was the context in which the mayor and city council of San Antonio hired two professional mediators and asked them to bring the parties in the Applewhite debate together to fashion a water plan that would be acceptable to all.

Before turning to the mediation effort, it is important to note the several unresolved and contentious issues that had surfaced in the earlier conflicts. Among the most central was the long-term interests of real-estate developers to construct upscale subdivisions in the hilly and scenic North Side of San Antonio, an area that also lay over the recharge zone of the aquifer. Such development posed a pollution danger to the aquifer. The resulting growth in impervious cover also cut back on the amount of water that could filter back into and recharge the aquifer. City council, at the behest of environmentalists, produced San Antonio's 1995 water-quality ordinance, which limits impervious cover on the recharge zone within the city and its extraterritorial jurisdiction. However, in the months before the ordinance was passed, so many development plats were filed that nearly 30 percent of the 81,920 acres of the recharge zone in the county was grandfathered.[17] Needless to say, growth over the recharge zone and water quality continued to be issues of debate.

Another issue was additional water sources for the city, whose sole source has been the aquifer. Legislative restrictions on pumping, enacted in 1993, gave impetus to the search for additional sources of potable water. Given that voters twice rejected the building of a surface reservoir, the San Antonio City Council directed the San Antonio Water System (SAWS) to participate in the Authority's Irrigation Suspension Program, which would pay farmers on the western reaches of the aquifer not to irrigate, and to approach farmers to sell their aquifer pumping rights to the city. Water activists criticized the buying of pumping rights as very costly, as compared with recharge and spring augmentation. They also argued that the city council's decision to have SAWS build a wastewater recycling system that could serve the nonpotable water needs of local industries was not cost-effective and would have to be subsidized by ratepayers. These were the major issues that water activists brought into the mediation process.

The Mediation Effort Begins

Three characteristics of the Mayor's Citizens Committee on Water Policy distinguished it from previous water committees. First, it would include all the players in the former water wars, as well as prominent community leaders and neighborhood groups. The diversity on the committee was to ensure public trust in the process and the credibility of the outcome of the process—two characteristics not associated with the previous water committees. Second, the MCCWP would involve the use of professional mediation to forge, through consensus, an equitable water plan for the city. Third, the mediators and the committee would have their own support staff independent of SAWS. SAWS would be part of the process, but not direct it.

The mediators played an important role in the selection process for the committee members. They spent two months interviewing some seventy potential participants. In June 1996 they presented a list of twenty-four to the city council, who added ten more prominent citizens and representatives from neighborhood citizens' groups.

Several issues were at hand in the initial stages of the formation of the committee: the concerns about San Antonio's credibility as a responsible player in the ongoing water debate in the area; the lack of information about the aquifer as San Antonio's sole potable water source; and the lack of a reasoned water plan, and criteria by which to gauge the costs and benefits of water projects and so to prioritize them.

The Actors

Several institutional actors participated in the Mayor's Citizens Committee on Water Policy. Among them were several chambers of commerce, Greater San Antonio, North San Antonio, South San Antonio, the Hispanic and the Women's Chamber. The real-estate developers chose not to participate, but, in the words of one of the mediators, felt that their interests were represented in several "fresh faces." Other actors included the U.S. Armed Services, which have five major facilities in the San Antonio area; environmentalists who had been active in water-quality issues; citizen water activists who had been successful in the twice-defeated referenda on the Applewhite reservoir; a social concerns group made up of religious and civil-rights leaders; several persons prominent in the political life of the city; and representatives of several neighborhood groups. At the beginning of the process the mediators felt that they had all points of view on water issues seated at the table.

Goals

The mediation effort was essentially one of "consensus building." There was no chairperson since that would endow one of the constituencies with more power than the others. The mediators acted as facilitators to ensure that the group abided by the "ground rules," set agendas, met or changed deadlines they set for themselves, and generally moved toward their goal of completing their mission or charge. No votes were taken, but a topic was discussed until such time as everyone felt they could "live with the decision of the group" whether or not they agreed with everything that was said. One mediator commented that the process demanded that "people had to listen to one another."

The "Charge" of the committee (June 20, 1996) included seven items:

1. To take a fresh look at all issues relevant to a comprehensive water policy for the San Antonio area.
2. To consider the full diversity of water needs and develop a vision of the water future of the community.
3. To define criteria for the objective evaluation of water supply strategies.
4. To reach consensus on a water policy and plan of action that can be supported by the community.
5. To reach out to the public throughout the process.
6. To communicate with other water users in the greater Edwards Aquifer region.
7. To prepare a final report detailing the policies and action steps on which consensus had been reached as well as the full range of views where consensus was not possible.

The committee met thirty-six times between July 13, 1996, and January 15, 1997, with additional subcommittee meetings. The three subcommittees were charged with suggesting agenda items, arranging technical presentations, and keeping the city council and the public informed on the process.

The ground rules were simply that participants listen to each other, that participants not be presenters, that the meetings be open to the public, that press releases be handled through the city council, and that members not say anything outside the room that could jeopardize the cooperation realized within the group. The participants understood that "everything was on the table" and that nothing would go into the final report that had not been discussed within the group. Items on which consensus was not possible would be so noted.

The committee had a general deadline of January 1997 to report to the city council so that the city might have a plan in place before the 75th Texas Legislative Session that convened that same month. The committee submitted its final report, "Framework for Progress: Recommended Water Policy Strategy for the San Antonio Area," to the city council on January 23, 1997.

Criteria

Faced with the recent history of contention over water management, the committee members drafted a set of criteria to govern the evaluation of specific water policy and management plan alternatives. The criteria reflect the broad set of issues and interests found in the committee and upon which all could agree:

1. Trust and credibility in the water policy development process.
2. Community unity should be the means and the end of water development policy.
3. Availability and reliability of water sources including the aquifer and additional (not just alternative) sources.
4. Economic opportunity and sustainable growth in the area.
5. Protect and sustain the local and regional environment.
6. Ensure efficiency and affordability of water resources.
7. Fairness and equity of allocation of costs and benefits across the region.

Plan of Action

Based on the above criteria, the committee agreed on a recommended plan of action whose cornerstone was the optimization of the Edwards Aquifer. The plan of action laid out specific recommendations to be implemented on an ongoing basis, over the next twelve months, over the next one to five years, as well as several long-term actions. These included legislative and Edwards Aquifer Authority strategy and action that would preclude rules, such as severe pumping limits, that would in effect foreclose future water opportunities for San Antonio. Other actions would address the Texas Natural Resources Conservation Committee plans, the purchase of water rights for San Antonio, provision of the water needs of downstream users on the Guadalupe River, implementation of a water-recycling program in San Antonio, local conservation efforts, and water quality efforts. Immediate actions would also include completion of previously initiated studies, especially the Aquifer Recharge Enhancement Studies and the spring augmentation study, as well as new studies of aquifer optimization, endangered species refuges, temporary streamflow enhancement of the Comal River, and studies such as the Trans Texas Planning efforts.

Actions recommended for the short term (one to five years) included securing water rights, implementation of aquifer recharge and optimization projects, evaluation of surface-water projects, initiation of a saline water study, continued conservation measures, and creation of a "Sustainable Development Committee" which would examine the "issues surrounding appropriate and equitable long-term development in Bexar County and the capacity for continued development without further deterioration in the quality of life."[18]

Finally, long-term actions recommended included participation in Interbasin Transfers, surface-water projects and, if feasible, desalination "for using brackish or saline water from the Edwards Aquifer."[19] As inclusive and broad as the recommended actions were, five of the thirty-four participants refused to sign the final report. The reasons for both consent and dissent lie in the process to which we now turn our attention.

The Process

At the beginning of the mediation process two distinct positions existed among some committee members. The water activists felt that the aquifer's resources had hardly been tapped. Searching for an alternative source of water would be time and money wasted. Others, especially among the representatives of the Greater San Antonio Chamber of Commerce, and the San Antonio Water System, felt that surface-water alternatives to the aquifer had to be found. Their position had been strengthened by the pumping limits that S.B. 1477 had put on the aquifer to maintain spring flow in New Braunfels and San

Marcos. In fact, the Greater San Antonio Chamber of Commerce was reported to be furious with Mayor Thornton for having brought the water activists into the discussion. In the previous surface reservoir controversy the pro-Applewhite forces had labeled the activists as "radicals." Such was the climate in which the mediators had to begin their efforts.

The Role of the Mediators

The presence of two mediators itself presented a problem. There seemed to be some role conflict between the two. The one, a resident of San Antonio, knew first-hand the history of the water conflicts and, at times, was perceived by some in the committee as having his own agenda. His role as catalyst in the creation and formation of the committee was key, however. The outside mediator, with a long history in water conflicts, was perceived as being concerned with the process as much as the outcome. Early on, he encouraged the group to put "on the table" all their issues and concerns. As the group chose to take up an issue, he kept them focused and at important points offered summaries of where consensus had been reached. This allowed the group to move on to other issues still waiting to be discussed. In the words of one member, "Consensus was letting everyone articulate their point of view, listening with an open mind, discussing until the group reached a point where everyone could live with the decision, and not to go back and reopen discussion until the group wished to do so."

The mediation process itself can be looked at as a rite of passage with a definite beginning, transition, and ending. The early months had been spent educating the larger group to the issues at hand. About one-third of the group was well versed in the history of water conflicts in San Antonio and had clear opinions on the issues. Some expressed frustration that by the time everyone was up to speed, the committee's work was brought to a close.

The frequency of meetings allowed everyone to get to know one another and to begin to distinguish between individuals and their ideas. The technical presentations by two geologists were especially helpful in that regard. Their analysis of the structure and functioning of the aquifer lent credibility to the water activists' position, which until then, generally, had been dismissed. Another member characterized the early months of the process as learning a common language that included "optimization," "augmentation," and "recharge." Several committee members found that the group dynamic was such that people were able to "soften their positions" and in time a common ground of consensus emerged on most issues.

Outcomes

At the end of the process, the "bones of contention" were two. Did San Antonio have a "water problem" or a "water-management problem"? The first statement suggested that priority needed to be given to seeking additional water sources. The second implied that San Antonio had more than adequate water in the aquifer and that it should be managed well before millions of dollars were spent on pipelines to bring expensive surface water to the city.

The second issue was that of recycled water. The city council had allocated money for the building of a pipeline to pump water uphill from the wastewater-treatment plants in southern parts of the city to industrial, military, and recreational users (golf courses) in the central and northern parts of the city. At the beginning of the mediation, it was not clear to all the participants if recycled water was "on the table" for discussion. The water activists wanted it to be discussed; SAWS argued that the city council had already authorized them to begin the construction.

The mediators and several committee members felt that the committee simply ran out of time or this issue would have been discussed. As it turned out, the final report referred to the "water problem" and included recycled water as an option. The five water activists would refuse to sign the final report for those reasons.

The final month was characterized by much discussion over several drafts of the report, lobbying by the Greater San Antonio Chamber of Commerce, and a looming deadline. Several drafts of the report were prepared by members who attempted to summarize the group's thinking on the several issues before them. There was no unanimity on any of the drafts until a member, himself representing the military bases, assumed a facilitating role and organized the conflicting points and wording in such as way that the committee could "live with it." Like one of the mediators, he was an "outsider" to the conflict, having only recently moved to San Antonio. Members of the committee recognized that as an "outsider" he did not seem to have a personal agenda and seemed open on all the issues. He noted that the committee had not the time to develop both a water policy and a water plan. He agreed with the goal that the committee develop a general framework for policy in which everyone's position would be included. Yet, when his draft report was presented to the group on January 22, 1997, the day before the committee was to report to the city council, it included a laundry list of water-policy alternatives, not all of which had been discussed. This procedural failure was, in his opinion, why some did not sign the final report.

Another factor that played itself out in the committee was the mayoral race. One of the water activists who did not sign the final report was herself an unannounced candidate for mayor, as was the city councilman who initiated the mediation effort, a second city councilman who was an urban planner, and the incumbent himself who had authorized the committee in the first place.

We noted earlier that the Greater San Antonio Chamber of Commerce was angered with the mayor's decision to form the committee in the first place. In the words of one member, the last-minute lobbying by the Greater San Antonio Chamber of Commerce nearly "deep-sixed" the entire process. The Chamber, long an advocate of a surface reservoir, called a meeting of "its representatives" on the committee, plus some others, and tried to "strong arm" the Chamber's proposal for a surface reservoir. One of those invited to the meeting noted, "The Chamber would like to helicopter businessmen, contemplating a move to San Antonio, over the city, and show them 'our reservoir'; they can't show them 'our aquifer.'" Another concern of the Chamber was that the final report would undermine an existing agreement between them, environmentalists, and city council that allowed residential and commercial development over the recharge zone of the aquifer. Interestingly, the meeting had unintended effects. Chamber representatives on the committee were, in the words of one, "embarrassed" at the Chamber's action. Another felt that since the Chamber had no sense of the consensus process, their efforts were counterproductive. A third member was so angered that she, herself a businessperson, decided to run for public office in a water agency.

Finally, the looming deadline worked against the process. One committee member suggested that three more months were needed to bring the process to a fitting conclusion. As it was, she felt that many sensed a lack of closure.

Conclusion

In the end, a common ground had emerged on a water policy for the city of San Antonio. The SAWS agreed to establish the Citizen's Working Group, which on April 6, 1998, produced a series of "benchmarks" by which the policy goals of the MCCWP could be measured and evaluated. Even the dissenters to the Mayor's Committee Report in subsequent public comments referred to the "good parts of the report." One of them agreed to serve on the follow-up committee, the Citizen's Working Group. That thirty-two-member group met between October 1997 and March 1998 under the auspices of the San Antonio Water System. They produced a series of procedures for implementing and measuring the effectiveness of policy recommendations, recommended by a previous Citizen's Water Committee, and endorsed by the city council of San Antonio in January 1997.

More problematic, however, in terms of the outcome, was the manner in which the debate was phrased. Nearly the entire mediation focused on the issue of water quantity. Is there enough? Do we need more? Where do we get it most cheaply? How do we secure more water, be it through optimization of the aquifer or from additional surface sources? Lacking in much of the process was a comparable emphasis on water quality. Residential and commercial building over the recharge zone in Bexar County poses a direct threat to the quality of the aquifer water. While that issue was discussed, it was to a great extent "kept off the table" by overemphasis on water quantity. Such was the legacy of the earlier debate over the Applewhite Reservoir. While the reservoir was defeated twice in the polls, water quantity, be it surface water or aquifer water, continued to frame the actual terms of the debate. As building over the recharge zone continues, the danger that the aquifer will be polluted increases.

San Antonio may have to look elsewhere for its water, not just because of pumping limits, but also due to poor management of its "commons." Further complicating the issue is the fact that the "commons" in this case is water shared by a larger community than just the city. Very different definitions of water exist among the six-county users of that "commons"—domestic, industrial, agricultural, and recreational. As a resource, water is a hydrological given, but as a commons it must be constructed culturally. The mediation effort was an important step in the learning of a common language with which to talk about the management of the aquifer. Yet, other voices need yet to be heard before a true commons can be constructed. There are the voices of those who are as much concerned with the quality of water as with its quantity. Finally, the dialogue must include all the stakeholders from Kinney County in the west to Hays County in the east whose dependence upon a common water source reserves them a place at the table. The question remains: who will be the Bob Ross to offer the invitation to sit down and construct a cultural commons?

FIVE

Land Marks

10

✳

Lewis F. Fisher

Preservation of San Antonio's Built Environment

San Antonio is the birthplace of historic preservation in the United States west of the Mississippi. After the landmark saving of the Alamo in 1883, San Antonians maintained preservation leadership in some areas—saving the natural environment and "cultural preservation"—while falling behind in others. Notably, in the words of one astute observer, San Antonio preservation efforts were "long on inspiration and short on research."[1] The city's fragmented efforts gradually coalesced into a single effective pioneering organization—the San Antonio Conservation Society, formed by a cadre of artists—with direct lobbying links to government-sponsored agencies. The society is apparently the first group in the nation to concern itself not just with historic landmarks but with the natural environment as well.

The net result is that San Antonio's preserved historic setting is credited with providing the basis of a growing annual $3-billion tourist industry. Now the city's second-largest industry, and given the downsizing of the long-dominant military, tourism is projected to become the largest within a few years. In no other American city can

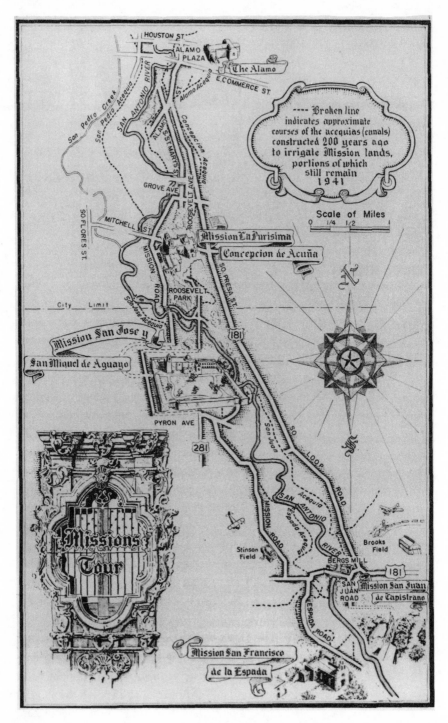

Fig. 10.1. San Antonio Mission trail (*Source:* San Antonio Conservation Society.)

such an economic impact be traced so directly to a single group of historic preservationists.[2]

San Antonio is "a city people want to come to visit," noted a consulting firm in 1995 in successfully recommending that the convention center, rather than being relocated to the suburbs, be expanded downtown, where it could remain within walking distance of "retail operations, businesses, entertainment offerings, cultural/historical attractions and restaurants." Added the report: "Historic preservation is built into the culture of San Antonio . . . with many historic and authentic attractions such as the Alamo, the River Walk, the Market Square area, La Villita and the Spanish missions, which offer exciting visitor destinations and experiences that cannot be duplicated."[3]

The depth of the historic preservation movement in San Antonio often comes as a surprise to the world outside, for most San Antonians would rather throw a fiesta than delve through dusty archives to sort out the historical record. Thus half-remembered stories have been embellished unimpeded into wide-ranging conjectures and then have been accepted as fact. Not surprisingly, common knowledge regarding two of San Antonio's top historic resources—the Alamo and the San Antonio River—has been so infected.

Historians remain confused over the old mission church called the Alamo, saved when a group of San Antonians convinced the Texas legislature to buy it in 1883. That was years before the purchase for preservation of any of California's missions, the Governor's Palace in Santa Fe, or anything else west of the Mississippi—and when Clara Driscoll, still hailed today as "Savior of the Alamo," was but two years old. Yet common knowledge still often picks 1905 as the year the Alamo was saved from destruction. That happens to be simply the year that the present chapter of Daughters of the Republic of Texas gained custody of the shrine instead of a rival chapter after a free-for-all over saving a related nearby structure, which its advocates thought could be saved if it were referred to as the Alamo.[4]

Even the existence of these Daughters—who organized in 1891 and remain a major statewide organization—was apparently quite unknown in the outside world. In 1955 the social historian Wallace Evan Davies in his *Patriotism on Parade* reported with great insight and detail on the "epidemic of Sons, Daughters and Dames" formed throughout the country in the 1890s. But there is no mention of those Daughters who guarded—in 1905 and 1955, as today—Texas's most hallowed shrine.[5]

Nor, ten years after Davies's book, did Charles Hosmer seem to be aware of San Antonio's pioneering preservation role when he completed *Presence of the Past,* the seminal book on the historic preservation movement in the United

States. San Antonio gets no mention. Hosmer made up for it in 1981 in his two-volume sequel, *Preservation Comes of Age,* when he wrote that "few cities in the Southwest have the charm and history that one can find in San Antonio, with its river bend park, Spanish missions and varied ethnic communities."[6] Then Hosmer swallowed whole a latter-day myth about the saving of the downtown San Antonio River, perhaps the most successful linear park in the nation, if not the world.

This still-resilient myth essentially holds that a misguided City Hall was about to pave over the river's Great Bend—"an open sewer"—for a flood-control project in 1924. But then, the story goes, a group of defiant ladies organized the Conservation Society solely to defeat the scheme and single-handedly convinced city fathers instead to adopt landscape architect Robert Hugman's plan for today's River Walk by presenting city fathers with a puppet show promoting the river.

In the classic style of such myths, however, each "fact" holds an element of truth and, when corrected, yields a quite different story. There had indeed been a plan to pave over the Great Bend, but it was formalized in 1911 by a group of businessmen, not by City Hall. And it was city leaders themselves who landscaped and beautified the river through downtown in 1913–14. The flood-control plan outlined in 1920 specifically spared the Great Bend. The Conservation Society was organized in 1924, but with the intent of saving the doomed Greek Revival Market House. Robert Hugman's plan was adopted in 1938 to modify the still-intact 1913–14 beautification project of the river, certainly not an "open sewer." The puppet show promoted the importance of preserving San Antonio's general ambiance—and barely mentioned the river; more than thirty years later the show's author wrote the river into a leading role in a revised script that even still serves as a trusted source for those like the hapless historian Charles Hosmer.[7]

San Antonio's Authentic Past

It is somehow fitting that such exaggerated myths would swirl about such a city as San Antonio. For San Antonio itself easily takes on mythical proportions, blessed as it is with the pervasive ambience of a truly heroic and authentic past. The king of Spain approved San Antonio's founding in 1718 as a waystation between Spanish missions on the Rio Grande and those in East Texas. The outpost soon had its own collection of missions, their architecture now deemed "extraordinary" for such a remote spot.[8] Here Davy Crockett really died at the behest of Santa Anna, Geronimo actually was held captive at Fort Sam Houston, and Theodore Roosevelt in fact recruited Rough Riders before taking them away to charge up San Juan Hill.

During the turbulent first two-thirds of the nineteenth century, San Antonio's parent government changed five times, and the city itself was a battleground more than once. But its stone and adobe buildings were not easily destroyed. On top of that, waves of European immigrants kept adding their interpretations of what buildings should look like. When Frederick Law Olmsted came through in 1856 he found that San Antonio's "jumble of races, costumes, languages and buildings, its religious ruins" left it vying only with New Orleans in "odd and antiquated foreignness."[9]

Another traveler, Richard Everett, coming through with a mule train bound for silver mines in Arizona, added:

> San Antonio is like Quebec, a city of the olden time, jostled and crowded by modern enterprise. . . . The narrow streets, the stout old walls which seem determined not to crumble away, the aqueducts, . . . the dark, banditti-like figures that gaze at you from the low doorways—everything, in the Mexican quarter especially, bespeaks a condition widely different from what you are accustomed to behold in any American town.[10]

Nearly all American cities were then being connected to other places by rail. But San Antonio continued evolving for another two decades in virtual geographic isolation, accessible only by horseback, stagecoach, or wagon. Goods from the outside were hauled overland in a tortuous journey from the Texas coast. San Antonio's population nevertheless had passed 12,000 when its isolation came to an abrupt end on February 19, 1877, with arrival of the Galveston, Harrisburg, and San Antonio Railway. Eight thousand citizens were on hand to greet the train. The party lasted two days.[11]

Civic leaders pressed forward with great zeal to modernize the place, sensitive to such barbs as that in a Houston newspaper reporting on San Antonio's railroad-inspired tourist boom: "Many came on pleasure only for a day to peep at the old town, and then go away to tell how queer it looked."[12] Richard Harding Davis sensed the general mood when he wrote fifteen years later: "The citizens of San Antonio do not, as a rule, appreciate the historical values of their city; they are rather tired of them."[13]

These comments came at a time when historic preservation meant saving landmarks or sites identified with military heroes or with the birth of the nation. It was happening, in fits and starts, primarily in New England and along the Atlantic coast. The notion that preservation might have broader applications across a wider urban landscape was yet basically unheard of—except in far-off San Antonio.

For a city so strikingly removed from mainstream America, and for one that seemed so eager to slough off its past and catch up with everywhere else, San Antonio could always muster an awareness of the significance of its physical makeup, however little its citizens could agree on what to do with it. During the next century or so the Alamo City would sometimes follow, sometimes lead, sometimes lag behind the rest of the country in concepts and techniques regarding preservation of its historic built environment. Its leading preservation organization even did things with a special flair, making at least one august preservation group in the Northeast suffer by comparison. That group, a member of both perceived, "took itself so terribly seriously. They did good work, of course, but they didn't have any fun. San Antonio took its conservation seriously, believe me, but they had fun doing it."[14]

By the time formation of the National Trust for Historic Preservation and related organizations brought the country's scattered preservation movements more or less into sync after the mid-twentieth century, what had already happened in fiesta-loving San Antonio would emerge as a landmark on the national scene.

Remembering the Alamo

While in 1877 San Antonians were getting ready for the party at the new train station, a sense of foreboding was voiced by none other than the railroad president himself, Thomas W. Pierce. He was from Boston, where citizens had just managed to save the Old South Meeting House after the bitter loss of John Hancock's home. Pierce gave forward-thinking *San Antonio Daily Express* editor James P. Newcomb an interview.

Perhaps the new station should be located farther away from downtown San Antonio, Pierce suggested, so a new city could grow up around it. That way the old city could be "left undisturbed with all its ancient quaintness, and the modern growth kept out of the old confines." Newcomb agreed, and suggested, presciently, that San Antonio might have trouble keeping up with better-located places in the race to become a "so-called genuine business city. . . . But with some of our old-time charming customs still preserved, some of our old buildings still standing, some of our old, narrow, crooked streets still left, we might still be, with our incomparable climate, the Mecca of the traveler."[15]

Such an idea of saving an entire landscape for future generations was, however, far ahead of its time for the United States, much less for San Antonio, and nothing more was heard of it. San Antonians were having a hard enough time simply absorbing the notion that a single landmark needed saving.

As the efforts in Boston indicated, nothing was stirring emotions of preservation-minded Americans more than landmarks of the American Revolution, then not that long ago. The first landmark purchased by a public body in America for preservation as a landmark was, in fact, Washington's headquarters in Newburgh, New York—the Hasbrouck House, bought by the New York State Legislature in 1850 for $9,000.[16] Some members of the New York legislature in 1850 were, no doubt, sons of Revolutionary War veterans anxious to preserve the memory of the triumphs of their parents' generation. Two decades later, sons of the veterans of another revolution—in Texas—were feeling the same way about the memory of their fathers' great deeds. No landmark symbolized the Texas Revolution more than the Alamo.

It was, in fact, the coming of the railroad that sparked the drive that saved the Alamo. Except for the few years of the Confederacy, the U.S. Army had used the Alamo complex as a quartermaster depot since Texas joined the United States, leasing it from the Catholic Church, the legal owner even after the old Spanish mission, founded with the city of San Antonio in 1718, was closed in 1793. Now that supplies could arrive easily and in far greater volume, the Army was building Fort Sam Houston outside of town as a central point to serve forts on the frontier. With the Army gone, the Catholic diocese sold parts of its Alamo property to individuals and the old mission convento to a wholesale grocer for use as a warehouse. There were strong Catholic parishes nearby, making the Alamo unnecessary as a church, but the diocese still held back on putting the Alamo ownership in secular hands.

Enter, in 1877, the *Daily Express,* aided by insight from the railroad president. "The 'Old South Church' of Boston, with all its hallowed memories that belong to it, is not yet crowded with the sad glory that surrounds the Alamo," the paper editorialized early in 1877.

> The proposition we suggest regarding the Alamo has been or is
> about to be done by the citizens of Boston, with the difference
> that, in their case, it is through private enterprise and liberality

that the old monument of Revolutionary fame is to be preserved.
It would be too much to ask of this city to bear all the expense
that the suggestion incurs, but it is not too much to ask that that
duty be performed by the State. . . . We hope that the proper authorities may move in the matter, and the Alamo, the glory of
Texas, will be insured from what will in time otherwise befall it,
absolute decay.[17]

In the industrial Northeast in 1876 Bostonians had to come up with
$400,000 to save the Old South Meeting House. They did, with private funds.
A single donor, Mary Hemenway, contributed $100,000.[18] But it was indeed
"too much to ask" for San Antonians alone to buy the Alamo, for Texas lacked
major industries to generate fortunes for philanthropy. Local money for chari-
table causes was hard to come by, even $20,000, paltry by New England stan-
dards, to buy the hallowed Alamo. The request to the state was made by the
Alamo Monument Society, chartered in 1879 under the presidency of San Antonio's Mary Adams Maverick, widow of Samuel Augustus Maverick, sent as a
delegate from the Alamo to sign the Texas Declaration of Independence and
whose unbranded cattle put his name in the English language. A legislative
delegation came down from Austin to look things over, and in 1883 the purchase was approved.[19]

The city of San Antonio assumed custodianship of the Alamo and hired a
Texas Revolutionary War veteran to keep an eye on it. Things perked along for
twenty years, despite regular complaints over the shabby condition of the
place, until the nearby convento came up for sale again. Then began one of the
great battles in the history of historic preservation, involving not just strong
personalities but a yet-unsolved conundrum of preservation itself.

Onto the preservation scene had come a young schoolteacher named
Adina De Zavala, granddaughter of Lorenzo de Zavala, first vice-president of
the Republic of Texas. Adapting the national fervor for revolutionary heroes,
she used her grandfather's name for the chapter of the Daughters of the Republic of Texas she organized in 1893. She helped mark the grave of Texan
martyr Ben Milan and began annual Texas Heroes Day observances at the
gravesite, cajoled her employer—the San Antonio School District—into re-
naming schools for Texas heroes and in 1902 began collecting funds and materials for the first restoration attempt at the fast-decaying San José Mission.[20]

"I consider historic shrines of inestimable worth," she explained of her effort to pull San Antonio into the preservation mainstream. "If people—especially children—could actually see the door through which some noble man or

woman passed . . . they'll remember. . . . Inevitably they'll be filled with high ideals, the desire to emulate."[21]

In 1903 news of the impending sale of the Alamo convento brought her patriotic instincts to the boiling point. The convento was to be cleared away for a park to provide a vista for a hotel planned across the street behind the convento. Desperate for purchase money, De Zavala, then forty-one, happened to meet Clara Driscoll, a well-traveled ranching heiress twenty years her junior. The two recruited others for a campaign of speeches, statewide fundraisers, even a larger national letter-writing campaign than the one De Zavala had tried to raise money for the San José. California missions preservationist Charles F. Lummis this time contributed $1. But the effort brought in less than $7,000. At the end, Clara Driscoll herself came up with the remaining $65,000. The advance was so amazing to Texans that, even though she was reimbursed a year later by an embarrassed legislature, Driscoll was made San Antonio's Fiesta Queen in three successive years and remains highly revered today.[22]

How the convento should look, however, soon split the Daughters of the Republic of Texas statewide into two camps—the De Zavalans and the Driscollites. The De Zavalans believed that the two-story building just purchased was essentially the original Alamo convento, the activity center for the priests and their mission Indian charges. It should, they thought, be restored as a Texas Hall of Fame, a sort of "Valhalla for Texas." But Driscoll soon reneged on her original agreement with De Zavala that—since more of the fighting in 1836 took place at the derelict mission convento than in the church—the convento rather than the church was the real Alamo. The existing two-story convento was actually a reconstruction, Miss Driscoll declared, and should be torn down so it did not overshadow the church, "which is, of course, the main feature in the Alamo mission." Then the whole convento area could become a park—the very goal of the hotel developers.[23]

As the upper floor of the building came down, De Zavala—who once barricaded herself inside for three days to dramatize its plight—was shown to have been correct. The bulk of the stones dated from mission days.[24] But even if historic preservation had by then developed to the point that entire groupings of buildings were being saved, there was much debate on exactly how the Alamo looked when it was a battleground, much less a mission. A San Antonio banker perhaps spoke for most San Antonians fed up with it all when he suggested that all that should remain was a low wall, "covered with ivy here and there," so as "to satisfy our wish for something beautiful without entirely doing away with something historic."[25]

Clara Driscoll Sevier reappeared on the scene in the 1930s as head of a state committee to oversee state purchase of the rest of the block and the clearing of post-battle landmarks—to the consternation of some other preservationists—in time for the Texas Centennial in 1936.[26] Under the continuing supervision of the Daughters of the Republic of Texas, the Alamo remains a shrine in a parklike setting rather than a historic reconstruction. It has never ceased to draw debates and conflicts over its variously perceived role even as it remained the top tourist attraction in Texas—at least until its primacy was challenged by a transformed San Antonio River.

A "genuine business city"

While the "Second Battle of the Alamo" was winding down in 1913, San Antonio, again the largest city in the largest state, was rushing headlong toward becoming a "genuine business city." In 1910 its population was more than 96,000, eight times the number only four decades earlier. Since its downtown remained around the old Spanish center, the old cityscape was threatened by new development.

A threat to landmarks even greater than replacement of small old buildings with larger new ones and of old homes for expanding commercial areas was the widening of charming downtown streets, most of them too narrow for regular carriage traffic, much less new automobiles. In a program that lasted for decades, building facades on one side were sheared off and the buildings shortened to accommodate the street widening, if the buildings were not removed altogether. Shrugged the *San Antonio Light* in 1912: "The old and obsolete must give way for the march of progress, and when the modern necessity demands, the historic and otherwise memorable must pass to give room for the modern and commercial."[27]

The archrival *Express* soon demurred, sensing the appeal that even then was boosting the city's economy:

> Monument after monument of the past is falling. The storm of
> progress is leveling them to be replaced by modern structures, but
> let us keep what we have. No longer let us be careless custodians
> of the goose that lays our golden egg. The tourist comes because
> he has heard of San Antonio's fame as a picturesque, historically
> interesting city. He brings millions of dollars annually.[28]

The city of San Antonio had already faced, in 1897, what must have been its first lawsuit over impending destruction of a landmark. The proceedings were to save the so-called Veramendi Palace, San Antonio's finest Spanish-era residence, threatened by the widening of Soledad Street. Citywide protest from a historic standpoint, however, was anemic, and the lawsuit served mainly to achieve a better financial settlement with the city for its owners. The last of the building came down in 1910.[29]

Meanwhile, progressive San Antonians were belatedly embracing the tenets of the national City Beautiful movement, with its full-blown urban reform agenda that stressed political activism as a means of accomplishing civic improvements, environmental awareness, and new principles of city planning.[30] In what was perhaps the most broadly based reform movement in San Antonio's history, a host of independent civic groups began working to build playgrounds, remove billboards, improve sanitation, adopt a new city charter, build a coliseum—and to beautify and drill wells to pump new water into the San Antonio River.

The beloved narrow, winding San Antonio River had historically supplied the city's water through a system of lateral acequias, until those were replaced a few years before by artesian wells that lowered the water table and reduced the river's flow as well. Long-time political boss and mayor Bryan Callaghan II resisted civic efforts to improve the river. When Callaghan died in office in 1912, City Beautiful reformers took control of City Hall. Within two weeks a new City Plan Committee was on task and hearkening to one reformer who declared, "No complete plan could be adopted that would not include the preserving and beautifying of the river, . . . [including] space along its banks for flowers, colonnades, pergolas, etc. in addition to the parks and plazas we now have [elsewhere]."[31]

A sudden flurry of proposals suggested ways to improve the river channel to allow walks and restaurants beside its banks. Architect Harvey Page foresaw a park in which "at night myriads of electric bulbs will shine from the trees while Mexicans dressed in the garb of Aztec Indians will paddle canoes, filled with tourists." One newspaper was sufficiently inspired to predict, presciently, "The San Antonio River may again be the pride of all San Antonio, and this stream may be made the most unique in the United States. . . . The famous canal of Venice will not compare with the San Antonio River, and tourists will come thousands of miles to see this city and this stream."[32]

City Hall decided to execute the project itself, assigning it to the city's river engineer, George Surkey. The muddy channel through downtown was defined with low walls, many of them built with rocks from historic buildings victimized by the incessant street widenings. Trees and shrubs were planted along the banks, and decorative electric lights were indeed strung from trees across the narrow stream. The mayor switched on the lights to unveil the completed river project from the new bridge over Commerce Street in 1914 at the time of the dedication of the two-year, six-mile widening of that historic business artery.[33]

Modern-day precepts of historic preservation, however, had not reached the horizons of early twentieth-century urban reformers, and City Beautiful contributions to San Antonio's historic built environment remained confined to the enhanced setting of the downtown riverbanks. Leadership in the salvation of historic landmarks would remain with individuals—mostly women—who were sufficiently single-minded to persevere until the general nationwide apathy and outright hostility to such efforts receded or until broadly based preservation groups emerged. During this interim, San Antonio had such a champion in the person of Adina De Zavala.

Still licking her wounds after the De Zavalans' ignominious departure from the ranks of the Daughters of the Republic of Texas, Adina De Zavala resurfaced in 1915 as head of Founder's Chapter No. 1—the De Zavala Chapter—of her newly created Texas Historical and Landmarks Association. The group may have had as many as a dozen chapters throughout the state at one time or another, but De Zavala was always its "unchallenged leader."[34] An educated schoolteacher of modest means and unburdened by a family, she was dogged in her pursuit and articulate in making her views known. Unfortunately, noted her biographer, L. Robert Ables, she also suffered from "her forthrightness, her tendency toward stubbornness which bordered upon intractableness if she thought she was right, [and] a quick tongue."[35]

Foiled in her plans for the old Alamo convento (only its roofless first-floor walls remained) she enlisted the energy of her allies toward another site for a Texas Hall of Fame, this one facing Military Plaza west of City Hall—the newly identified "Spanish Governor's Palace," previously known only as a nondescript, flat-roofed row of shops and saloons topped by billboards. Its keystone was dated 1749, certifying the structure as the last major Spanish-era residence remaining in Texas.

Though she could not find another Clara Driscoll to come up with enough money to save the Governor's Palace, Adina De Zavala remained possessive of her role as chief guardian of San Antonio's past, alienating those who could help and unable to understand what kept going wrong. When a group of artists came together on their own to save the Greek Revival Market House, De Zavala confronted one of them, Emily Edwards, at once. She "called me up and told me that that was her field . . ." [and that] there was just room for nobody else," recalled Edwards. "She was just furious." Then De Zavala headed for Edwards's house, but when she got there Edwards was gone. One of the new group's members visited De Zavala as an intermediary and reported back, "There were many tears, but we will be permitted to exist."[36]

Thus was one hurdle overcome in the formation, in 1924, of the San Antonio Conservation Society by a dozen artists in love with a colorful city that, in the race for "progress," seemed about to lose its soul. Looking beyond the significance of individual landmarks to frame an entire urban artistic scene, these ladies spread their palette with a breadth of objectives yet unattempted by any other single group in the nation. Even today the Conservation Society's mission statement targets not just physical but "cultural" preservation, including "the preservation of historic buildings, objects, places and customs relating to the history of Texas, its natural beauty and all that is admirably distinctive to our State."[37]

No matter that preservationists elsewhere were saving historic forts and meetinghouses and crumbling homes of dead military heroes, and gave little thought to historic commercial buildings. San Antonio's appeal was the charm of a multicultural heritage visible in the varied shapes and sizes of its built environment. Diminish this variety and the heritage becomes diminished. Contrasting colorfully—especially from an artist's point of view—with San Antonio's rugged low stone buildings of indigenous architecture were the various adaptations of European styles, in particular the delicate flutings and balanced classical proportions of Greek Revival architecture. The 1859 Market House was an excellent authentic specimen of Greek Revival, rare in a frontier outpost. The artists firmly believed it should not be sacrificed for a wider street.

Some well-meaning but ineffective men's groups made a cameo appearance in this preservation effort, City Hall was briefly sympathetic and by the time the Market House finally came down whole new alliances had been formed that would help carry San Antonio into the forefront of the national preservation movement.

The Conservation Society happened to have organized just in time to facilitate saving of the Spanish Governor's Palace. To the surprise of hardly anyone Adina De Zavala's plans to add an imagined second story to the building and create a "Texas Hall of Fame" had produced nothing but publicity. In 1924 its owners were considering a purchase offer from New York developers. De Zavala's group was making yet another noisy appeal when two representatives of the powerful City Federation of Women's Clubs, alerted by De Zavala's Texas

Historical and Landmarks Association but apparently loathe to be allied with it, approached City Hall on their own. With that, funds to purchase the building were appropriated as part of a municipal bond issue and the city of San Antonio found itself in the business of historic preservation.[38]

Next the mayor asked six historical organizations to each appoint three delegates to a committee to oversee the Governor's Palace restoration, completed in 1931. Two of the groups were controlled by Adina De Zavala, the Landmarks Association and the Daughters—and Sons—of the Heroes of Texas. That gave her six votes, four short of a majority. She complained bitterly to the press and presented the mayor with another petition, this one signed by sixty of her supporters attesting that the whole process wasn't fair. But she failed to persuade the mayor, marking a turning point for San Antonio: promoting preservation by legalistic petitions had given way to achieving preservation by personal contacts and consensus. From then on Adina De Zavala, then in her late sixties, would be a peripheral figure on the local preservation stage.[39]

The young Conservation Society became the unifying force on the Governor's Palace restoration committee, since the majority of representatives of the designated member groups happened to also be members of the Conservation Society. The committee was chaired by Rena Maverick Green, widow of a state senator, granddaughter of pioneer Alamo preservationist Mary Adams Maverick, artist, civic activist, demonstrator in Washington for woman suffrage.[40]

But Green's greatest contribution to preservation, for San Antonio and the nation, was her work with the four Spanish missions that moldered along alternate sides of a six-mile stretch of the San Antonio River just south of town. They were rapidly being encroached upon as new development spread south. Mrs. Green was a frequent visitor to England, where Britain's National Trust, formed in 1895, stressed preservation not just of landmarks but also of their historical settings. She determined to save not just the mission churches but their secular compounds and surrounding landscapes as well and turn them all into a national or state park, perhaps with the old mission irrigation systems rejuvenated to grow crops for demonstration farms.[41]

When Rena Green and Emily Edwards cofounded the Conservation Society, Mrs. Green was chairing the missions committee of the local Daughters of the Republic of Texas. She had struck up a correspondence with California's leading missions preservationist—the venerable Charles F. Lummis—and was involving everyone from the governor to Congressman John Nance Garner in her quest. Green immediately transferred her energies to the Conservation Society. Once the society lost its founding goal with the razing of the Market

House, the organization made saving of the missions its top priority, placing on its official seal the tower of Mission San José, "Queen of the Missions of New Spain."[42]

For four years the Conservation Society sought to replicate the method of the Landmarks Club of California by securing leases on the derelict mission churches from local Catholic authorities—Adina De Zavala had been granted one in 1902 for Mission San Juan—and then undertaking private fundraising and restoration. But San Antonio's Catholic hierarchy equivocated. Finally the Conservation Society struck out on its own, focusing not on the churches but on the surrounding mission compounds, by then split up among many private owners. The initial target was Mission San José.[43]

"Our first step was to buy pieces of land—a few feet at a time—surrounding the mission and granary and save the buildings from threatened encroachments of little homes, stores, filling stations . . . and factories," recalled Amanda Taylor, another leader in the society's quest. "What I couldn't buy we just fenced, since nobody seemed to own it." Conservation Society members had bought a third of the once barrel-vaulted but then roofless stone granary across from the San José when the owner of the rest raised his price to as much as $25,000. One March morning in 1931, however, he phoned Mrs. Taylor. He'd been arrested for gambling and bootlegging, and needed $5,000 to stay out of jail. The ladies got their reluctant husbands to cosign a note and the granary was theirs.[44]

The WPA

The Depression provided San Antonio preservationists with a bonanza—federal subsidies for much of the necessary restoration work. Three wide-ranging projects benefited most: restoration of San José, an effort downtown that saved not just one building but an entire neighborhood, and a rebeautified San Antonio River. Moreover, San Antonio benefited from a shift in attitude as the nation was captivated by the Rockefeller-sponsored restoration of Colonial Williamsburg, which had begun in 1926. Historic preservation, to use the words of Charles Hosmer's title, had "come of age." The "original popular romantic phases of preservation," as exemplified by Adina De Zavala's plans for the Alamo and the Spanish Governor's Palace, were giving way to "the new age of professionalism and planning," as exemplified by the work beginning at San Antonio's missions.[45]

The ink was hardly dry on the National Park Service's authorization in

1933 of the Historic American Buildings Survey when the project's Texas district, headed by San Antonio architect Marvin Eikenroht, began its most extensive project of the time—the measured drawings of San Antonio's missions.[46]

Mission efforts also benefited from the architectural work of Harvey Partridge Smith, who began his longtime San Antonio missions restoration work overseeing the Conservation Society's restoration of San José's vault-roofed granary. Smith, architect for the Spanish Governor's Palace restoration, had come to San Antonio in 1915 from California, where he witnessed early restoration of that state's Spanish missions. At San José he also oversaw reconstruction of the San José compound perimeter walls, the Indian quarters, and the roofless church, on which the Catholic diocese had made some repairs. An underground room uncovered during excavations turned out to be the lower level of the mission's mill. The mill was rebuilt under the direction of Ernst Schuchard, an engineer for a local milling company who was also an accomplished artist.[47]

Yet the reach of preservationists for the highest levels of excellence exceeded their grasp. Rena Maverick Green, chairing the society's missions committee, was also in charge of archaeology. She asked the University of Texas for professional help, but was told they could give none. She wrote the Smithsonian, which replied that it could not afford to send an archaeologist but there might be one who could come after he finished a project in Georgia, though he probably "would not be available without some compensation."[48]

Green insisted that workmen sift the soil for artifacts as they dug, which they did, but since there was no place to put them, many were just picked up by tourists. While work was going on concurrently at Mission San Juan, Green got a call that a seven-foot skeleton had just been found in the octagonal foundation of San Juan's unfinished baptistry. By the time she arrived at the site, the bones were in a bushel basket, with no photographs or drawings having been made. Remembered one of her daughters of the whole archaeological experience: "That just drove Mama crazy."[49]

As the initial labors of the Civic Works Administration were shifted to the more tightly organized Works Progress Administration, Washington took a closer look at the missions project and decided that finishing restoration of the San José church, owned by the Catholic archdiocese, was not a proper use of public funds. Work stopped, the roof and dome still unfinished. Then the archbishop, who had previously insisted that the church had "no funds for preservation or restoration, but only for saving souls," had a revelation. "Every soul with a living faith," he now decided, would be inspired "to see this monument to religion restored to some at least of its past glory and dedicated anew to its original sacred purpose." Work resumed, this time on the payroll of the archdiocese, with a boost from state-appropriated Texas Centennial funds. The nearly restored church was rededicated during a Solemn Pontifical Mass on April 18, 1937.[50]

The Conservation Society had already celebrated completion of the rest of the mission complex with a party in the mission plaza, followed the next fall with an "Indian Harvest Festival," for which the ladies used their imaginations to recreate what they thought must have been an original event around the missions. Historical dramas were performed in a new outdoor amphitheater nearby and Mexican arts and crafts went on sale in the restored Indian quarters to help draw tourists to the missions from downtown. Using all the negotiating skills developed during the previous decade, in 1941 the Conservation Society drew the other owners of mission compound properties—Bexar County and the Catholic Church—to a table with representatives of the Texas State Parks Board all signed an agreement establishing San José Mission State Park. Foreshadowing a future development, a National Park Service representative was also drawn in on an advisory basis.[51]

As soon as San Antonio's homegrown preservation movement could draw on support from newly evolving federal programs, one of the city's most colorful and best-known politicians jumped into the fray. He was Maury Maverick, another grandchild of Alamo preservationist Mary Adams Maverick. Only eleven days after he took his oath as a congressman in 1935 he was lobbying to get San José Mission into the National Park System. Two months later he introduced the pioneering Historic Sites Act into the House, two weeks after it was introduced in the Senate by Virginia's Harry F. Byrd. Until this act passed, the United States was "the only major nation in the western world" without a national policy on historic preservation.[52]

Four years later, Maverick was back in San Antonio as the newly elected mayor. Again he wasted no time coming up with plans to preserve the city's heritage. Now he focused on a near-downtown neighborhood known as La Villita, which dated to the early days of the city but was badly rundown, if still colorful. Architect O'Neil Ford began his distinguished career in San Antonio with this project, later developing a modern regional architecture based on such styles as La Villita's, which he thought more stimulating than those of

New Orleans or Cape Cod. Ford saw La Villita's restoration as demonstrating the evolution of San Antonio architecture, creating "one general atmosphere of cool shady places of profuse banks of blossoming native trees and shrubs . . . [with] no sharp separation of the things that make houses and grounds and furniture one fine whole."[53]

Using his friendship with President Franklin D. Roosevelt and others in Washington, Mayor Maverick soon had the money for the National Youth Administration to hire local workers to clean the place up and to locate artisans. An open space was named Juarez Plaza to honor a former president of Mexico, Benito Juarez. One street was named Calle Hidalgo in honor of Mexican independence martyr Father Miguel Hidalgo y Castillo, and the seven houses were named for various South American countries and national heroes. Maverick wangled a grant from the Carnegie Corporation to build a community building named for South American patriot Simón Bolívar. Celebrities ranging from Eleanor Roosevelt to H. G. Wells came to watch the progress.[54]

Maverick characteristically came up with a grab-bag of compelling reasons for supporting the project: seven picturesque but decaying homes could be restored, unemployed artists and artisans could be hired to do the furniture and Spanish-style ceramic and ironwork details, and, in those perilous times, the whole project could be given a Pan-American theme to promote "peace, friendship and justice between the United States of America and all other nations of the Western Hemisphere, as well as nations of the world." The mayor dismissed the National Park Service's suggestion that the city hire an archaeologist, then in the face of problems with historical accuracy expressed great frustration over the Park Service's refusal to name La Villita a National Historic Site. He even announced that La Villita was "superior in its historical value" to Colonial Williamsburg.[55]

Such a scattershot approach led preservation historian Charles Hosmer to conclude that in San Antonio—with the exception of "a few harried husbands," Maury Maverick and architects Harvey Smith and O'Neil Ford—that

> It was a woman's world with a pleasant admixture of Latin culture that the Park Service people avoided when proposals resembling La Villita were presented to them. When one compares the writings of Mayor Maverick and the statements of the founders of the Conservation Society, it is clear that Maverick was in the mainstream of San Antonio thinking—long on inspiration and short

on research, with a highly developed sense of historical reality but
with little appreciation of the need for professional assistance.[56]

Indeed, the wide-ranging enthusiasm that landed a Carnegie grant to build
Bolivar Hall to promote world peace contrasts sharply with the more-focused
Carnegie grant won not long after by preservationists in Charleston, South
Carolina, to inventory eleven hundred historic buildings. When danger came,
Charlestonians had the knowledge to mount a quick defense. In San Antonio
such research would take a back seat for a few more decades, too often leaving
San Antonians still trying to figure out a landmark's history even as a bulldozer
was finishing it off.[57]

The tradeoff for lack of intense focus on the details was that conservationists were free to shift their attention quickly to crises in areas not limited to the
traditional purview of preservationists but that had an important impact on the
broader scene on the canvas—the appearance and health of the surrounding
urban environment, for example. While the Conservation Society was negotiating with the Catholic Church to restore the mission churches, helping organize the first city museum, and sponsoring essay contests and conducting
tours to promote historical awareness, significant energy was also channeled
toward directing the physical growth of San Antonio. Its downtown was becoming choked by overbuilding while outward growth was sprawling
unchecked.

As San Antonio preservationists went straight, if futilely, to the top for help
in restorations—to leading universities, the Smithsonian, and the National
Park Service—neither did they shirk in searching for competent outside help
to bring order to the city itself. The Conservation Society considered itself the
decisive factor in the city's hiring in 1929 of topflight urban planner Harland
Bartholomew of St. Louis to prepare San Antonio's first master plan. The hiring
came at the expense of the mayor's cut-rate alternative plan, which included an
imaginative proposal by a young architect named Robert H. H. Hugman to re-
beautify the San Antonio River. In his final report, Bartholomew recommended
keeping the downtown river strictly as an urban park, without Hugman's proposed commercial intrusions.[58]

But the Depression intervened, and Bartholomew's plan went on the shelf.
In 1938 businessmen led by hotelier Jack White revived Hugman's plan and,
with WPA funding secured in part through the influence of Congressman
Maury Maverick, the flood-protected Great Bend of the river was drained and

transplantable landscaping temporarily removed. Workmen slogged through the mud building imaginative limestone walls and walkways, sharply arching bridges and a theater, its stage on one side of the river and seats on the other, on a steeply sloping bank leading up to La Villita.

Conservationists who urged preservation of natural beauty and thus backed Bartholomew's recommended use of the downtown river as a natural park were dismayed at the limestone fantasyland their beloved stream seemed to be turning into. Rena Maverick Green, a member of the city committee that hired Bartholomew, solicited comments. One came from eminent San Antonio architect Atlee B. Ayres, who complained, "With few exceptions, it is a most unwise expenditure and will be a source of ridicule to our tourist friends and others. I do hope that we won't have any more of this mis-named river beautification."[59]

Mrs. Green sent this and similar assessments from conservationists to her cousin Maury Maverick, the former two-term congressman who was elected mayor in 1939. He was unable to get Hugman to shift the emphasis from stonework to simple landscaping. Finally, Hugman was unanimously fired by the oversight committee, headed by Hugman's erstwhile backer Jack White. Further stonework was halted, though Hugman's design by then unmistakably defined the mile-long River Walk. For the next quarter century the River Walk was maintained as a park but had little use, until hotel development along the River Walk for a world's fair in 1968 made it commercially viable and it evolved into an internationally known attraction—just as Hugman's overall plan had predicted it would.[60]

Postwar Growth

Though at the start of World War II preservation of the river as mostly green space seemed assured, by the end of the war street-level city parks were under assault from seemingly every direction. Again the Conservation Society rose to the defense.

Downtown merchants throughout the nation were desperate to find new parking space as an alternative to the immense parking lots of new shopping malls in the suburbs. In San Antonio, by the 1950s a dozen parks faced mortal threats from surface or underground parking proposals, which promoted bomb shelters as a secondary advantage. In 1953 the Conservation Society uncovered a city plot to turn Travis Park—a block from the main downtown shopping street—into a three-level underground garage, with the Confederate war memorial in the center hoisted onto a pedestal to mark escalator entrances. Then grass and trees would be planted on the ground-level roof so it could still be called a park. This was to be only the first of four city-sponsored garages. The others would be under the old Spanish Main Plaza and parts of Alamo Plaza and La Villita.[61]

Unlike other major cities, where ad hoc organizations had to be formed to fight noxious proposals, the San Antonio Conservation Society was in place, ready to rise up on a moment's notice. The battle cry was sounded by none other than Rena Green, then seventy-nine: "It's an old story with us, saving parks and monuments," she reminded assembled conservationists who had just heard a defense of the Travis Park project by the mayor—none other than the reviver of Hugman's river project, Jack White. "We have saved them before. We shall save them again."[62]

By the time the Conservation Society was through, four years later, the city was vanquished in court and developers had lost interest in all similar projects. The rest of the parks were safe—except for the city's largest, which engineers planned to nick with an expressway headed through a floodplain which some conservationists declared was an official park. The North Expressway battle, joined in 1960, lasted ten years, dividing friends and families, draining public and private coffers, confounding judges and sparking inspired maneuvering all the way to the floor of the U.S. Senate.[63]

When it was completed as the McAllister Freeway—for nearly $30 million more than it would have cost originally—preservationists and politicians had to heal a rift that had essentially paralyzed the preservation movement in the city. The paralysis had disastrous consequences. In 1960 National Park Service architectural historian John C. Garner Jr. estimated that San Antonio had one thousand buildings "of historic and vintage character," but by the end of the decade, when he directed San Antonio's Historic American Buildings Survey, he could count no more than 300.[64] San Antonio's preservationists had been locked in a death grip over an expressway with the very politicians they could have been sweet-talking into saving historic buildings. But, not armed with the sort of hard data researched by their counterparts in Charleston, the preservationists had only a vague idea of what was being lost.

An old neighborhood several times the size of La Villita, for example, was razed in 1947 for a department store parking lot after no one could provide specific information on the picturesque homes to justify their preservation. So the Conservation Society president asked the membership to come up with a list of surviving "interesting homes and buildings." Six years later, as a past president, she finally got something to pass around.[65]

Inspiration once again creatively substituted for research in a postwar campaign that guaranteed media coverage: Six Flags Over Texas. Overwhelmed by the vastness of San Antonio's undocumented historic resources, conservationists focused on saving one landmark from the era of each of the six nations that once ruled over some part of Texas. The campaign was thrown together in 1951 to tap local Southern sentiments by placing under the protective flag of the Confederacy the Vance House, threatened with replacement by a Federal Reserve bank building. One architectural historian termed the Vance House "not only the paradigm of the antebellum mansions in Texas but intrinsically one of the best domestic buildings ever erected in the state." The preservation movement was maturing nationally, and reinforcements could be called upon for such local crises. But the bitter pitched battle began too late to convince the bankers to pay attention to any idea of saving the structure. By the time the fledgling National Trust for Historic Preservation's Frederick J. Rath Jr. arrived from Washington to back up San Antonio preservationists, he had to speak beside a Confederate flag, draped in black crepe, flying at half mast above the rubble of the Vance House.[66]

The memorial service could, however, adjourn for a happier event a few blocks away—the first public viewing of a three-story mansion newly donated to the Conservation Society for restoration on King William Street, the centerpiece for surrounding blocks of elegant Victorian homes. The historic neighborhood, an easy walk from downtown, had gotten a little down at the gills, but remained virtually intact. In 1968 the Conservation Society—working, given the poisonous expressway politics of the time, in quiet support of a neighborhood organization—helped make the King William area the first zoned historic district in San Antonio and in Texas.

That same year marked a pivotal point in the history of San Antonio—the hard-won opening of a world's fair, Hemisfair '68. The fair's near-downtown neighborhood site was transformed in part with federal urban renewal funds, which helped build a badly needed convention center complex on the fairgrounds. Handicapped by their adversarial relationship with City Hall, preservationists could save only two dozen of the site's 117 structures they deemed historic. Local politicians later had to grudgingly recognize that of all the attractions of the fair, it was the incorporation of these authentic structures as restaurants or mini-pavilions that most captured visitors' imaginations. "Without their special local flavor," wrote Ada Louise Huxtable in the *New York Times*, "this would be just another, smaller carbon copy of the flashy commercial formula that has become overly familiar to 20th century fair hoppers."[67]

Hostilities from the expressway furor began fading into memory once a divided Conservation Society dismissed in 1970 all its expressway-related litigation. Preservationists and politicians had developed a healthy respect for their respective powers and began to renew the working relationship they had enjoyed in the earlier times of a smaller city when all sides were kin. Aware of the fast-growing appeal of historic preservation and of the fact that in cities such as New Orleans it was governmental or quasi-governmental bodies that were carrying out studies of historic resources, the city of San Antonio took the pioneering step of hiring a Conservation Society activist, Pat Osborne, as its first historic preservation officer. City government and preservationists closed ranks to win the final drive to create San Antonio Missions National Historical Park, which needed the political clout of both forces to overcome obstacles of separation of church and state before the park could open in 1983.

More historic districts were created, some landmarks were lost, new financing techniques and tax credits saved others and tempers at both ends of the spectrum often flared. Professional inventories of historic resources came to pass. Yet the San Antonio Conservation Society has kept the freewheeling, sociable outlook of its founders, as manifested in an inspired four-night Fiesta extravaganza: A Night in Old San Antonio, a sort of "cultural preservation," which each spring brings 100,000 celebrants to crowd the streets of La Villita and enjoy ethnic foods and entertainment reminiscent of various points in the city's past. Net annual proceeds hover around $700,000, making this the largest single event benefiting historic preservation in the nation.[68]

San Antonio has sometimes led, sometimes followed, other times ignored the course of the national preservationist movement. As elsewhere, local philosophy has evolved from piecemeal preservation to salvation of the urban fabric, led at first by individual volunteers, then by volunteer organizations, then by many with professional training in the field. But in San Antonio, more than in most places, preservation activism remains colored by a fiesta spirit that often subordinates the dry details while propelling achievement to—most of the time—new levels. Research may be fine and necessary, but San Antonio shows how inspiration can pay the bills.

11

✳

John Hutton

Elusive Balance

Landscape, Architecture, and the Social Matrix

Throughout 1997 developers and the local press hailed San Antonio's new Alamo Quarry Market as an ideal blend of commercial space and artful landscaping. A representative of Trammell Crow Central Texas, Inc., the builders, boasted of a 460-acre site that would provide more than seventy stores for a wide range of tastes and needs: "You can meet here, eat, drink, go to a movie, browse in a bookstore, have a pastry or sit in a plaza and listen to music."[1]

The project was praised for its site and design. Built on the location of a former cement plant, the Quarry Market adapted the huge "clinker" shed into a multiscreen cineplex, health club, and bookstore. Five smokestacks that had marked the site were repaired and refurbished; the crusher building was converted into a restaurant, while the dilapidated generator building was demolished and replaced with a near duplicate, housing upscale shops. Signs and equipment from the cement factory were scattered around the site to maintain a visual link to its past.

Most important, the market was to fulfill the promise of a balanced mix of shops, landscape, and pathways to make the center a sort of commercial park. The example of Naples, Florida, was repeatedly invoked for that town's blend of shops, restaurants, streets, and pedestrian walkways through dispersed islands of greenery.[2] At a meeting of real-estate professionals in March 1997 the Quarry Market was discussed in terms of a new aesthetic in San Antonio architecture: developers were becoming "better stewards of their land," dedicated to water conservation and xeriscaping, and, above all, careful landscaping. The city's new tree-preservation ordinance was particularly identified as a critical factor in increasing shade and encouraging pedestrian traffic.[3]

As sections of the market began to open in late 1997, however, praise gradually shifted to open dismay. Richard Garison, president of the San Antonio chapter of the American Institute of Architects, asserted that the entire project had developed into a "planning disaster, disoriented, pedestrian unfriendly and uncoordinated," marked by cookie-cutter megastores located hundreds of feet from one another, separated by acres of asphalt parking lot devoid of shade, clear pathways, or rest areas. Early talk of "oases" in the center region proved in practice to refer to lone trees on tiny islands scattered across the lots. The ten vehicular entrances to the market coordinated badly with the existing roads, traffic flow, and traffic lights. In spite of promises to finish the buildings on all sides, many large buildings were oriented in such a manner that motorists faced only the blank and featureless rear ends of the shops, marked by loading docks and service entrances. "Walkways," where they existed at all, meant in practice only unmarked gaps between parking rows. The scattered sidewalks sometimes failed to end in ramps for strollers or wheelchairs. The few trees were too young and isolated to provide shade, a major flaw in a city where summer temperatures can hover above 100 degrees for more than a month at a time. An architectural columnist for the *Express-News,* the city's daily newspaper, lamented that instead of picturesque, tree-shaded paths, "[w]hat we got was a ring of chain stores around a big parking lot." Any potential for synergy between the mix of retail centers, he added, was lost in the vast automotive landscape. Another writer for the same paper warned, "Parking lots already resemble anthills of cars moving a few yards from store to store." This would only worsen "when summer sets in about March" and "the bubbling asphalt will add to the uphill climb."[4] There would be no plazas filled with consumers enjoying live music; there were, in fact, no plazas at all, no place to play music (except perhaps the parking lot), and no one willing to sit in 100-degree heat to hear it in the first place.

Only along the northern and, to a much lesser degree, the eastern boundaries of the market can we find hints of what was originally promised, with blended landscaping, attractive and hardy local foliage, and large, outward-facing windows on shops producing a harmonious and inviting aspect to the market site. The western boundary, on the other hand, all too visible from the highway, reveals the Alamo Quarry Market in a far less attractive guise of a vast parking lot, screened off only by "restaurant row," a boundary wall of structurally similar chain restaurants.[5] (A portion of the central parking lot is shown in fig. 11.1.)

The problems with the Alamo Quarry Market are emblematic of landscape architecture in San Antonio as a whole. The fate of the project cannot be understood without situating its construction in terms of the climate, and the geographical and social/political contexts of San Antonio's historic development. The Alamo Quarry was, typically for the city, an attempt to restore and redevelop a site with both a rich past and a history of neglect.[6] Its final form was shaped by city politics, decades of debate over reclamation, development, and tree preservation, and by the power of local developers and national chain stores to determine land-use patterns. Examining the intersection of these forces offers an opportunity to discuss the wider efforts in San Antonio to shape (in the words of a 1997 "strategic plan" for the city) a "safe, secure,

Fig. 11.1. The Quarry Market parking lot (*Source:* Courtesy of Rebecca Bridges.)

friendly, and green environment," marked by increasing greenspace and a determination to make local neighborhoods "more accessible and less intimidating."[7]

"Landscape architecture," in this context, will be defined broadly as the aestheticization of architecture in a landscape,[8] particularly as it takes shape in practice—not just in builders' plans, but on the ground, as part of an ongoing social process. Critic Anne Whiston Spirn notes,

> architects' drawings show no roots, no growing, just green lollipops and buildings floating on a page, as if ground were flat and blank, the tree an object not a life. The maps which planners employed showed no buried rivers, no flowing, just streets, lines of ownership, and proposals for future use, as if the city were merely a human construct, not a living, changing landscape.[9]

To determine why so few "green lollipops" showed up in practice in the Quarry Market project—indeed, why there was so little greenery at all—requires a careful analysis of San Antonio's efforts at landscape architecture, and the social and geographical mix that shaped those initiatives.

Climate and History

San Antonio was founded as San Antonio de Valero, a Spanish Franciscan mission, in 1718; other missions followed in the next decade. San Fernando Cathedral was built from 1738–58, while a governor's palace was erected in 1749.[10] When the Spanish inspector-general recommended that settlements be pulled back to more defensible positions in the late-eighteenth century, San Antonio and Santa Fe became Spanish frontier outposts.

After Mexico won its independence from Spain in 1820, Mexican authorities encouraged immigrants from the United States to populate Texas. The settlers, who were supposed to adopt Catholicism (and abandon the slave system), soon outnumbered Spanish-speaking Texans ten to one, though most settled in eastern portions of the territory. In 1835 they rebelled and set up the Republic of Texas.

After the Mexican War of 1846–48 and the annexation of Texas to the United States, San Antonio was left with a contradictory legacy. On the one hand, it was one of a handful of U.S. cities, along with St. Augustine, Santa Fe, and Santa Barbara, to retain significant remnants of its Spanish colonial heritage; important sites included five colonial missions (including the Alamo), the Governor's Palace, and San Fernando Cathedral. On the other hand, the city would become best known for Fiesta, a ritual celebration of the Battle of the Alamo—a defeat, albeit a heroic one, at the hands of the Mexican army under General Santa Anna.[11] Meanwhile, by the early-twentieth century, its Anglo civic leadership sought a "progressive" reputation built on not only ignoring but largely effacing its past. A 1949 popular account of the city's history quoted an 1877 witness, Harriet Spofford, on the backwardness of post–Civil War San Antonio: "The streets in the old part of the city," she wrote, "are exceedingly narrow and by no means clean. And the sidewalks are narrower yet and worn in ruts by the tread of many feet." Streets were blocked by the detritus of daily life, from uncut blocks of stone to "clumsy Mexican wagons." The author of the 1949 guide then sighed: "Old ways and customs gave way slowly and reluctantly before the march of progress."[12] An 1854 magazine essay was far blunter: the city, it argued, was being "developed under the brighter auspices of Anglo-Saxon energy and enterprise. . . . The Mexican will soon disappear altogether."[13] A history of the San Antonio Conservation Society notes that the arrival of the railroad in 1877 posed a threat to the city's historic roots, with an "era of prosperity and exuberance that threatened to sweep all before it." By 1920, with a population of 161,000, San Antonio was the largest city in the state, in which pat phrases about "progress" and "commerce" were the dominant rhetoric.[14]

Inevitably, in this context, major architectural projects involving significant landscaping were described and defended on the basis of restoration and reclamation. The city was dotted with numerous Spanish colonial landmarks, but they were in increasingly dilapidated form. The Alamo served as an army warehouse, the adjoining "Long Barracks" as a partly gutted store; the battered remnants of the site were surrounded by a modern business district that pressed in from all sides. By 1902 a survey of the four other Spanish missions revealed most to be in a ruinous state: San Jose's north wall, dome, and most of the roof had collapsed in the 1860s and '70s, while the chapel of San Juan was entirely roofless.[15]

Private restoration projects (sponsored by such civic groups as the Daughters of the Republic of Texas, and Catholic organizations) secured these sites, though the Alamo survived only in its small chapel, surrounded by hotels and shops. Others were lost, including the Veramendi Palace (residence of the vice-governor of Bexar); the Garza House, another Spanish-era residence reduced to housing a saloon, was torn down in 1912. It was not until the New Deal—and the reform administration of Mayor Maury Maverick—that the city became an active participant in ambitious projects to restore (and, in part, to reinvent) commercial and residential areas. The restoration of La Villita (a residential area built to house Spanish soldiers on the site of a Coahuiltecan Indian village) marked a major landmark in this process. Maverick announced that the reconstruction of La Villita would promote "peace, friendship and justice between the United States of America and all other nations of the Western Hemisphere." To that end, the central plaza was renamed for Mexican revolutionary Benito Juarez, and a library/community center honored Simon Bolivar. The architect, O'Neil Ford, promised a synthetic recreation of the La Villita site as a model of diversity and indigenous sophistication. The goal was a mixture of housing, community centers, and greenery, a "general atmosphere of cool shady places of profuse banks of blossoming native trees and shrubs with no separation of the things that make houses and grounds and furniture all one fine whole." Houses surrounding the area were employed as craft centers and design studios.[16]

The development of the Paseo del Rio—San Antonio's River Walk—was also a major design and reclamation project from this era. Initially interested in flood control, San Antonio leaders in 1929 built a seventy-foot flood channel to divert walls of water that periodically had devastated the downtown region during flood seasons. They fended off attempts by developers to use similar channels to bypass and drain the river altogether (their rare opposition to developers fueled by vocal outrage from citizens' groups) and began to refurbish the banks and walls lining the river. By 1941, with considerable support from the Works Progress Administration, the work was essentially complete: 17,000 feet of new walkways, with thirty-one stairways and three check dams, lined the river. The walkways and banks were covered with more than 4,000 trees, shrubs, and other plants.[17]

In all these endeavors, several facts remained evident. First, San Antonio municipal leaders supported, and in some cases initiated, these projects, but federal money and employees finished them. There was no urban infrastucture in San Antonio to coordinate, much less complete such work; this remained true in the coming decades. Second, all of these projects came with well-defined, if sometimes contradictory, social and political agendas. Political leaders such as Maverick wanted highly visible developments that could selectively employ the Spanish history of the city to pursue a political agenda (most often an emphasis on ties between San Antonio and Mexico, which provided much of the city's trade). Catholic leaders wanted to emphasize the religious nature of the early missions, including the Alamo; to the Daughters of the Republic of Texas, the significance of the Alamo lay not in its roots as a Spanish Catholic mission but as the "the shrine of Texas freedom" in a war fought against Mexico. Local business interests were primarily interested in economic outcomes but were willing to mix in a dash of restoration and landscaping if it could help turn a profit.

Finally, in every case most of this work was only tangentially connected with landscape architecture. An American landscape architect has joked that most people consider his profession's sole task as coming in after the architects have completed their work to plant some shrubbery and set down the odd potted plant. So it was with all of these San Antonio public works; landscape elements were often an afterthought, designed to soften the raw edge of construction. Yet landscape architecture, in the words of one scholar, is the sustained effort to "create and preserve beauty in the surrounding of human habitations and in the broader natural scenery of the country," and to promote "the comfort, convenience, and health of urban populations [who] urgently need to have their hurrying workaday lives refreshed and calmed by the sights and sounds which nature, aided by the landscape art, can provide."[18] For San Antonio's major architectural projects, by contrast, the emphasis was always elsewhere—directly functional issues (such as flood control), political aspirations (La Villita), or on what could be portrayed (however plausibly) as restoration and preservation. The architectural unity and total effect of a site was not merely a lesser issue, but most often a question of "finishing off" a project in a pleasing manner.

This disregard for landscape architecture became even more evident in the 1940s, a consequence of an odd combination of factors: by this time, San Antonio had been bypassed in population by Houston and Dallas and never developed a business climate comparable to either city. Its hinterland's agricultural and ranching economy was not financially strong, and it lacked significant oil resources. San Antonio thus remained a relatively impoverished city; the predominantly Hispanic West and South Sides, in particular, comprised neighborhoods in which streets, electrical, and sanitation services remained rudimentary. Even the wealthier North Side lacked, as a rule, sidewalks, adequate streetlights, and (at least until the 1980s or early 1990s), adequate rain sewers. This relatively undeveloped economic environment had the ironic effect of generating a political climate dominated by business (especially development corporations), intent on "modernizing" the city and expanding it. From 1955 to 1975 the Good Government League, a closed coalition of business leaders, dominated local politics. Organized on a platform of "clean government" that would put an end to political corruption, the GGL consciously emphasized "pro-growth" policies that rejected even minimal regulatory controls of new construction. Few could challenge this system, for the GGL was almost entirely insulated from popular control and input; it made its decisions in private sessions known as "bat roosts," and candidate lists were drawn up by secret caucuses of select powerbrokers.[19]

For the GGL, issues of preservation, restoration, or beautification were not part of its "clean government" reform program. On the contrary, in 1955, when the Conservation Society asked candidates for mayor and city council to pledge to "oppose any infringement or encroachment on our parks and plazas by private and any other interests," to support "extension and beautification of the San Antonio River," and to back "a program to save the historical, cultural, and architectural landmarks of the city," the pledge was immediately supported by every member of the "corrupt" old guard People's Ticket and most independent candidates—but by not one member of the GGL slate.[20] Not surprisingly, one result of the GGL's sweeping victory was a persistent assault on parklands and other historic sites. The GGL also helped initiate a construction environment that produced a legacy of new malls and corporate edifices in a depressingly uniform style: essentially, a huge building (or collection of buildings) set in the midst of a vast parking lot, with no shade or protection for automobile or pedestrian from the San Antonio sun. The campus of San Antonio College, established in 1951, exemplifies the type: nineteenth-century neighborhoods close to the near-downtown campus were casually obliterated, along with their complex of social, political, and geographical connections. The bulldozers left behind a scarred and gutted landscape dominated by ever-widening circles of parking lots.

In such a social and political context, serious attempts at an integrated, harmonious mix of architecture and greenspace had to develop outside the city's and local corporate structures.[21] Many of these reflect the determined efforts of one or two dedicated individuals or are personal legacies.

Typical—if only in its eccentricity—is the Sunken Garden. The garden was part of an eleven-acre site deeded to the city of San Antonio in 1915 and attached to Brackenridge Park; it was directly adjacent to an abandoned quarry. The City Parks commissioner, Ray Lambert, had the inspiration to flood the quarry and proclaim it a lily pond. From 1917 to 1918 he constructed the site, nearly always outside the structures (and the tiny budget) of the park system.

He employed teams of convict laborers to landscape the site, and his plans for stone bridges and a pseudo-pagoda necessitated persuasion in place of nonexistent city funds. Local residents donated bulbs, more exotic plants were obtained from a local plant nursery, and the electrical utility company donated lights. Local palm trees were uprooted to provide a roof for the pagoda. In all, Lambert spent only $7,000 for the entire project. Redubbed the Japanese Tea Garden, the project gradually became a bewilderingly eclectic site, complete with an adjoining village of (assertedly) Japanese huts selling Mexican arts and crafts. In 1926 a Japanese artist was invited to move into the garden site, operating a small restaurant until the artist's family was evicted in the midst of anti-Japanese hysteria in 1942.²² (It was renamed the Chinese Tea Garden until the 1950s, when Cold War tensions made China politically unacceptable as well; it became the Sunken Garden until the 1980s, when Japanese Tea Garden was restored as its formal name.) It exists today as a tourist site (close to the San Antonio zoo) in uneasy balance with a poorly maintained site for small concerts.

Although the Sunken Garden was primarily the result of a single man's determination and drive, it was officially the product of municipal efforts, under municipal authority. By contrast, the Marion Koogler McNay Art Museum was from the outset a private project, the consequence of the will and wealth of a private individual. When McNay, a wealthy collector, died in 1950, she willed her collection, her residence, and two-thirds of her fortune for the establishment of an art museum; the museum (and the twenty-three-acre gardens) opened in 1954. Additions and renovations followed, from the opening of the Brown Wing in 1970 to the Leeper Auditorium in 1996, but throughout the museum planners maintained a sense of unity and of a carefully designed space. Though the museum presents a rather forbidding presence from the street—all sight of the museum is blocked by a tall, thick hedge—the grounds, with winding paths, fountains, and streams, provide not only cool shade but the seemingly chance vistas and harmonious settings so striking by their absence in most San Antonio architectural projects.²³ The result has been an acceptance of the museum and its environs; it is, for example, a major site for wedding photos in the city.

This harmony of architecture and site is not to be taken for granted in San Antonio. The development of the San Antonio Museum of Art (SAMA) demonstrates the downgrading of landscaping and siting even in art-related projects. SAMA purchased the grounds of the former Lone Star Brewery, just north of downtown, in 1973. Aided by a large grant in 1977 SAMA opened its doors in the new location in 1979. Over the next decades, the museum acquired and renovated outlying brewery buildings, including the brewhouse and hop-house; in 1988 it obtained the old boiler and engine rooms. The museum spaces created through this purchase and renovation are impressive, but nothing was done to make the cluster of structures into a unified site; landscaping was mostly limited to planting grass between structures (and not always then). More seriously, although located on the south bank on the San Antonio River, the SAMA complex nowhere takes advantage of the setting; the river can be seen through some museum windows, but opportunities to use the riverfront for benches and plazas—or even tables with awnings—were ignored.[24] Unlike the McNay, SAMA takes no interest in its surroundings or nearby communities; its orientation is entirely inward-focused on interior spaces, while external space is conceived of as intrusive, to be walled off and screened out.[25]

Projects such as the Sunken Garden, in all its mutations, and the McNay Museum, were generally small-scale and strongly dependent upon the ingenuity and/or the wealth of a single, forceful individual. They did not alter the city's lack of interest in or commitment to landscape design. Though the Sunken Garden set a precedent for the adaptation of abandoned quarries, there were limited opportunities and even more limited funding for such development. (Maintenance has also presented continuing problems. A report on the Sunken Garden site noted major difficulties with graffiti and general disrepair.)[26] The social and economic climate in San Antonio did not shift significantly from the prodevelopment stance of the GGL years; in fact, the Good Government League was defeated not by a populist revolt but by a secession of younger, more aggressive real-estate interests, who sparked the breakaway Northside Chamber of Commerce. Development—whether in the form of restoration or (as at San Antonio College) obliteration of existing sites and structures—remained almost entirely in the hands of corporate developers and land speculators. It was they who would be central to the changes that would come to Cementville.

A Malled Village

The spatial growth of San Antonio after World War II was explosive; its limits surged from 36 square miles in 1940 to more than 450 by 1999. This growth left behind many (if scattered) remnants of an older, undeveloped city. Among those remnants was the community that was to become the location of the Quarry Market—the small, poor neighborhood known as Cementville.[27] Housing employees of the Alamo Cement Company since 1914, the community had remained secluded, bordering on the affluent suburb of Alamo Heights but lacking modern roads, sewers, and other urban amenities. It fostered a sense of Mexican identity and culture; the local Unión Fraternal Mexicana sponsored song and poetry, while the on-site Bluebonnet School maintained both the Spanish language and cultural activities. With the loss of the plant and the adjoining quarry, the community dwindled and died. The location—sited midway between downtown and the airport—became increasingly valuable real estate; a large shopping center sprang up, swallowing much of the grounds on which the community had existed. A new subdivision, Lincoln Heights, began to fill the area with expensive homes; the former quarry became a landscaped golf course. Two affluent assisted-living centers took over more space, then a huge Methodist church (promptly dubbed the "Methodome"), followed by new apartment complexes. Cementville's small parish church, St. Anthony of Padua, was all that remained of the former neighborhood. (The priest of St. Anthony's joked to the press that "I used to say we're by Cementville, but now I say we're in Lincoln Heights by Alamo Heights Methodist.")[28] As plans for the Alamo Quarry Market progressed, the area became surrounded by more commercial property: a strip of expensive shops, an office building, and a bunker-like apartment block that boasted of the highest rent per square foot of any rental unit in the city.

One of the factors that shaped the character of the Alamo Quarry's development was the persistent tendency of San Antonio's most prominent design projects to present themselves to the public as "restoration" campaigns; in this case, developers (beginning with their project's name) spoke repeatedly of their intent to save the "heritage" of the Alamo Cement Company. "Preservation" and "restoration" of existing sites have come to take on some special meaning in recent years. Anne Whiston Spirn has noted that most "reconstructions of past landscape—Sturbridge Village in Massachusetts, Williamsburg in Virginia, and Disney's Main Street take their authority from the past, but present a sanitized, sentimental version of past and present." She observes that the same is true for places like the Alamo Quarry, "from which the past has been selectively stripped," and then cites as an example Philadelphia's Independence National Park, in which restored structures "are scattered like headstones in a cemetery." In a parallel critique, the Australian political scientist Donald Horne has explored the phenomenon of touristic restoration, in which restored structures are ripped from any context and original significance. The observer is presented with "objects transformed into 'monuments'—they commemorate persons, social classes, events, epochs, styles, ideas" in a particularly barren way: "Now, though, they are like dead coral that has been painted; they have become something else."[29]

Horne makes an extensive analysis of what he terms "the tourism of industrialism," the selective gutting, stuffing, and mounting of certain industrial landmarks. He stresses that "[t]ourist programmes can pay special honour to a 'tower,' or some office construction of strange shape. . . . This is really honouring the idea of industrialism as a safe and amusing toy, like the museum exhibits in which children are encouraged to push the buttons." As such, "one learns nothing of the social processes of the factory or of the effects history has on people's lives."[30]

In this process, scattered, partial relics are inevitably jumbled together with reconstructed elements (however fanciful) and the brand-new. The result is a mixture of what Italian semiotician Umberto Eco has described as "kitsch reverence" and "crèche-ification" of the preserved structures and materials, all stamped by a "mortuary chill that seems to enfold the scene."[31]

The Alamo Quarry Market feels similarly embalmed. Although local reporters and columnists generally praised the attempt to preserve aspects of the original cement plant, it exists at best in uneasy relationship with its historical predecessor, quite unlike the Japanese Tea Garden (which intended quite openly to completely transmute its quarry site into something utterly different). It is also quite distinct from La Villita, which was intended to resurrect a previously extant community.[32] At the Alamo Quarry bits and pieces of the original site were salvaged (as with the "clinker" building) or replaced by simulacra. The five site smokestacks were restored; some were promptly incorporated (with the addition of plate-glass windows) into a store for camping equipment. Perhaps feeling left out, designers of a nearby building added false stumps of smokestacks aping a ruinous state that the actual stacks never attained (see fig. 11.2). Signs and tokens from the original plant and its heavy machinery were dropped around the site, most often in traffic roundabouts. (Markers designed to convey a sense of the space and its past proved generally useless, however, as none could be read by drivers in fast-moving cars.) A miniature engine and length of track were carefully installed between a Borders bookstore and an ice-cream shop. Outlying buildings incorporated partial walls of rusticated stone to suggest that they were actually built on the foundations of the original structures. The slide into kitsch was always imminent—most obviously in the multiscreen cineplex, in which meaningless fans constantly spun and in which a huge internal combustion engine was maintained (outwardly) intact. At regular intervals, the engine would begun to vibrate and roar, simulating its original operation. Although no pistons and gears would ever move again, spurts of false "steam" appear on cue. (As the machinery—more properly, the sound system—begins to roar, a public announcement carefully explains to puzzled theatergoers what is happening.) The whole strikes a false note, as part of an equally false ensemble.

The issue is not falsification per se: as Spirn points out, any restoration necessarily involves some form of falsification, if only one of decontextualization of the structures restored. The problem with the Alamo Quarry is that the extent and character of the falsification is so extreme that the reduction of a working-class factory into an elite mall is so jarring. More to the point, the isolated elements of the former factory are deliberately and uniformly stripped of even the slightest reference to the once-vibrant community that formerly surrounded and lived in symbiosis with the factory. The Alamo Quarry Market may be dotted with tokens of the former Alamo Cement Company, but no vestige of Cementville has been left—no sign, no marker, no street names. The homes and school have been so thoroughly effaced that no one in any of the new homes or apartment blocks would have the slightest notion of the older community underlying their homes. St. Anthony of Padua Church survives as a collection of small, adobe-walled structures, its function as the religious heart

Fig. 11.2. The Quarry Market smokestacks (*Source:* Courtesy of Rebecca Bridges.)

for the area supplanted (though not, of course, for its parishioners) by the nearby Alamo Heights Methodist and St. Luke's Episcopal Churches.

The reduction of the cement plant to a nostalgic curio is connected as well to the political and legal climate in which the Alamo Quarry was built. Since the late 1980s new superstores and markets have been springing up across the North Side of San Antonio (but virtually never the poorer South Side). The new Wal-Marts, multiscreen cineplexes, and mega-bookstores have a depressing sameness about them: large slabs of architecture in the midst of a sea of parking spaces, just like the Alamodome, the city's sports stadium and some-time-convention hall, which sets a bleak tone in this regard. The pro-growth climate, however, was not without challenge: in addition to partly successful efforts in the 1970s and '80s to prevent development in the recharge zone of the Edwards Aquifer, two city codes were proposed to shape and to limit and define what would be constructed: the "1 percent for art" ordinance and the tree-preservation ordinance.[33] One passed, but was then repealed; the other passed, but in a form that largely limited its effectiveness.

The "1 percent for art" ordinance, modeled on those already in effect in other cities, called for a set-aside in major design and construction projects of 1 percent of the total budget for art broadly defined as painting and sculpture, but also landscape architecture. The ordinance was enacted in 1996 but ran into a steady barrage of criticism from local developers and conservative city council representatives who denounced the ordinance both for its intrusion into the "free market" and as a kind of job-protection racket for artists. Not only was the ordinance reversed, but a new city council majority moved in against arts funding in general, arguing that only those arts programs that could be demonstrated to pull in significant numbers of tourists should be funded at all. Arts institutions received a 15 percent across-the-board cut; at least one institution was totally defunded.[34]

Though this reversal was defended in terms of "helping the people" and a frugal, "nuts and bolts" budget, its vanguard was a trio of city council members from Districts 8, 9, and 10—the affluent, expanding northern and northwestern sides of the city. Districts 8 and 10 in particular, occupying territory north of "the loop" (Interstate 410), help to define the aridity of San Antonio's recent expansion: clumps of walled and gated communities squatting between strip malls and multi-screen cineplexes. Former councilman Robert Marbut (District 8) led the charge, calling the "1 percent for art" program a symbol of "government pork and waste." Marbut, a one-time mayoral hopeful, also introduced the proposal to base arts funding on how many tourists the museum or gallery could attract; he fought successfully to eliminate all city funding to the Esperanza Peace and Justice Center for its radical views (particularly its exhibition of gay and lesbian artworks).[35]

The swing against arts funding (and "beautification" proposals specifically) took place almost simultaneously with the citywide debate over a tree-preservation ordinance. Environmental groups, long disturbed by the city's tolerance of clear-cutting sites for new construction, were spurred into action when K-mart bulldozed a massive lot on the North Side; some of the toppled oaks had been more than a century old. Citizens worked diligently through the 1990s to pass limits on how and where trees could be cut (and the circumstances under which they had to be replaced). A tree-preservation ordinance passed in 1996, drafted by a committee that included elected officials, environmental activists, and land developers. The compromise hammered out in 1996 almost immediately began to unravel, however; a watchdog committee set up to evaluate the ordinance met just once in 1997 and was immediately disbanded, as spokespeople for both sides disagreed angrily about just what the ordinance entailed.[36] Shortly after enactment, new protests were raised about continued clear-cutting: an automobile dealership justified its need for a tree-less lot on the grounds that trees brought birds, which left unpleasant deposits on their cars; a pharmacy construction involved the cutting of one hundred trees. Critics stressed that the continued destruction was linked directly to loopholes incorporated into the ordinance from the outset: included was a "grandfather clause" exempting any property platted or included even in a preliminary development plan in either March (commercial) or May (residential) of 1997. Even for those properties on which the ordinance was binding, there were broad exemptions, involving the diameter of the trees, zones around houses, changes in the grade of the land, and (for apartments) exclusion of broad "strips" within which the buildings are to be located. As a representative of an engineering firm acknowledged, even following the letter of the law would save very few trees.[37]

Commercial and residential development in the late 1990s was deeply affected by the nature and outcome of the debates over both ordinances. A few commercial development projects had attempted, however timidly, to meet demands for a pedestrian-friendly, landscaped project, with provision for ample greenery and shade.[38] But as the Alamo Quarry Market demonstrates, the city leaders' revolt against aesthetic and environmental regulation played a key role in creating relatively drab and sterile commercial landscapes. One analysis of the Quarry Market's failings pointed to the role of national chain stores: "Major national retailers typically demand a big parking lot at the front door and direct exposure to the high traffic volumes of major arterial streets and expressways." That demand, however, is directly antagonistic to the needs of the market as a whole. As in malls, outdoor markets thrive when there is space and the encouragement for strolling, for spending leisure time on site. The longer potential shoppers stay, the more they will tend to buy; the exception to that marketing truth is the norm at the Quarry Market: people tend to drive in, stop at a single store, then exit as quickly as possible so as to avoid the traffic snarls of the market's interior spaces.[39] Whatever the original intent and preferences of the market's designers, they did not withstand the demand of the long-sought-after major chain stores to fit into a preferred format designed for stand-alone stores, especially in the absence of a civic support for and regulations concerning the form and content of local construction projects. The result is a shopping complex both bleak and unattractive.

The lack of a meaningful landscape or tree-preservation ordinance (coupled with the national chain stores' insistence on huge frontal parking lots) doomed the well-intentioned efforts of the sites' landscape architect to produce a harmonious blend of structure and nature. In the northern and northwestern border fringes, which met the original goal of "all-round" buildings with hidden loading docks, Elorriaga and Grounds Control planted a careful blend of high-color vegetation well adjusted to San Antonio's heat and sunlight, from green cloud sage and esperanza to varieties of yucca and ornamental grasses. The problem is not with the xeriscaping, which is impressive, but with the vast central area, all but devoid of vegetation at all. The lone trees on tiny islands were selected to live in blinding sunlight and high heat; they provide no shade for less hardy pedestrians as they trudge across the melting asphalt of the endless parking lot.[40]

The market and its surroundings have already begun to fray along the edges. A small strip mall just north of the Quarry Market opened just before the larger complex. It has never been fully occupied; three restaurants have already come and gone. Nonetheless, the surrounding area continues to fill with more shopping centers; a satellite "Quarry Crossing Market" is nearing completion just across the street. InverWorld, an international stockbroking firm, took up space just north of the Quarry Market; months after opening its new, multistoried headquarters, it was threatened with lawsuits and involuntary bankruptcy. In July 1999 the Powerhouse, a vast restaurant/entertainment complex intended to anchor the northern half of the Market, was itself forced to declare bankruptcy and close its doors. Its two upper stories, intended for an exclusive private club and a cigar bar, were never completed.[41]

The developers' failure of imagination reflects a broader problem. San Antonio is a poor city with dreams of becoming a nationally prominent one. The combination of its social climate and the surrounding environment, its hopes of attracting commerce and its fear of setting limits or even basic parameters for controlling growth, combine to produce a lasting paradox: an attractive, decentralized city increasingly surrounded by and filled in with monotonous office and shopping blocks, devoid of imagination, bare of the slightest shade, and virtually identical to analogous sites across the country.

Char Miller

City Limits

An Afterword

The paradoxes of place captured the imagination of one nineteenth-century visitor to San Antonio. The city's "history, population, climate, location, architecture, soil, water, customs, costumes, horses, cattle, all attract the stranger's attention," observed poet Sidney Lanier in 1873, "either by force of intrinsic singularity or of odd juxtapositions." Long a small village—it "was a puling infant for a century and a quarter, yet has grown to a pretty vigorous youth in a quarter of a century"—this frontier town had by the mid-1870s become a bustling melange of peoples. Its "inhabitants are so varied that the 'go slow' directions over its bridges are in three languages, and the religious services in its churches held in four." Since the Civil War, San Antonio's physical growth and economic development had been significant, particularly in light of its marked isolation: "it stands with all its gay prosperity just on the edge of a lonesome, untilled belt of land one hundred and fifty miles wide, like *Mardi Gras* on the austere brink of Lent."[1]

As sharp a demarcation separated the city's social classes. For all San Antonio's new wealth, there were everywhere signs of an ancient poverty with its attendant ills. Heading west along Commerce Street lined with new limestone edifices, and crossing San Pedro Creek into the section of town the Spanish first platted in the early eighteenth century, Lanier entered a domestic landscape crowded with *jacals,* thatched-roofed housing built of mesquite stakes, interlaced with twigs, a wattle often covered with an adobe-like surface. Here he found "astonishing numbers" of Mexicans "huddled" in what he described as "a kennel whose door has to be crawled into." Not coincidentally, the level of disease in this dense and impoverished neighborhood was high: "typhus-fevers and small-pox are to be found among such layers of humanity. People are not sardines."[2]

The weather only complicated their lives. "The thermometer, the barometer, the vanes, the hygrometer oscillate so rapidly, so frequently, so lawlessly, and through so wide a meteorological range," the wide-eyed traveler asserted, "that the climate is simply indescribable." These abrupt shifts had on-the-ground consequences: the region's "soil is in wet weather an inky-black cement, but in dry a floury-white powder." Flood and drought wracked the land, further compromising the city's already thin supply of potable water: "it is built along both banks of two limpid streams, yet it drinks rain-water collected in cisterns." Grasping for a metaphor, the bewildered poet concluded after his two-month residence that if "peculiarities were quills, San Antonio de Bexar would be a rare porcupine."[3]

It bristles still, although some of the "striking idiosyncrasies and *bizarre* contrasts" Lanier noticed have moderated over the past 125 years. Gyroscopic weather patterns continue to astound, although the city is insulated from some of the consequences through advances in meteorological forecasting; as for the legendary mud and dust, these largely have been paved over.

Yet these changes may be a matter of degree, not of kind. Set within a river valley and sprawling out over its surrounding hills, San Antonio will not—because it cannot—fully escape the convergence of climate and geography that produces the kind of powerful thunderstorms and rampaging waters that regularly have scoured the floodplain on which the city has been built. New evidence for this came in October 1998 when a series of upper-level disturbances moved slowly over southcentral Texas, pulled moisture up from the Gulf of Mexico, and from the remnants of two Pacific hurricanes, all of which collided with a stalled cold front. This unusual pattern produced record rainfall: on October 17 San Antonio was drenched with 11.27 inches, and over a three-day period up to 22 inches soaked a super-saturated landscape. Despite the millions of dollars spent in the preceding two decades on the construction of a network of channels, ditches, and dams, and on two underground tunnels that diverted excess flow in the San Antonio River away from the central core, the sheer volume of water overwhelmed parts of these interlocking structures. Along the Cibolo and Salado Creek watersheds, which drain the city's North and East Sides, neighborhoods were swiftly overrun, homes battered beyond repair. Other creeks and streams were equally dangerous: innumerable cars were swept away at the city's many low-water crossings, one of the major freeways was inundated, and little of the urban infrastructure escaped damage. The tally for cleanup mounted into the hundreds of millions of dollars, but no amount of money could reclaim the eleven people who lost their lives in Bexar County. True, the devastation from the Flood of '98 would have been unimaginable had not flood controls been in place, but San Antonians also rediscovered how quickly natural forces can overwhelm human energy and capital.[4]

The city remains baffled by another conundrum that it has faced since Sidney Lanier toured the town. He had wondered why an environment blessed with such beautiful rivers had to rely on rainfall for its drinking water. Had he lingered longer he might have understood the need for cisterns: they were in place to catch late winter precipitation as a supplement to the irregular, and often unsanitary, flow of the San Antonio River and San Pedro Creek, and were of particular import during the drier months of the summer and fall. Still, even though early-twenty-first century residents know what Lanier and his contemporaries did not—that the city sits above the remarkably productive underground cistern, the Edwards Aquifer—the essential dilemma remains. How does a community, which for so long has depended on this sole source of potable water, sustainably manage this essential supply?

It has not yet resolved this question. At least earlier San Antonians who set out cisterns recognized the compelling need to stretch the available resource, a conservationist agenda that disappeared when in the late nineteenth century the first artesian wells gushed forth a seemingly limitless stream of water. It would not be for another hundred years that conservation would reemerge as a partial response to a diminished aquifer. Only in the 1990s, after extended dry periods forced the region to realize it must regulate competing human claims on the Edwards—a realization further sharpened when it was confronted with Endangered Species Act lawsuits in defense of salamanders and grasses extant within the underground reservoir and its springs—did south Texas initiate strict controls. For the first time, limits were set for agricultural, industrial, and urban pumping. This created the demand for new water markets, leading to the laying down of a system to distribute "gray water," or treated effluent, for use on golf courses, parklands, and corporate and university campuses. This new regulatory regime also spawned "water ranching," a process whereby the San Antonio Water System (SAWS) is permitted to purchase a portion of the pumping rights allotted to other users, notably farmers or ranchers in the surrounding counties. To expand its supply, and thus its access to water sources well beyond the Edwards Aquifer, SAWS has commenced as well buying rights to water stored in distant reservoirs and aquifers. This has generated considerable controversy—slaking San Antonio's growing thirst may mean others will go dry.[5]

As with the politics of water, common ground has been in short supply in other areas of public policy. Take Lanier's depiction of the stark disparities in income, housing, and public health in the 1870s. His was not the first such commentary, and certainly was not the last. Throughout the twentieth century, local investigations and national exposés repeatedly revealed the substandard wages, debilitating working places, and pestilential environment in which the bulk of the population was mired. In this respect, much had changed by 1985 when another visitor, English essayist Stephen Brook, toured the city; beginning in the 1940s some of the worst slums were cleared, and by the 1970s sewage and water lines had been extended throughout much of the metropolitan area. Even so, Brook was struck by the social and economic inequalities evident when he compared North Side, and "predominately Anglo enclaves" studded with Spanish "styles of architecture," and impoverished neighborhoods to their south and west: there "the vast majority of the Hispanic population lives in more abject circumstances in what must be one of the largest barrios in the United States."[6]

Its size and enduring presence are a further reflection of San Antonio's dismal record in delivering basic public services. Its failure is magnified by the fact that the city has been, and remains, one of the poorest in the nation; its relative poverty will continue unabated for the foreseeable future, to judge from a discouraging U.S. Census Bureau report released in July 2000. It indicated that of the nation's fifty most populated counties, Bexar County ranks forty-ninth in average wages earned; new job creation offered little hope for improvement, as much of the increase in local employment occurs in the lower-skilled sectors of construction, telemarketing, and tourism. At the dawn of the twenty-first century, San Antonio essentially was where it had been at the opening of the twentieth.[7]

That the past is prologue is a direct result of the city's commercial character. So argued Ramiro Cavazos, director of San Antonio's Economic Development Department, in response to the Census Bureau data: "We've been a big military town for over a century," he contended, and this reality has shaped economic prospects: "We have never had to rely on the open marketplace because we have had a huge segment of the population employed through civil service, state and local government and the schools." Although not entirely accurate—civil service employment on the military bases became a substantial factor only in the 1940s—Cavazos's argument dovetailed with one that Keith Phillips of the Federal Reserve Bank of Dallas advanced. For him, there was a direct link between the pool of available skilled labor (and the larger paychecks such abilities can command) and levels of education in a given population. "The spread between the average wage of a high school dropout and the average wage of a college student has been widening for over a decade," he affirmed, an affirmation containing ominous news for San Antonio, which "has a higher percentage of dropouts than many parts of the country."[8]

Instructive, these assessments do not fully explain why the city has for so long been a low-wage town built on the cheap. Once it was fashionable to lay this off on the demographic composition of the metropolitan area. Many nineteenth- and twentieth-century observers knew who to blame for San Antonio's economic backwardness and social lethargy—its large, and largely undereducated, Hispanic population. Just how little explanatory power ethnic stereotypes contain is abundantly manifest in the Mexican American community's drive to elevate its economic condition, expand its political rights, and improve its social status. In the Great Depression, for instance, Hispanics were at the forefront of efforts to unionize unskilled labor, leading to the explosive Pecan Sheller strikes of the late 1930s. These were forcibly repressed in affirmation of Anglo prejudice and paternalism. A public official who vigorously opposed the demand for higher wages argued that if the shellers "earned more than $1 a day, they'd just spend their money on tequila and on worthless trinkets in the dime store." One pecan operator was similarly blunt about why he had no intention of increasing the pay of those in his employ: "You can't make a Mexican work a whole week if they have money enough to live on."[9]

They did not have enough to live on, of course, which is precisely why thousands took advantage of the quick expansion of civilian defense work on the city's five military bases in the years before, during, and after World War II. Like their white and African American peers, Hispanics in San Antonio recognized that these jobs—the numbers of which dramatically escalated during the Cold War—represented an extraordinary opportunity for social mobility; over time, the salaries, benefits, and status these civilian defense jobs conferred enabled many to claim middle-class standing. Their determined initiative turned warfare into welfare, at once improving their lives and that of the commonweal.[10]

The notion that the oppressed can bend the world to their design runs counter to the once-prevailing racial narratives that gave structure to San Antonio's culture, politics, and society. That human beings, whatever their station, are active agents in the growth and development of their communities also complicates another kind of faith—that geography is destiny. Certainly place matters, and almost every page of this anthology contains evidence of the degree to which climate, location, and site have shaped the human experience in south Texas. But geographical context does not alone determine the kinds of cities that humans have constructed, as becomes evident in a brief comparison of San Antonio and its rival urban centers to the east and north.[11]

Neither Houston nor Dallas became powerful industrial cities because of the logic of place, unless a siting within fetid bayous (Houston) or the dry, hot High Plains (Dallas) are somehow conducive to sustained, robust economic development. They grew despite their locale, grew indeed as a result of a consistently aggressive entrepreneurial class that since the late nineteenth century has dominated city government and used it as a lever to raise private and public funds to underwrite expansion; that they fought with and off nearby cities with similarly elevated aspirations—Galveston and Fort Worth—only added to their competitive impulses. Whether investing in railroads, automobile production facilities and airline manufacturing plants, or maneuvering in Congress for federal funds to construct a ship channel, petrochemical industry, and NASA headquarters, the actions of Houston and Dalls exemplify what Harvey Molotch has called the urban "growth machine." By the mid-twentieth century, these cities' relentless efforts and staggering success, which often came at the expense of the poor and dispossessed, catapulted them into dominance of the Lone Star State's urban hierarchy and into national prominence.[12]

San Antonio, the oldest city in the state, and the one with the most pronounced geographical *raison d'être,* was left in the lurch. In the 1920 Census it had been the largest city in the state, but by the next decade it had slipped to third, and continued to fall behind in population and production. This decline was at once relative to the expansion of Dallas and Houston, and a consequence of the Alamo City's inability and unwillingness to compete. Its civic elite and political leadership had been at odds since the early twentieth century, and were therefore incapable of devising a unified plan for economic growth. The one thing they could agree on was the necessity of keeping taxes at very low levels, which prevented them from using this crucial mechanism for raising capital to fund urban development and thus contend with their in-state rivals.[13]

San Antonio's parsimony reached new heights early in World War II when the federal government proposed to construct an aircraft manufacturing plant in town, an unparalleled chance to expand the then-limited manufacturing sector, diminish dependence on agricultural production, and boost earnings. Mayor Maury Maverick was fully in support of the project, but the Chamber of Commerce spurned the proposal: it did not want to raise taxes to pay for the necessary extension of public utilities to the facility and was worried that this new work would somehow disrupt the city's entrenched relationship with the U.S. Army; "it would be extremely difficult to move any of these factories . . . to San Antonio," H. M. Van Auken, general manager of the Chamber reported, "largely on account of this being a great military reservation and in the Army's 'theatre of operation.'" These businessmen were not adverse to growth—they were eager to expand the city's function as a purchasing center and mail-distribution point for the new "Army cantonments and flying fields in Texas"—but they would only support it if it occurred on their terms. The industrial revolution would have to wait.[14]

Their terms were exclusive, based on segregationist politics, and bound up in a conception of San Antonio that was fractured along lines of class, ethnicity, gender, and race. Because local powerbrokers did not conceive of the community *as* a community, they refused to acknowledge the human connection between themselves and the 50 percent of the population who were Mexican and African Americans, many of whom were leading lives of quiet destitution. The studied and stunning indifference of the elite was not simply a matter of impoverished imaginations. It was also a result of their "somewhat peculiar p[s]ychology." They embraced a "'defeatist' attitude" which "admits that bad conditions exist," according to the authors of a 1939 U.S. Public Health Service report on San Antonio, but then assured themselves "that nothing constructive can be done about them." Symptomatic of the ability of well-off whites to distance themselves from threats to the public health was their

> smugness . . . concerning the prevalence of venereal diseases. This attitude allowed no recognition of the presence of gonorrhea or syphilis in the city exclusive of Negro and Latin American groups. Apparently, no cognizance is taken of the public health axiom that "communicable diseases are no respecters of persons."[15]

To have accepted that truism would have required an enlarged sense of civic obligation and social responsibility that neither this generation of the elite, nor their grandparents, nor their subsequent children, possessed. Among the disturbing legacies of this long-standing sense of disengagement are the continued immaturity of San Antonio's economy, the preponderance of low-skill work and wages, and the ongoing necessity to repair still-neglected built and natural environments. Of the city's many odd quills, this inheritance is surely one of the most peculiar.

NOTES

Introduction

1. *San Antonio Light,* July 12, 1937, 3A; Lewis F. Fisher, *Crown Jewel of Texas: The Story of San Antonio's River* (San Antonio: Maverick Publishing, 1998), 9.

2. William Cronon, "The Trouble with Wilderness: Or, Getting Back to the Wrong Nature," in *Out of the Woods: Essays in Environmental History,* ed. Char Miller and Hal K. Rothman (Pittsburgh: University of Pittsburgh Press, 1997), 39–41; Anne A. Fox and Cheryl Lynn Highley, "History and Archaeology of the Hot Wells Hotel Site, 41 BX 237," Center for Archaeological Research, University of Texas at San Antonio, Archaeological Survey Report no. 152 (1985), 4–19.

3. George E. Waring Jr., *Report of the Social Statistics of Cities,* part 2 (Washington, D.C.: Government Printing Office, 1887), 329.

4. *San Antonio Express,* July 7, 1883, and August 1, 1883; Wayne Cox, "The Development of a Sewer System," unpublished manuscript, 198–218, in author's possession.

5. Donald Everett, *San Antonio: The Flavor of Its Past, 1845–1898* (San Antonio: Trinity University Press, 1976), 55–56, 59; Waring, *Report of the Social Statistics of Cities,* 332.

6. Everett, *San Antonio,* 142; Waring, *Report of the Social Statistics of Cities,* 330.

7. Char Miller, "Flood of Memories," *Texas Observer,* September 27, 1996, 16–17.

Chapter 1. San Antonio

1. Daniel D. Arreola, "The Texas-Mexican Homeland," *Journal of Cultural Geography* 13 (Spring/Summer 1993): 61–74; Jeffrey B. Roet, "Site and Situation: A Historical Geography of San Antonio," in *A Geographic Glimpse of Central Texas and the Borderlands: Images and Encounters,* ed. James F. Petersen and Julie Tuason (Indiana, Pa.: National Council of Geographic Education, 1995), 41–50.

2. Nevin M. Fenneman, *Physiography of Western United States* (New York: McGraw-Hill, 1931), 51, 53, 55.

3. Roet, "Site and Situation," 41–50; Donald W. Meinig, *Imperial Texas: An Interpretive Essay in Cultural Geography* (Austin: University of Texas Press, 1969).

4. Bureau of Business Research, *Texas Fact Book* (Austin: University of Texas, 1989); C. W. Thornthwaite, "An Approach Towards a Rational Classification of Climate," *Geographical Review* 38 (1948): 55–59.

5. Wladimir Köppen, *Die Klimate der Erde: Grundekriss der Klimakunde* (Berlin: De-Gruyter, 1923). Note: Köppen's climatic classification is the most commonly used system on maps that depict world climatic types.

6. Richard A. Earl and Troy Kimmel, "Means and Extremes: The Weather and Climate of South-Central Texas," in *Geographic Glimpse of Central Texas and the Borderlands*, ed. Petersen and Tuason, 31–40.

7. NOAA, San Antonio: Climate and Records (*www.srh.noaa.gov/ewx/html/sclidata.htm*).

8. Earl and Kimmel, "Means and Extremes," 31–40.

9. Texas Parks and Wildlife, *Preserving Texas' Natural Heritage*, Policy Research Report no. 31 (Austin: LBJ School of Public Affairs, 1978); William Marsh and Nina Marsh, "Juniper Trees, Soil Loss, and Local Runoff Processes," in *Soils, Landforms, Hydrologic Processes, and Land-Use Issues: Glen Rose Limestone Terrains, Barton Creek Watershed, Travis County, Texas,* ed. C. M. Woodruff and William M. Marsh (Austin: Field Report and Guidebook, Society of Independent Professional Earth Scientists, Central Texas Chapter, 1992).

10. James F. Petersen, "Along the Edge of the Hill Country: The Texas Spring Line," in *Geographic Glimpse of Central Texas and the Borderlands*, ed. Petersen and Tuason, 20–30.

11. Marsh and Marsh, "Juniper Trees, Soil Loss, and Local Runoff Processes," in *Endangered and Threatened Animals of Texas*, ed. Linda Campbell (Austin: Texas Parks and Wildlife Press, 1995), 4-1–14.

12. Mike Kingston, ed., *Texas Almanac, 1994–1997* (Dallas: Dallas Morning News, 1993).

13. E. G. Wermund, "Environmental Units in Carbonate Terranes as Developed from a Case Study of the Southern Edwards Plateau and Adjacent Interior Coastal Plain," in *Approaches to Environmental Geology,* ed. E. G. Wermund (Austin: University of Texas, Bureau of Economic Geology, 1974), 52–78.

14. Petersen, "Along the Edge of the Hill Country," 20–30.

15. Thomas R. Hester, "Early Human Population Along the Balcones Escarpment," in *The Balcones Escarpment,* ed. Patrick J. Abbott and C. M. Woodruff Jr. (Boulder, Colo.: Geological Society of America, 1986), 55–62.

16. C. M. Woodruff Jr., "Geology and Physiography of Glen Rose Limestone Terrains, Barton Creek Watershed, Central Texas," in *Soils, Landforms, Hydrologic Processes, and Land-use Issues,* ed. Woodruff and Marsh, 3-1–8; Petersen, "Along the Edge of the Hill Country," 20–30.

17. Peter T. Flawn, "The Everlasting Land," in *A President's Country: A Guide to the Hill Country of Texas,* ed. Jack Maguire (Austin: Alcade Press, 1964), 67.

18. Ferdinand Roemer, *Roemer's Texas, 1845–1847* (1849), translated by Oswald Mueller for the German Heritage Society (Austin: Eakin Press, 1983), 110–11, 175.

19. Petersen, "Along the Edge of the Hill Country," 20–30.

20. Ibid.

21. Frederick Law Olmsted, *A Journey Through Texas: or, A Saddle-Trip on the Southwestern Frontier,* reprint (Austin: University of Texas Press, 1978), 156–57; Richard Everett, "Things in and about San Antonio," *Frank Leslie's Illustrated Newspaper* 7, no. 163 (January 15, 1859).

22. Gunnar Brune, *Major and Historical Springs of Texas* (Austin: Texas Water Development Board, 1975), 69–76.

23. Petersen, "Along the Edge of the Hill Country," 20–30.

24. Peter R. Rose, "Pipeline Oil Spills and the Edwards Aquifers, Central Texas," in *The Balcones Escarpment*, ed. Abbott and Woodruff, 163–83.

25. Victor R. Baker, "Flood Hazards along the Balcones Escarpment in Central Texas: Alternative Approaches to Their Recognition, Mapping, and Management," in Circular 75-5 (Austin: University of Texas Bureau of Economic Geology, 1975), 1–22; Petersen, "Along the Edge of the Hill Country," 20–30.

26. NOAA, San Antonio: Climate and Records (*www.srh.noaa.gov/ewx/html/sclidata.htm*).

27. S. Christopher Caran and Victor Baker, "Flooding along the Balcones Escarpment," in *The Balcones Escarpment*, ed. Woodruff and Abbott, 1–14; George W. Bomar, *Texas Weather* (Austin: University of Texas Press, 1983), 56–69; Raymond M. Slade, "Large Rainstorms along the Balcones Escarpment in Central Texas," in *The Balcones Escarpment*, ed. Woodruff and Abbott, 15–20.

28. Baker, "Flood Hazards along the Balcones Escarpment in Central Texas," 1–22.

29. Caran and Baker, "Flooding along the Balcones Escarpment," 1–14.

30. Char Miller, "Flood of Memories," *Texas Observer,* September 27, 1996, 16–17; John L. Davis, *San Antonio: A Historical Portrait* (Austin: Encino Press, 1978).

31. Petersen, "Along the Edge of the Hill Country"; Lewis F. Fisher, *The Crown Jewel of Texas: The Story of San Antonio's River* (San Antonio: Maverick Publishing, 1997).

Chapter 2. "A Fine Country with Broad Plains"

1. *Anglo American* is here defined as the English-speaking population that began to immigrate into Texas early in the Mexican post-independence period.

2. *Hispanic* is defined in this chapter as the Spanish-speaking population of New Spain, including acculturated Indians and people of African ancestry.

3. First and second quotes, Robin W. Doughty, *At Home in Texas: Early Views of the Land* (College Station: Texas A&M University Press, 1987), 6; see also 14–15; Doughty, *Wildlife and Man in Texas: Environmental Change and Conservation* (College Station: Texas A&M University Press, 1983).

4. In December 1836 the congress of the nascent Republic of Texas declared its borders to stretch from the mouth of the Rio Grande to its source thence to the Adams-Onís Treaty line in present-day southern Wyoming, thus including the eastern half of New Mexico, and parts of Colorado, Kansas, and Oklahoma in its boundaries.

5. "The Expedition of Don Domingo Terán de los Rios into Texas (1691–1692)," trans. Mattie Austin Hatcher, *Preliminary Studies of the Texas Catholic Historical Society* 2, no. 1 (January 1932): 14; Juan Antonio de la Peña, "Peña's Diary of the Aguayo Expedition," trans. Rev. Peter P. Forrestal, *Preliminary Studies of the Texas Catholic Historical Society* 2, no. 7 (January 1935): 24.

6. The early expeditions, from the 1680s to the 1720s, following different routes, during different seasons, often confused the names of streams. The modern names of those Texas streams with Spanish names were established by the end of the eighteenth century.

7. Fray Isidro Félix Espinosa, "Ramón Expedition: Espinosa's Diary of 1716," trans. Rev. Gabriel Tous, *Preparing the Way: Preliminary Studies of the Texas Catholic Historical Society* 1,

Studies in Southwestern Catholic History 1 (Austin: Texas Catholic Historical Society, 1997), 75–76.

8. Domingo Ramón, "Captain Don Domingo Ramón's Diary of His Expedition into Texas in 1716," trans. Rev. Paul J. Foik, *Preliminary Studies of the Texas Catholic Historical Society* 2, no. 5 (April 1933): 11; Fray José de Solis, "The Solís Diary of 1767," trans. Rev. Peter P. Forrestal, in *Preparing the Way*, 140.

9. Cayetano María Pignatelli Rubí Corbera y San Clement, "Itinerary of Señor Marqués de Rubí, Field Marshal of His Majesty's Armies, in the Inspection of the Interior Presidios that by Royal Order He Conducted in this New Spain, 1766–1768," trans. David McDonald, in *Imaginary Kingdom: Texas as Seen by the Rivera and Rubí Military Expeditions, 1727 and 1767*, ed. Jack Jackson (Austin: Texas State Historical Association, 1995), 132; "Expedition of Don Domingo Terán," 43; "Barreiro Provincial Descriptions of Coahuila-Nuevo León and Texas, 1727–1728," trans. Ned F. Brierley, in *Imaginary Kingdom*, ed. Jackson, 58.

10. Juan Agustín Morfi, *History of Texas, 1673–1779*, trans., intro., and annotations by Carlos E. Castañeda, 2 parts (Albuquerque: The Quivira Society, 1935) 1:48.

11. William C. Foster, in his *Spanish Expeditions into Texas, 1689–1768* (Austin: University of Texas Press, 1995), has cataloged the fauna and flora mentioned in the diaries, journals, and reports on eleven different expeditions to Texas. The two appendixes are an invaluable tool for anyone wishing to begin the process of studying biological distribution in early Texas. Two other appendixes list the documented epidemic diseases in northern New Spain from the late sixteenth to mid-eighteenth centuries, and Indian groups reported by the expeditions discussed in the book. Discussion of the fauna and flora in this and the following paragraphs is based on Foster unless otherwise noted.

12. "Expedition of Don Domingo Terán," 17.

13. "Peña's Diary," 24.

14. "Domingo Ramón's Diary," 14; Morfi, *History of Texas,* 1:67.

15. Fray Isidro Félix Espinosa, "The Espinosa-Olivares-Aguirre Expedition of 1709," trans. Rev. Gabriel Tous, in *Preparing the Way*, 61.

16. Juan Bautista Chapa, *Texas and Northeastern Mexico, 1630–1690: The First Official History of Texas*, ed. and intro. William C. Foster (Austin: University of Texas Press, 1997), 165; "Domingo Ramón Diary," 20; "Solís Diary of 1767," 125.

17. "Espinosa-Olivares-Aguirre Expedition," 61.

18. Jackson, ed., *Imaginary Kingdom*, 42; Morfi, *History of Texas,* 1:49.

19. "Solís Diary of 1767," 135.

20. Los Adaes, which is located near present-day Robeline, Louisiana, was abandoned in 1773, following the advice of frontier inspector the Marqués de Rubí. Hispanic residents were removed to San Antonio, but many of them returned to East Texas the following year, settling first at the Camino Real crossing of the Trinity River, and in 1779 at the former mission site of Nacogdoches.

21. Carlos E. Castañeda, *The Mission Era: The End of the Spanish Regime, 1780–1810*, vol. 5 of *Our Catholic Heritage in Texas, 1519–1836* (Austin: Von Boeckmann-Jones Co., 1942), 177.

22. "Espinosa-Olivares-Aguirre Expedition," 55.

23. "Ramón Expedition," 74.

24. Juan Agustín de Morfi, *Viaje de indios y diario del Nuevo México*, annotations by Vito Alessio Robles (Mexico: Manuel Porrúa, 1980), 357–58.

25. Padrón de Texas, September 26, 1778, Archivo San Francisco del Grande, Biblioteca Nacional de México, transcript in Spanish Material from Various Sources, vol. 32, Center for American History, University of Texas at Austin (hereafter cited as ASFG). For further discussion see Jesús F. de la Teja, *San Antonio de Béxar: A Community on New Spain's Northern Frontier* (Albuquerque: University of New Mexico Press, 1995), 92.

26. "Diario de la conquista y entrada a los thejas," *Universidad de México* 5 (1933): 233.

27. José Padrón v. Juan Leal Goraz, June 25, 1733, Bexar Archives, Center for American History, University of Texas at Austin (hereafter cited as BA); Notary protocols, March 22, 1738, and September 15, 1747, ibid; Testamentary proceedings for Francisco Hernández, Oct. 5, 1751, ibid. See also de la Teja, *San Antonio de Béxar,* 46–47.

28. Testament of Francisco Delgado, February 7, 1764, Spanish Archives of Bexar County, Bexar County Clerk's Office, San Antonio, Texas; "Solís Diary of 1767," 122.

29. Gov. Ripperdá to viceroy, April 20, 1776, in Correspondencia con el Gobernador de Texas, Barón de Ripperdá, en los años de 1774 hasta 1777 inclusive, Carpeta 2a., ramo Provincias Internas vol. 99, Archivo General de la Nación de México, microfilm reel 93, Benson Latin American Collection, University of Texas at Austin (hereafter cited as AGN:PI).

30. Noticia que el Capitán D. Rafael Martínez Pacheco, gobernador Interino, y Comte. de las armas de dha. Proa. manifiesta del tpo. que se ha experimentado en ella, 30 June 1787, BA; Martínez Pacheco to Ugalde, January 30, 1789, ibid; Martínez Pacheco to Ugalde, March 30, 1789, ibid.

31. Martínez to Viceroy Revilla Gigedo, June 6, 1790, BA.

32. Except where otherwise noted, the following discussion on ranching is based on de la Teja, *San Antonio de Béxar,* 97–117. For a narrative political history of Spanish ranching, see Jack Jackson, *Los Mesteños: Spanish Ranching in Texas, 1721–1821* (College Station: Texas A&M University Press, 1986).

33. "Expedition of Don Domingo Terán," 55.

34. *Bexareños* refers to Hispanic residents of the jurisdiction of San Antonio de Béxar.

35. "The Texas Missions in 1785," trans. J. Autrey Dabbs, in *Preliminary Studies of the Texas Catholic Historical Society* 3, no. 6 (January 1940): 18; De la Teja, *San Antonio de Béxar,* 113–14.

36. "Solís Diary of 1767," 120; Morfi, *History of Texas,* 1:49.

37. Causa formada pr. el Govr. de esta provincia Baron de Ripperdá, contra Francisco Xavier Rodríguez, Juan José Flores, y Nepomuceno Travieso, vecinos de la villa de Sn. Fernando, sobre extracción de reses orejanas, 7 March 1777, BA.

38. Carta de Fray Mariano Francisco de los Dolores, respecto a quejas de los indios contra los habitantes de San Fernando de Béxar, 1758, legajo 95, no. 28 ASFG; Padrón de Texas, September 26, 1778, ASFG.

39. Bando de buen gobierno expedido por el Sñr. Come. Gral de estas Proas. Internas, January 11, 1778, BA; De la Teja, *San Antonio de Béxar,* 109.

40. Gov. Ripperdá to viceroy, December 19, 1775, Carpeta 2a; Martínez Pacheco to Juan de Ugalde, November 11, 1787, BA; questionnaire concerning the commandant general's order, May 21, 1789, BA.

41. Contiene tres vandos sobre el buen régimen que deven observar estos vezinos en las corridas del ganado orejano, February 15, 1794, BA.

42. Petition of Manuel Delgado, April 3, 1796, BA.

43. Cabildo to viceroy, August 4, 1772, in Correspondencia con el ayuntamiento de la

Villa de San Fernando y con various individuos en distintos años desde el de 1771 hasta el de 1793, incluyendose un informe sobre la Prova. del Gobernador que fue de ella D. Jacinto de Barrios, Carpeta 8a, microfilm reel 93, AGN:PI.

44. Petition of citizenry, January 29, 1788, BA.

45. Gov. Ripperdá to viceroy, February 8, 1773, vol. 100, microfilm reel 94, AGN:PI.

46. Petition of Francisco Bueno, April 16, 1796, BA.

47. Quoted in de la Teja, *San Antonio de Béxar,* 112.

48. Tomás Felipe de Winthuisen to [viceroy], August 19, 1744, BA.

49. Gov. Ripperdá to viceroy, April 5, 1775, Carpeta 2a; Causa criminal contra soldado Juan Chirinos por dar muerte a el soldado Cristóbal Carabajal, January 16, 1772, BA; Bernardo Fernández to Gov. Muñoz, January 6, 1791, ibid.; Petition of Manuel de Arocha, et al., February 8, 1792, ibid.

50. Appeal of Tomás Travieso of murder conviction, Guadalajara [1777], BA.

51. Manuel Espadas to Martínez, May 6, 1790, BA; Petition of Antonio Baca, March 30, 1791, ibid.; Petition of Manuel Rodríguez, November 7, 1792, ibid; License by Muñoz, January 2, 1793, ibid.

52. Quoted in Vito Alessio Robles, *Coahuila y Texas en la época colonial,* 2nd ed. (Mexico: Editorial Porrúa, 1978), 608.

Chapter 3. Where the Buffalo Roamed

1. Jesse Clements, "South Texas Trail Riders Shatter Myths of the Old West," *San Antonio Express-News,* January 28, 1997, 1, 3B.

2. Ibid.; Ihosvani Rodriguez, "Trials of the Trail Ride: Rookie Sees Traditionalists Aren't Horsing Around," *San Antonio Express-News,* February 3, 1999, 1, 7A; Anita McDivitt, "Day on Trail Leaves Lasting Impression," *San Antonio Express-News,* February 7, 1998, 1, 7D; these articles almost constitute a subgenre of reportage—call it the "ride of passage".

3. The quantities of food prepared are staggering: "10,000 biscuits, 200 gallons of gravy, 500 pounds of bacon, 400 pounds of hash browns, 15,000 tortillas and 800 gallons of coffee" were on the menu for the the Year 2000 Cowboy Breakfast; Edmund Tijerna, "Cowboy Breakfast Aiming for Record," *San Antonio Express-News,* January 13, 2000, 8B; Alexander Wiley, "Country People: Cowboy Breakfast Kicks Off Weekend of Stars," *San Antonio Express-News,* January 25, 1998; "Cowboy Breakfast Set to Dish It Out," *San Antonio Express-News,* January 24, 1997.

4. Descriptions of events at the San Antonio Stock Show and Rodeo are drawn from the *Express-News,* February 7, 1997, 1, 8A.

5. Char Miller and David R. Johnson, "The Rise of Urban Texas," in *Urban Texas: Politics and Development,* ed. Char Miller and Heywood Sanders (College Station: Texas A&M University Press, 1990), 3–29.

6. Frederick Law Olmsted, *A Journey Through Texas; or, a Saddle-Trip on the Southwestern Frontier,* reprint (New York: Burt Franklin, 1969), 135–36; others shared his high opinion of the grass: Gideon Lincecum, "Native or Indigenous Texas Grasses," *Texas Almanac, 1861,* 141–42.

7. Ibid., 162, 271–72; on the enduring hostility that emerged in this period see Arnoldo DeLeon, *They Called Them Greasers: Anglo Attitudes Towards Mexicans in Texas* (Austin: University of Texas Press, 1983); Jack Jackson, *Los Mesteños: Spanish Ranching in Texas, 1721–1821* (College Station: Texas A&M University Press, 1986), 584–617.

8. Jackson, *Los Mesteños,* 614–15; to the south and west of the San Antonio River, especially along the Rio Grande, Mexican Americans' ranching presence was far more pronounced (613–14).

9. Ibid., 590–98.

10. There is considerable scholarly debate about the influences of the Spanish and Mexican livestock industry within and beyond Texas; compare Jackson to Terry G. Jordan, who argues that south Texas was not the cradle of the western American cattle industry, and that "the case for Hispanic influence in the Great Plains has been consistently overstated": *Trails to Texas: Southern Roots of Western Cattle Ranching* (Lincoln: University of Nebraska Press, 1981), 150–57; Terry G. Jordan, *North American Cattle-Ranching Frontiers* (Albuquerque: University of New Mexico Press, 1993), 208–40; Cabeza de Vaca reported in 1540s that Gulf Coastal Indians burned the landscape for hunting purposes: "The Narrative of Alvar Nunez Cabeza de Vaca," in *Spanish Explorers in the Southern United States, 1528–1543,* ed. Frederick W. Hodge (New York: Scribner's Sons, 1907), 67; Vinton Lee James, *Frontier and Pioneer Recollections of Early Days in San Antonio and West Texas* (San Antonio: Artes Graficas, 1938), 155, also reports that Native American people burned the prairie, but he did not recognize the relationship between the annual "immense fires" the Indians would touch off each fall, blazes that "would sweep the entire country until stopped by a river or some natural barrier, leaving an appearance of utter desolation," and the creation of a "treeless prairie, covered with a rank growth of grass almost waist high" that became "pasture ground for immense herds of deer, graceful antelope, wild horses and the uncouth and ponderous buffalo." William Cronon, *Nature's Metropolis: Chicago and the Great West* (New York: W. W. Norton, 1991), 213, argues that fires on the northern plains "destroyed the woody stems of trees (mainly oaks and hickories) that might otherwise have dominated the terrain, and gave the abundant root growth of the grasses an injection of nutrients that accelerated their recovery." The same held true on the Gulf Coastal Plain, and the Edwards Plateau, both of which have become much more heavily wooded due to the suppression of fire; on the similarities between buffalo, and cattle and sheep grazing, see ibid., 220.

11. Olmsted, *Journey Through Texas,* 239, 273–75; Brownson Malsch, *Indianola: The Mother of Western Texas* (Austin: State House Press, 1988), 27–30, 39–50; Ferdinand von Roemer, *Texas, with Particular Reference to German Immigration and The Physical Appearance of the Country* (San Antonio: Standard Printing, 1935), 130–31; Wayne R. Austerman, *Sharps Rifles and Spanish Mules: The San Antonio-El Paso Mail, 1851–1861* (College Station: Texas A&M University Press, 1985), details another major transportation development emanating from San Antonio; Sidney Lanier, who lived in San Antonio in the early 1870s, also commented on the city's role as a supply depot for the U.S. Army and northern Mexican states: Sidney Lanier, *Florida and Miscellaneous Prose,* Centennial Edition (Baltimore: Johns Hopkins Press, 1945), 233; Kenneth L. Stewart and Arnoldo De León, *Not Room Enough: Mexicans, Anglos, and Socio-economic Change in Texas, 1850–1900* (Albuquerque: University of New Mexico Press, 1993), 25; Ike Moore, ed., *The Life and Diary of Reading W. Black* (Uvalde, Tex.: El Progreso Club, 1934), passim, confirms the intense wagon traffic in the region; Donald E. Everett, *San Antonio: The Flavor of Its Past, 1845–1898* (San Antonio: Trinity University Press, 1975), 72.

12. Jesús F. de la Teja, *San Antonio de Béxar: A Community on New Spain's Northern Frontier* (Albuquerque: University of New Mexico Press, 1995), 110–13, 119–38; Jesús de la Teja and John Wheat, "Béxar: Profile of a Tejano Community," in *Tejano Origins in Eighteenth-*

Century San Antonio, ed. Gerald E. Poyo and Gilberto Hinojosa (Austin: University of Texas Press, 1991), 17–21; Félix D. Almaráz, *Tragic Cavalier: Governor Manuel Salcedo of Texas, 1803–1813* (Austin: University of Texas Press, 1971), 18–21; Kenneth W. Wheeler, *To Wear a City's Crown: The Beginnings of Urban Growth in Texas, 1836–1865* (Cambridge: Harvard University Press, 1968), 42–46.

13. Cronon, *Nature's Metropolis,* 216–17; Everett, *San Antonio,* 72.

14. Cronon, *Nature's Metropolis,* 218–24; Jordan, *North American Cattle-Ranching Frontiers,* 215–27; Frank W. Jennings, *San Antonio: The Story of an Enchanted City* (San Antonio: San Antonio Express-News, 1998), 226.

15. Karen E. Stothert, "The Archaeology and Early History of the Head of the San Antonio River," Southern Texas Archaeological Association Special Publication no. 5, and Incarnate Word College Archaeological Series no. 3, San Antonio, 1989, 1–39; W. W. Newcomb, *The Indians of Texas: From Prehistoric to Modern Times* (Austin: University of Texas Press, 1960), 131–40; T. N. Campbell, "The Payaya Indians of Southern Texas," San Antonio: Southern Texas Archaeological Association Special Publication no. 1, San Antonio, 1975, 1–2.

16. Campbell, "Payaya Indians of Southern Texas," 1–2, 23–26; Newcomb, *The Indians of Texas,* 136; David La Vere, *Life Among the Texas Indians: The WPA Narratives* (College Station: Texas A&M University Press, 1998), 14–22 argues that the Tonkawa of Central and Eastern Texas offered considerable resistance to Spanish missions and missionaries, unlike the bands living on the Edwards Plateau.

17. Olmsted, *Journey Through Texas,* 188–89; Terry G. Jordan, *German Seed in Texas Soil: Immigrant Farmers in Nineteenth-Century Texas* (Austin: University of Texas Press, 1966), 147–51.

18. Olmsted, *Journey Through Texas,* 193–202, 223–26; roughly 90 miles to Olmsted's west, Reading W. Black, founder of Uvalde, Texas, documented his daily hunting in his diary: over November and December 1854 he bagged 82 ducks, fifteen of which he shot on December 27, "10 in one shot"; goose, quail, and turkey also graced his table, as did deer, panther, wild cattle, and mustangs. *The Life and Diary of Reading W. Black,* arranged by Ike Moore (Uvalde, Tex.: El Progreso Club, 1934), 59–64.

19. Reading Black shared Olmsted's perception of the forts' ability to disrupt the movement and raiding of the Comanche, Kickapoo, Lipan, and Tonkawa in southwest Texas; Black to Governor Throckmorton, January 10, 1867 in *Life and Diary,* 22–23; but he also knew, as Olmsted did not, that the forts were economic hubs, and that as markets they had a decidedly different impact on native peoples than the simply punitive one Olmsted ascribed to them. Black records extensive trade between Indians, the U.S. Army, and himself; on September 25, 1854, for instance, he "got 200 skins" in trade (*Life and Diary,* 53). As Robin Doughty points out, these military posts, and their paired European settlements, provided "economic incentives for hunting and killing off mammals and birds [that] resulted in sizable declines in populations of many species, and in contractions in aboriginal ranges." He cites botanist Jean Louis Berlandier's calculation that "Indians carried perhaps as many as 40,000 deer hides, 1,500 bear skins, and 1,200 other pelts to Nacogdoches [Texas] in less than a year"; Doughty, "Settlement and Environmental Change in Texas," *Southwestern Historical Quarterly* (April 1986): 440–41; German geologist Ferdinand von Roemer also noted the brisk trade in pelts and bear oil in the markets of Fredericksburg; Roemer, *Texas,* 232;

Newcomb, *The Indians of Texas*, 138; La Vere, *Life Among the Texas Indians*, 13–14, 25, 31. These and other accounts suggest the complex response the Plains Indians had to the presence of new economic opportunities; that they had a hand in setting up the conditions of their own demise is a pattern replicated elsewhere in North America; William Cronon, *Changes in the Land* (New York: Hill and Wang, 1983), 82–107.

20. Kendall's letters appeared in the *San Antonio Herald* and the *New Orleans Picayune* and are reproduced in Harry James Brown, ed., *Letters from a Texas Sheep Ranch* (Urbana: University of Illinois Press, 1959), 12–14; Although Kendall supported the Confederacy, other sheep owners, especially Germans located in Gillespie County, just to the west of Kendall's spread, did not: "to these Germans, secession meant war, war meant the withdrawal of troops from local military posts, and that in turn meant the loss of a major market for agricultural produce as well as the removal of protection against the Comanche Indians"; Jordan, *German Seed in Texas Soil*, 183. The forced exodus to Oklahoma in the mid-nineteenth century is explored in La Vere, *Life Among the Texas Indians*, 37–43.

21. Paul H. Carlson, *Texas Woollybacks: The Range Sheep and Goat Industry* (College Station: Texas A&M University Press, 1982), 36–41; Fayette Copeland, *Kendall of the Picayune* (Norman: University of Oklahoma Press, 1943).

22. Brown, ed., *Letters from a Texas Sheep Ranch*, 72–73.

23. Ibid., 84–85; other transportation costs also escalated as the temperatures rose: "Three weeks ago I paid a man $1.00 per 100 lbs. for bringing up a load of salt to my sheep: to-day he would not stir for a step for another for $10.00 a 100—no, not for $20.00. The trip would inevitably involve the loss of every ox in his team" (85).

24. Herbert M. Mason Jr. and Frank W. Brown, *A Century on Main Plaza: A History of the Frost National Bank* (San Antonio: The Frost National Bank, 1968), 16–22; Carlson, *Texas Woollybacks*, 77–78, 197–98; *San Antonio Express*, February 20, 1888, 11.

25. "Gideon Licecum," "The Indigenous Texian Grasses," *The Texas Almanac*, 1868, 76–77; Jordan, *North American Cattle-Ranching Frontiers*, 215–21.

26. Sidney Lanier, commenting on the ecological transition from grassland to brush country in 1872, offered this contemporary insight as to why the mesquite tree came to dominate the plains to the city's south: "It appears to have spread over this portion of Texas within the last twenty-five years, perhaps less time. The old settlers account for its appearance by the theory that the Indians—and after them the stock-raisers—were formerly in the habit of burning off the prairie-grass annually, and that these great fires rendered it impossible for the mesquit shrub to obtain a foothold; but that now with the departure of the Indians, and the transfer of most of the cattle-raising business to points farther westward, have resulted in leaving the soil free for the occupation of the mesquite"; Lanier, *Florida and Miscellaneous Prose*, 244; Carlson, *Texas Woollybacks*, 48–67, 101–20, 188–204; a large number of Rio Grande Plain sheep were trailed even farther north, into the Rocky Mountain region. For the growth of the goat industry, see Douglas E. Barnett, "Angora Goats in Texas: Agricultural Innovation on the Edwards Plateau, 1858–1900," *Southwestern Historical Quarterly* (April 1987): 347–72; with this surge onto the Edwards, the practices of Spanish/Mexican sheep and goat raising now predominated; material culture—the use of palisado corrals and ranchstead housing, occupational differentiation, and nomenclature all reflect the degree to which "the Mexican plateau abounds in Texas": Jordan, *North American Cattle-Ranching Frontiers*, 150–52; Carlson, *Texas Woollybacks*, 56–57.

27. Copeland, *Kendall of the Picayune*, 277.

28. Stephen Gould, *The Alamo City Guide* (New York: MacGowan and Slipper Printers, 1882), 71–72; Donald Everett, "San Antonio Welcomes the 'Sunset'—1877," *Southwestern Historical Quarterly* (July 1961): 48; Everett, *San Antonio*, 134–35, 137–38.

29. George Waring Jr., compiler, *Report of the Social Statistics of Cities* (Washington, D.C.: Government Printing Office, 1887), 332; Everett, "San Antonio Welcomes the 'Sunset,'" 59; Gould, *Alamo City Guide*, 71–72.

30. "Cattleman Square," An Urban Design Study of a Part of the Vista Verde TEX R-109 Urban Renewal Area, San Antonio, Texas, Phase One Report, Design Analysis, January 1980, 2–4; "Houston Street," *San Antonio Express*, February 20, 1888, 16.

31. Gould, *Alamo City Guide*, 133–35; Maria Watson, "San Antonio on Track: The Suburban and Street Railway Complex Through 1933," M.A. thesis, Trinity University, 1982, 7–14, 35–42; Donald E. Everett, *San Antonio's Monte Vista: Architecture and Society in a Gilded Age* (San Antonio: Maverick Publishing, 1999), 1–26; the role of trolleys in the development of residential and commercial districts is detailed in Sam Bass Warner, *Streetcar Suburbs: The Process of Growth in Boston, 1870–1900* (New York: Atheneum, 1976).

32. Gould, *Alamo City Guide*, 71–75, 133–35; Everett, *San Antonio's Monte Vista*, passim.

33. *San Antonio Express*, February 20, 1888, 2–3.

34. Gould, *Alamo City Guide*, 72; Crosby A. Houston, "San Antonio's Railroads in the Nineteenth Century," M.A. thesis, Trinity University, 1963, 23–115, charts the development of the various lines that crisscrossed the city and its hinterland; regional newspapers also editorialized in favor of San Antonio build tracks linking it to secondary and tertiary markets (93–95).

35. S. G. Reed, *A History of the Texas Railroads* (New York: Arno Press, 1981), 243–49; J. L. Allhands, *Railroads to the Rio* (Salado: Anson Jones Press, 1960), 15–47; *Corpus Christi: 100 Years* (Corpus Christi: The Corpus Christi Caller-Times, 1952), 99–104; Paul Schuster Taylor, *An American-Mexican Frontier: Nueces County, Texas* (New York: Russell and Russell, 1971), 78–83; *San Antonio Express*, February 20, 1888, 2–3, 9, 11; *Bee County Centennial, 1858–1958* (Beeville: Beeville Centennial, 1958), 17–18, 31–32, 35; C. L. Patterson, *Nixon (Gonzalez County) Texas: A Progressive Diversified Agricultural Haven* (San Antonio: Sid Murray and Sons Printers, 1938), 18, recounts the changes the railroad brought to local turkey growers: before its arrival, they used to drive their herds more than forty miles to San Antonio slaughterhouses; by the 1930s the dressing plants had been spun out to Nixon so that "most of the turkeys die near home."

36. Houston, "San Antonio's Railroads," 108–10.

37. Bob Bennett, *Kerr County, Texas: 1856–1956* (San Antonio: Naylor Company, 1956), 230–34, shows how Kerrville's commercial axis shifted toward the new depot and away from the traditional business center along Water Street; Carlson, *Texas Woollybacks*, 77–78; Winifred Kupper, *The Golden Hoof: The Story of Sheep in the Southwest* (New York: Knopf, 1945), 161–69; Gene Hollon, "Captain Charles Schreiner, the Father of the Hill Country," *Southwestern Historical Quarterly* (October 1944): 145–68; there is anecdotal evidence that Schreiner refused to loan funds to those who did not run sheep and goats, a mechanism designed to tighten the link between his capital investments and wool-commission profits.

38. S. G. Reed argues that the rail line to Kerrville "was not expected to much of a freight producer" implying that passenger business had been the impetus for the line's construction;

Reed, *History of the Texas Railroads*, 246. If so, then why did it take three years before the company began running passenger service? Reed also argues that SAP abandoned plans to extend its lines from Kerrville to the Texas Panhandle due to prohibitive construction costs. To be more precise, Kerrville was the end of the line because SAP directors concluded that expansion would not recover the high costs due to the scant population and small markets that lay between the Hill Country and the Panhandle. That is why SAP directors voted instead to extend lines north from San Antonio to Waco, along the thickening line of population that hugged the Balcones Escarpment, and east across the densely populated Southern Plains into Houston; Houston, "San Antonio's Railroads," 110–12; Guido E. Ransleben, *A Hundred Years of Comfort in Texas: A Centennial History* (San Antonio: Naylor Company, 1954), notes the opening of a branch of San Antonio's Steve's Lumber Company in Comfort, increases in grain, cotton, and hog production, and the construction of tourist facilities, each of which depended on the SAP for its development, 59–60, 101, 185; on summer camps, Ransleben, *A Hundred Years of Comfort in Texas*, 60; Bennett, *Kerr County,* 245–46; Virginia Bradley, *Functional Patterns in the Guadalupe Counties of the Edwards Plateau* (Chicago: Geography Department, University of Chicago, 1949), 77–95.

39. Ransleben, *Hundred Years of Comfort in Texas*, 101.

40. "Stephen Crane in Texas," January 6, 1889, in *Stephen Crane: Tales, Sketches, and Reports,* ed. Fredson Bowers (Charlottesville: University of Virginia Press, 1973), 468–73.

41. *Great Short Stories of Stephen Crane* (New York: Harper and Row, 1965), 313.

42. Ibid., 313–15, 320–24; Christopher Benfey, *The Double Life of Stephen Crane* (New York: Knopf, 1992), 231–34; David Halliburton, *The Color of the Sky: A Study of Stephen Crane* (New York: Cambridge University Press, 1989), 227–35; Frank Bergon, *Stephen Crane's Artistry* (New York: Columbia University Press, 1975), 122–24.

43. For comparative information on the kind and number of each city's petrochemical refineries, and their productive capacity, see Elmer H. Johnson, *The Basis of the Commercial and Industrial Development of Texas* (Austin: Bureau of Business Research, 1933), 120–28; Stanley A. Arbingast, *Texas Resources and Industries: Selected Maps of Distribution* (Austin: Bureau of Business Research, 1955); on trucking, Bradley, *Functional Patterns in the Guadalupe Counties,* 9–13; Peyton Green, *San Antonio: City in the Sun* (New York: McGraw-Hill, 1946), 1–20; on the livestock industry's difficulties, Carlson, *Texas Woollybacks,* 188–214; on the shifts in the state's urban hierarchy, Miller and Johnson, "Rise of Urban Texas," 3–32; Char Miller, "Sunbelt Texas," in *Texas Through Time,* ed. Robert Calvert and Walter Buenger (College Station: Texas A&M University Press, 1991), 279–309.

44. Fort Worth and Dallas had recently built coliseums, and Houston's "Fat Stock Show" was the model against which San Antonio expected to be judged; *San Antonio Express,* February 2, 1947, 2A; *San Antonio Light,* February 16, 1950, 4B; Wiley Alexander, "Looking Back on 50 Years of History," *San Antonio Express-News,* February 5, 1999, 2J; Chuck McCullough, "Stock Show Eyes 50th Party," *San Antonio Express-News,* February 23, 1998, 1A.

45. *San Antonio Light,* February 16, 1950, 1, 5A, 1C; *San Antonio Express,* October 10, 1949, 1B.

Chapter 4. Parks, Politics, and Patronage

1. Jesse Clements, "Salas Working to Become 'Parks Guru' of East Side," *San Antonio Express-News,* April 16, 1998, 1B.

2. Ibid.; Chuck McCullough, "The Newest Road to City Hall: Candidates Find Neighborhoods Provide Fast Lane to Public Office," *San Antonio Express-News*, May 26, 1999, 1H.

3. Stewart King, "Little Known Important Facts about Our Parks," February 6, 1950, San Antonio Vertical File, "Parks," San Antonio Central Public Library.

4. Frederick Law Olmsted, *A Journey Through Texas: or, A Saddle-Trip on the Southwestern Frontier,* reprint (Austin: University of Texas Press, 1978), 150-51; Nic Tengg, *Visitor's Guide and History of San Antonio, Texas* (San Antonio: n.p., 1908), 66-77.

5. Homer Hoyt, *One Hundred Years of Land Values in Chicago* (New York: Arno Press, 1970), p. 99.

6. *San Antonio Express*, August 3, 1919, Real Estate section, p. 4.

7. Char Miller, "Flood of Memories," *Texas Observer,* September 27, 1996, 16-17.

8. "A Comparison of Data, Cities in Texas, 1963" (table), in *Parks Master Plan* (San Antonio: Department of Parks and Recreation, 1964), 3-7.

9. *Parks Master Plan.*

10. Tengg, *Visitor's Guide,* 69-77; Edwinna K. Janert, "San Pedro Springs," master's thesis, Trinity University, 1968, passim.

11. George E. Waring, *Report of the Social Statistics of Cities* (Washington, D.C.: Government Printing Office, 1887), part 2, p. 330; City of San Antonio, *Master Plan of 1951* (San Antonio: City of San Antonio, 1951), 209-11; Dora Crouch, Daniel S. Gann, and Axel I. Mindigo, *Spanish City Planning in North America* (Cambridge: MIT University Press, 1982), 23-65; Janert, "San Pedro Springs," 78-90; *San Antonio Express*, September 1, 1877, Vertical File, "Parks," San Antonio Public Library.

12. *San Antonio Express*, September 1, 1877, and May 1, 1897, Vertical File, "Parks," San Antonio Public Library; Janert, "San Pedro Springs," 78-80; *San Antonio Express*, April 9, 1903, and February 10, 1908; *San Antonio Light*, February 6, 1910, Vertical File, "Parks," San Antonio Public Library.

13. William H. Wilson, *The City Beautiful Movement in America* (Baltimore: Johns Hopkins University Press, 1989), 1; San Antonio, The Annual Mayor's Message and Financial Report for the Fiscal Year Ending May 31, 1904, Texana Collection, San Antonio Central Public Library, 3, 14-15.

14. San Antonio, Annual Message of Bryan Callaghan and Review of Reports of City Officers, for Fiscal Year Ending May 31, 1910, 14, on file in the Texana Collection, San Antonio Central Public Library; *San Antonio Express*, July 23, 1919, 6.

15. *San Antonio Light,* February 20, 1907, and February 21, 1907, Vertical File, "Parks," San Antonio Public Library; additional information on parks acquisition drawn from an analysis of historical data compiled by the City of San Antonio, Parks and Recreation Department, 1981.

16. David R. Johnson, John A. Booth, and Richard J. Harris, eds., *The Politics of San Antonio: Community, Progress, and Power* (Lincoln: University of Nebraska Press, 1983), 3-27.

17. *San Antonio Express*, July 23, 1919, 6.

18. Ibid.; *San Antonio Express*, November 28, 1923, 2, and November 29, 1923, 3. Galen Crantz, *The Politics of Park Design: A History of Urban Parks in America* (Cambridge: MIT Press, 1982), 183-85, addresses some of this language, but assumes that this was part of the patronizing rhetoric park reformers employed. That may have been true elsewhere, but in San Antonio in the 1920s this was the language that machine bosses and their media sup-

porters used to encourage working-class and minority voting in favor of the bonds (and thus of the parks), a rather different scenario than that Crantz has established; see also Daniel M. Bluestone, "From Promenade to Park: The Gregarious Origins of Brooklyn's Park Movement," *American Quarterly* 4 (1987): 529–50; Roy Rosensweig, "The Parks and the People: Social History and Urban Parks," *Journal of Social History* (Winter 1984): 289–95; Jon A. Peterson, "The Evolution of Public Open Space in American Cities," *Journal of Urban History* (November 1985): 75–88.

19. *San Antonio Express*, August 3, 1919, Real Estate section, p. 4.

20. Ibid.; *San Antonio Express,* November 23, 1923, 1, for similar discussions concerning who would pay for much-needed flood-control measures; *San Antonio Express*, December 3, 1923, 1, addresses the split between suburbanite and working-class interests in bond elections.

21. Park Acquisition data published by the City of San Antonio, Parks and Recreation Department, 1981.

22. Bradley Rice, *Progressive Cities: The Commission Government Movement in America, 1901–1920* (Austin: University of Texas Press, 1977), 84–99 and passim; Johnson, Booth, and Harris, eds., *Politics of San Antonio*, chap. 1; *San Antonio Light*, May 20, 1928, 1, and May 8, 1930, 1, 6. The vote margins in other Black precincts were not as great as in precinct 54, but most provided comfortable enough margins that helped carry the election. Some of the Hispanic West Side precincts were even more helpful: Precinct 10, which the *San Antonio Light* indicated had been "a machine stronghold for years, and whose voters primarily are Mexicans, gave the bonds the greatest majority in any one precinct. The vote there stood 412 for and 60 against." *San Antonio Light*, May 8, 1930, 6. The machine clearly needed every Hispanic and Black vote it could garner to win this particularly close election. Richard Garcia, *Rise of the Mexican American Middle Class: San Antonio, 1929–1941* (College Station: Texas A&M Press, 1991), 204–17.

23. *San Antonio Express*, May 11, 1927, 1, 5; Parks Commissioner Ray Lambert rolled up similar margins in precinct 54, and the other East Side precincts.

24. Ralph Maitland, "San Antonio: The Shame of Texas," *Forum* (August 1939): 52; Owen P. White, "Machine Made," *Collier's*, September 18, 1937, 32–33; Judith Kaaz Doyle, "Maury Maverick and Racial Politics in San Antonio, Texas, 1938–1941," *Journal of Southern History* (May 1987): 194–224.

25. Ralph J. Bunche, *The Political Status of the Negro in the Age of FDR* (Chicago: University of Chicago Press, 1973), 464–66; Kenneth Mason, *African Americans and Race Relations in San Antonio, Texas, 1867–1937* (New York: Garland Publishing, 1998), 265–82; Maitland, "San Antonio," 53. Bellinger's success in acquiring public improvements may have also paid a more tangible, and personal, reward. Maitland notes allegations that Bellinger had bought up low-priced land on the East Side "before he began asking for improvements and that his real estate doubled and tripled in value when the improvements came." If so, his actions were like political bosses everywhere. But his actions, and electoral successes, were different from his counterparts on the Hispanic west side. There emerged no comparable organization, and thus no comparable gains in infrastructure benefits. As sociologist Jack E. Dodson observed in the 1950s: "the belief is common in San Antonio that there had been, on occasion, considerable 'buying' of Mexican-American votes by local political bosses when needed in a close election. This participation in politics is on a lower level of political con-

sciousness than that of the Negroes: among the latter, the vote may be delivered, but for concrete goods, by the leaders; in the Latin-American group, the vote is not exercised or is often given by the individual in return for money, with no advantage accruing to the group." Jack E. Dodson, "Minority Group Housing in Two Texas Cities," in *Studies in Housing and Minority Groups*, ed. Nathan Glazer and Davis McEntire (Berkeley: University of California Press, 1960), 103–5; Robert Caro makes similar claims about Hispanic voting behavior in the late 1940s in *The Years of Lyndon Johnson: Means to Ascent* (New York: Knopf, 1990), 305–7; Richard Henderson, *Maury Maverick: A Political Biography* (Austin: University of Texas Press, 1970), 178–79; Garcia, *Rise of the Mexican American Middle Class*, 204–17, suggests that west side Hispanics were less politically cohesive and thus did not receive the kinds of political payback that the East Side secured.

26. On the GGL, see Johnson, Booth, and Harris, eds., *Politics of San Antonio*, 24 and passim.

27. "United States Participation in Hemisfair 68 Exposition," Hearing before the Subcommittee on International Organizations and Movements of the Committee of Foreign Affairs, HR, 89th Congress, 1st sess., Aug. 19, 1965, 2–8.

28. On the NAACP's concerns, see *San Antonio Light*, January 27, 1964, 4, and January 29, 1964, 1, 4, 12. As Kenneth Mason points out in *African Americans and Race Relations in San Antonio*, 265–79, there was a vocal segment of the local black political leadership who supported the GGL in hopes that it would break the Bellinger family's hold on East Side political life. This happened, to some extent. But the GGL's exclusionary form of governance set the stage for a continued de-emphasis on the citizenry's political participation in the city's critical fiscal decisions. This is ironic, for beginning in 1973 with the establishment of court-mandated single-member council districts in San Antonio, the city's Black and Hispanic citizens have wielded greater power, power that culminated in the election of Henry Cisneros as the River City's first Hispanic mayor. Since then, hundreds of millions of dollars have been lavished on downtown improvements but these have been funded though certificates of obligation, a funding instrument that has enabled the political leadership to evade public evaluation. The voting booth, it seems, is no longer an acceptable means by which to determine the content and character of public spending.

29. *San Antonio Light*, January 29, 1964, 1, 12.

Chapter 5. The Landscape of Death

1. See, e.g., Nikki Meredith, "The Murder Epidemic: Public Health Officials Are Setting Out to Conquer Violence in America as Though It Were a Virus," *Science* (December 1984): 43–48; Colin Loftin, "Assaultive Violence as a Contagious Social Process," *Bulletin of the New York Academy of Medicine* 62, no. 5 (June 1986): 550–55; James A. Mercy and Linda E. Saltzman, "Fatal Violence among Spouses in the United States, 1976–85," *American Journal of Public Health* 79, no. 5 (May 1989): 595–99; Malcolm Gladwell, "The Tipping Point: Why Is the City Suddenly So Much Safer—Could It Be That Crime Really Is an Epidemic?" *New Yorker* (June 3, 1996): 32–38.

2. Norbert Elias, *The Civilizing Process: State Formation and Civilization*, trans. Edmund Jephcott (Oxford: Blackwell, 1994). Elias first published his theory in 1939. For examples of historians who have applied Elias's theory to the incidence of homicide, see Ted Robert Gurr, "Historical Trends in Violent Crime: Europe and the United States," in *Violence in America*,

ed. Gurr (Newbury Park: Sage Publications, 1989): 1:21–54; Roger Lane, *Violent Death in the City: Suicide, Accident, and Murder in Nineteenth-Century Philadelphia* (Cambridge: Harvard University Press, 1979); Eric A. Johnson, *Urbanization and Crime: Germany, 1871–1914* (New York: Cambridge University Press, 1995); Eric A. Johnson and Eric H. Monkkonen, eds., *The Civilization of Crime: Violence in Town and Country Since the Middle Ages* (Urbana: University of Illinois Press, 1996).

3. Owen White, "Machine Made," *Collier's,* September 18, 1937, 32–33. John A. Booth and David R. Johnson, "Power and Progress in San Antonio Politics, 1836–1970," in *The Politics of San Antonio: Community, Progress, and Power,* ed. David R. Johnson, John A. Booth, and Richard Harris (Lincoln: University of Nebraska Press, 1983), 15–17.

4. David R. Johnson, "Frugal and Sparing: Interest Groups, Politics, and City Building in San Antonio, 1870–1885," in *Urban Texas: Politics and Development,* ed. Char Miller and Heywood Sanders (College Station: Texas A&M University Press, 1990): 35–36; Richard A. Garcia, *Rise of the Mexican American Middle Class: San Antonio, 1929–1941* (College Station: Texas A&M University Press, 1991), 38–39; Kenneth Mason, "Paternal Continuity: African-Americans and Race Relations in San Antonio, Texas, 1867–1937," Ph.D. diss., University of Texas at Austin, 1994.

5. Char Miller and David R. Johnson, "The Rise of Urban Texas," in *Urban Texas,* ed. Miller and Sanders, 3–29; David R. Johnson, "The Failed Experiment: Military Aviation and Urban Development in San Antonio, 1910–1940," in *The Martial Metropolis: U.S. Cities in War and Peace,* ed. Roger Lotchin (New York: Praeger, 1984), 89–108.

6. Garcia, *Rise of the Mexican American Middle Class,* 29.

7. Division of Research, Work Projects Administration, *The Pecan Shellers of San Antonio: The Problem of Underpaid and Unemployed Mexican Labor* (Washington, D.C.: U.S. Government Printing Office, 1940), 23–52; Garcia, *Rise of the Mexican American Middle Class,* 72–73.

8. K. E. Miller, "Abstract of U.S. Public Health Service Survey of Health Service, City of San Antonio, Texas" (San Antonio: San Antonio Chamber of Commerce, 1935), 2, 7.

9. Benjamin S. Bradshaw, Kenneth S. Blanchard, and George H. Thompson, "Postneonatal Diarrhea Mortality of Mexican American and Anglo American Infants: Trends and Context," *Population Research and Policy Review* 5 (June 1996): 7.

10. Garcia, *Rise of the Mexican American Middle Class,* 206, 210.

11. Kenneth Mason, "Black San Antonio and the Politics of Accommodation, 1867–1937," unpublished manuscript in the possession of David R. Johnson, 24–29.

12. White, "Machine Made," 35.

13. Examples include William B. Taylor, *Drinking, Homicide, and Rebellion in Colonial Mexican Villages* (Stanford, Calif.: Stanford University Press, 1979); W. Parker Frisbie and Rodolfo C. Pineiro, "Violent Deaths: Ethnic and Life-Cycle Differential Among Mexican Americans, Mexican, Mexican Immigrants, and Anglos, 1970–1980," *Frontera Norte* 4, no. 7 (May-June 1992): 131–56; June Nash, "Death as a Way of Life: The Increasing Resort to Homicide in a Maya Indian Community," *American Anthropologist* 69 (October 1967): 455–70; Ira Rosenwaike, "Homicide Patterns in Mexico and among Mexicans in the U.S.," unpublished paper in the possession of Benjamin Bradshaw, August 1991; Donna Shai and Ira Rosenwaike, "Violent Deaths among Mexican-, Puerto Rican- and Cuban-Born Migrants in the United States," *Social Science Medicine* 26, no. 2 (1988): 269–76; Lola R. Schwartz,

"Conflict without Violence and Violence without Conflict in a Mexican Mestizo Village," in *Collective Violence*, ed. James F. Short Jr. and Marvin E. Wolfgang (Chicago: Aldine-Atherton, 1972), 149–57; Fox Butterfield, *All God's Children: The Bosket Family and the American Tradition of Violence* (New York: Knopf, 1995); Roger Lane, *Roots of Violence in Black Philadelphia, 1860–1900* (Cambridge: Harvard University Press, 1986); Clare McKenna Jr., "Seeds of Destruction: Homicide, Race, and Justice in Omaha, 1880–1920," *Journal of American Ethnic History* 14, no. 1 (Fall 1994): 65–90. Also see sources in n. 2 above.

14. *San Antonio Express*, January 1 and December 27, 1940; *San Antonio Light*, June 11, 1941; Green Peyton, *San Antonio: City in the Sun* (New York: McGraw-Hill, 1946), 161–67.

15. Diana Schiller, "The Fight to Clean Up San Antonio's Mexican Corrals, 1930–1950," *Friends of the Patrick I. Nixon Medical Historical Library Annual Bulletin* 15 (Fall 1986): 1–13.

16. Bradshaw, Blanchard, and Thompson, "Postneonatal diarrhea mortality of Mexican American and Anglo American Infants," 8; Benjamin S. Bradshaw and David P. Smith, "The Decline of Tuberculosis Mortality in an Urban Mexican Origin Population, 1935–1984," unpublished paper in the possession of Benjamin Bradshaw, 11.

17. *San Antonio Register*, January 20, 1939; June 7 and December 20, 1940; February 4, 1941; October 6 and November 24, 1944.

18. Donna Dewberry, "Black Homicide in San Antonio, 1935–1954," unpublished paper in the possession of David R. Johnson, 9.

19. Mason, "Paternal Continuity," 222.

20. *San Antonio Register*, April 6, 1951, quoted in Dewberry, "Black Homicide in San Antonio," 4.

21. Booth and Johnson, "Power and Progress in San Antonio Politics," 19–25; David R. Johnson, "San Antonio: The Vicissitudes of Boosterism," in *Sunbelt Cities: Politics and Growth since World War II*, ed. Richard Bernard and Bradley Rice (Austin: University of Texas Press, 1983), 235–54.

22. Johnson, "San Antonio" 246–47; Jack E. Dodson, "Minority Group Housing in Two Texas Cities," in *Housing and Minority Groups*, ed. Nathan Glazer and Davis McEntire (Berkeley: University of California Press, 1960), 85–88, 92–98. Also Heywood Sanders, "Empty Taps, Missing Pipes: Water Policy and Politics," chapter 7 in this volume.

23. George S. Perry, "Rumpled Angel of the Slums," *Saturday Evening Post* 22 (August 1948): 32–47; San Antonio Housing Authority, *Our Slum and Blighted Areas* (San Antonio: SAHA, 1957); Bradshaw, Blanchard, and Thompson, "Postneonatal diarrhea mortality of Mexican American and Anglo American Infants," 14.

24. Bradshaw and Smith, "Decline of Tuberculosis Mortality," 12, 14; Bradshaw, Blanchard, and Thompson, "Postneonatal diarrhea mortality of Mexican American and Anglo American infants," 8, 14.

25. San Antonio Housing Authority, *Our Slum and Bighted Areas*, 25.

26. See H. H. Brownstein and P. J. Goldstein, "A Topology of Drug-Related Homicides," in *Drugs, Crime, and the Criminal Justice System*, ed. R. Weisheit (Cincinnati: Anderson, 1990); P. J. Goldstein, H. H. Brownstein, P. J. Ryan, and P. A. Bellucci, "Crack and Homicide in New York City: A Conceptually Based Event Analysis," *Contemporary Drug Problems* 16 (1989): 651–87.

27. Lawrence J. Redlinger, "Dealing in Dope: Market Mechanisms and Distribution Patterns of Illicit Narcotics," Ph.D. diss., Northwestern University, 1969, 139–42.

28. Booth and Johnson, "Power and Progress in San Antonio Politics," 23–25.

29. James L. Turbon, "Glory Be to the Father: The History of the San Antonio Neighborhood Youth Organization," master's research project, Trinity University, 1988; Sister Frances J. Woods, *The Model Cities Program in Perspective: The San Antonio, Texas, Experience*, report to the Subcommittee on Housing and Community Development of the Committee on Banking, Financing and Urban Affairs, House of Representatives, 97th Congress, 1st sess. (Washington, D.C.: U.S. Government Printing Office, 1982), 76, 78–79, 115.

30. Woods, *Model Cities Program in Perspective*, 258; Andre E. Bacon, ed., *City of San Antonio, Department of Model Cities, Four Action Years: A Graphic Illustration of the Spending of 87 Million Dollars on the Westside of San Antonio* (San Antonio: Department of Model Cities, 1973).

31. Joseph D. Sekul, "Communities Organized for Public Service: Citizen Power and Public Policy in San Antonio," in *Politics of San Antonio*, ed. Johnson, Booth, and Harris, 180–84.

32. Robert Brischetto, Charles Cotrell, and R. Michael Stevens, "Conflict and Change in the Political Culture of San Antonio in the 1970s," in *Politics of San Antonio*, ed. Johnson, Booth, and Harris, 75–94.

33. *San Antonio Express-News*, February 10, 1985; interview by David R. Johnson with Kevin Moriarity, Director of the Department of Human Resources and Services, City of San Antonio, September 11, 1989.

34. Derral Cheatwood, "Black Homicides in Baltimore, 1974–1986: Age, Gender, and Weapon Use Changes," *Criminal Justice Review* 15 (1990): 192–207.

35. Wilson McKinney, *Fred Carrasco: The Heroin Merchant* (Austin: Heidelberg Publishers, 1975), is a journalistic but very useful account of Carrasco's career.

36. For an excellent review and discussion of the connections between geography and violence, see Keith D. Harries, *Serious Violence: Patterns of Homicide and Assault in America* (Springfield, Ill.: Charles C. Thomas, 1990), esp. chap. 2.

Chapter 6. Battlefields

Note: We would like to thank the history offices of the San Antonio Air Force bases for their time and assistance in researching this chapter. We are also indebted to the two anonymous reviewers for the constructive comments on a previous draft.

1. John L. Davis, *San Antonio: A Historical Portrait* (Austin: Encino Press, 1978), 37.

2. U.S. Army, Headquarters Forces Command, *Environmental Assessment: Overall Mission, Fort Sam Houston Texas* (San Antonio: U.S. Army, 1991).

3. Jerry Needham, "Kelly-Area Health Woes Cited: Higher Rates of Cancer Found in Southwest Side Neighborhoods," *San Antonio Express-News*, August 25, 1999, 1A, 6A.

4. Michele S. Gerber, *On the Home Front: The Cold War Legacy of the Hanford Nuclear Site* (Lincoln: University of Nebraska Press, 1992), and William L. Graf, *Plutonium in the Rio Grande: Environmental Change in the Nuclear Age* (Oxford: Oxford University Press, 1994).

5. Seth Schulman, *The Threat at Home: Confronting the Toxic Legacy of the U.S. Military* (Boston: Beacon Press, 1992) and William Thomas, *Scorched Earth: Military's Assault on the Environment* (Gabriola, B.C.: New Society Publisher, 1995).

6. Shulman, *The Threat at Home*, 25–26, 84–89.

7. U.S. Environmental Protection Agency, *Progress Toward Implementing Superfund* (Springfield, Va.: National Technical Information Service, EPA 540R95147, 1994).

8. James H. Ware, "San Angelo and San Antonio: A Comparative Study of the Military

City in Texas, 1865–1898," master's thesis, Southwest Texas State University, 1993; Sam Wolford, ed., *San Antonio: A History for Tomorrow* (San Antonio: Naylor Company, 1963); Davis, *San Antonio,* 37.

9. Wolford, ed., *San Antonio,* 96; USAF, *A History of Military Aviation in San Antonio* (San Antonio: USAF, 1996).

10. Heywood Sanders, "Building a New Urban Infrastructure: The Creation of Postwar San Antonio," in *Urban Texas: Politics and Development,* ed. Char Miller and Heywood T. Sanders (College Station: Texas A&M University Press, 1990), 154–73; David R. Johnson, "San Antonio: The Vicissitudes of Boosterism," in *Sunbelt Cities: Politics and Growth since World War II,* ed. Richard M. Bernard and Bradley R. Rice (Austin: University of Texas Press, 1983); Stacy R. Miller, "Determinants of Population Growth in San Antonio, Texas: 1970–1990," master's thesis, Southwest Texas State University, 1996; Davis, *San Antonio,* 1; and Wolford, *San Antonio,* 95.

11. Miller, "Determinants of Population Growth"; F. A. Sanders, "Combating Oil and Metal Plating Waste Problems at Kelly Air Force Base," *Proceedings of the Seventh Industrial Waste Conference* (Lafayette, Ind.: Purdue University, 1952), 382–94; David R. Johnson, "The Failed Experiment: Military Aviation and Urban Development in San Antonio, 1910–40," in *The Martial Metropolis: U.S. Cities in War and Peace,* ed. Roger W. Lotchin (New York: Praeger, 1984), 89–108; Richard C. Jones, "San Antonio's Spatial Economic Structure, 1955–1980," in *The Politics of San Antonio: Community, Progress, and Power,* ed. David R. Johnson, John A Booth, and Richard J. Harris (Lincoln: University of Nebraska Press, 1983), 28–53; Char Miller, "Sunbelt Cities," in *Texas Through Time,* ed. Walter L. Buenger and Robert A. Calvert (College Station: Texas A&M University Press, 1991), 279–309; Rossi L. Selvaggi, "A History of Randolph Air Force Base" master's thesis, University of Texas, 1958; Sanders, "Building a New Urban Infrastructure," 154–73.

12. U. S. Army, *Environmental Assessment,* iii.

13. USAF, *Brooks Air Force Base Installation Restoration Program Site Visit* (San Antonio: USAF, 1995); Booz, Allen and Hamilton, Inc., *Management Action Plan: Lackland Air Force Base, Texas* (San Antonio: Booz, Allen and Hamilton, 1996); USAF, *Management Action Plan for Environmental Restoration at Kelly Air Force Base* (San Antonio: USAF, Contract #F41650-95-D-2005-5017, 1997); USAF, *Installation Restoration Program Final Basewide Groundwater Assessment Report for Randolph AFB, Texas* (San Antonio: USAF, Contract #F41624-95-D-8003-0013, 1997), and Alamo Area Council of Governments, *Regional Development: Existing Land Use,* Background Paper No. 1 (San Antonio: Alamo Area Council of Governments, 1969).

14. The action at Kelly is part of a national base-closure process that is causing economic upheaval in all host cities.

15. Ann K. Hussey, *The History of Aircraft Maintenance at Kelly Air Force Base* (San Antonio: Kelly Air Force Base, Office of History, 1998); U.S. Environmental Protection Agency, Office of Solid Waste and Emergency Response, *Guidance for Evaluation of Federal Agency Demonstrations that Remedial Actions are Operating Properly and Successfully Under CERCLA Section 120(h)(3)* (Washington, D.C.: USEPA, 1996), 2; USAF, *Final Programmatic Environmental Impact Statement, V. 1: Disposal of Kelly Air Force Base, Texas* (San Antonio: USAF, 1997); and Robert T. Lee, "Comprehensive Environmental Response, Compensation and Liability Act," in *Environmental Law Handbook,* ed., Thomas Sullivan (Rockville, Maryland: Government Institutes, 1997), 430–80.

16. See C. E. Colten and P. N. Skinner, *The Road to Love Canal* (Austin: University of Texas Press, 1996), 139–42.

17. Ferenc M. Szasz, "The Impact of World War II on the Land: Gruinard Island Scotland, and Trinity Site, New Mexico as Case Studies," *Environmental History Review* 19, no. 4 (1995): 15–30.

18. Robin W. Doughty, *Wildlife and Man in Texas: Environmental Change and Conservation* (College Station: Texas A&M University Press, 1983); U.S. Army, *Final Environmental Assessment: Overall Mission Fort Sam Houston, Texas* (San Antonio: U.S. Army, 1991); and Victoria Clow, Lila Knight, Duane Peters, and Sharlene Allday, *The Architecture of Randolph Field, 1928–31* (Plano, Tex.: Geo-Marine, 1998).

19. U.S. Army, *Final Environmental Assessment*, 82–85; USAF, *Management Action Plan*, 23–26; USAF, *Installation Restoration Program*; Selvaggi, "History of Randolph Air Force Base," 48–49; and Clow et al., *Architecture of Randolph Field*, 1–2; USAF, *Final Programmatic Environmental Impact Statement*, 13; The Conservation Foundation, *Groundwater Protection* (Washington, D.C.: The Conservation Foundation, 1987). The Ogallala Aquifer is a large water-bearing formation that extends from the Dakotas to north Texas that is no longer replenished by current precipitation. Water extracted from this formation is "mined," unlike the Edwards Aquifer which still receives recharge water.

20. U.S. Army, *Tank Units Field Manual 17-15 Platoon, Company and Battalion* (Washington, D.C.: U.S. Army Headquarters, 1966), and U.S. Army, *Final Environmental Assessment*, 32.

21. U.S. Army, *Final Environmental Assessment*, 26.

22. U.S. Army, *Field Manual 23-90: 81-MM Mortar M29* (Washington, D.C.: U.S. Army Headquarters, 1958).

23. USAF, *Management Action Plan*, 1–9; USAF, *Installation Restoration Program*; USAF, *Brooks Air Force Base Installation Restoration Program Site Visit* (San Antonio: USAF, 1995); Booz, Allen and Hamilton, *Management Action Plan*.

24. USAF, *Installation Restoration Program*; and "Brooks Pollution Irks Homeowners," *San Antonio Express-News*, April 8, 1996, 9A.

25. U.S. Army Corps of Engineers, *National Historic Context for Department of Defense Installations, 1790–1940: V. II* (Baltimore: U.S. Army Corps of Engineers, Baltimore District, 1995).

26. *Monthly Maintenance* 284 (1976); National Safety Council, *Industrial Safety Council* (Chicago: National Safety Council, 1948): and American Society for Testing and Materials, *Metal Finishing Handbook* (Philadelphia: American Society for Testing and Materials, 1962).

27. USAF, *Maintenance of Permanently Installed Petroleum Storage Systems: Air Force Manual 85-16* (Washington, D.C.: Department of the Air Force, 1956); War Department, *Sewage Treatment Plants and Sewer Systems at Fixed Installations* (Washington, D.C.: War Department, Technical Bulletin TB ENG 70, 1945); U.S. Army, *Final Environmental Assessment*, 2–3; USAF, *Brooks Air Force Base*, 3–8; USAF, *Management Action Plan*, 3-3–5; USAF, *Installation Restoration Program*; Booz, Allen and Hamilton, *Management Action Plan*, 1-1–2.

28. U.S. War Department, *Regulations for the Army of the United States, 1913* (Washington, D.C.: War Department, 1918); and U.S. War Department, *Refuse Collection and Disposal Repairs and Utilities: Technical Manual 5-634* (Washington, D.C.: War Department, 1946).

29. USAF, *Management Action Plan*, 1–12; and U.S. Army, *Final Environmental Assessment*, 11-87–90.

30. USAF, *Sewerage, Refuse, and Industrial Waste: Technical Manual 88-11* (Washington, D.C.: USAF, 1960), 3.

31. Sanders "Combating Oil and Metal Plating Waste," 382–84.

32. Raymond A. Ferrara, William G. Gray, and George F. Pinder, *Groundwater Contamination from Hazardous Wastes* (Englewood Cliffs, N.J.: Prentice-Hall, 1984).

33. USAF, *Management Action Plan*, 3–4; Booz, Allen and Hamilton, *Management Action Plan*, I-2; and U.S. Army, *Final Environmental Assessment*, I-14–24.

34. USAF, *Sewage, Refuse and Industrial Waste*, 27; USAF, *Installation Restoration Program*, 1997; and Booz, Allen and Hamilton, *Management Action Plan*, I-1–11.

35. For example see *Clark v. U.S.*, 660 Fed Supp 1164 (1987).

36. USAF, *Installation Restoration Program*, 1–2.

37. U.S. EPA, *Progress Toward Implementing Superfund*; and Kelly Air Force Base Advisory Board, Minutes, Meeting of May 8, 1996, San Antonio, Texas.

38. U.S. Army, *Final Environmental Assessment*, II-11–14; Ferrara, Gray, and Pinder, *Groundwater Contamination*, 1984.

39. U.S. Army, *Final Environmental Assessment*, II-12.

40. Ibid.; USAF, *Installation Restoration Program*; and USAF, *Brooks Air Force Base*, 3–8.

41. Booz, Allen and Hamilton, *Management Action Plan*, 6-6.

42. USAF, *Management Action Plan*, 1–6; Hussey, *History of Aircraft Maintenance*; Sanders, "Combating Oil and Metal Plating Wastes," 382–94.

43. U.S. EPA, *CERCLIS Hazardous Waste Sites* (*http://www.cpa.gov/superfund/sites/cursites/c3tx/s0603590.htm*); USAF, *Management Action Plan*, 1-2.

44. USAF, *Management Action Plan*, 1-9–10.

45. "Kelly-Area Health Woes Cited," 1A, 6A.

46. Kelly Air Force Base, *Environmental Community Relations Plan* (San Antonio: Kelly Air Force Base, 1998), and Committee for Environmental Justice Action, "Community Groups File Civil Rights Complaint Pertaining to Activities at Kelly Air Force Base," media packet, Committee for Environmental Justice Action, San Antonio, 1999.

Chapter 7. Empty Taps, Missing Pipes

1. Executive Committee, San Antonio Chamber of Commerce, meeting minutes, October 10, 1947.

2. Ibid., April 9, 1948.

3. Ibid., August 24, 1951.

4. Ibid., November 13, 1951.

5. "Majority Report of the Investment Bankers Committee," in Minutes of the Board of Directors, San Antonio Chamber of Commerce, October 14, 1952.

6. Board of Directors, San Antonio Chamber of Commerce, meeting minutes, September 28, 1943.

7. Ibid., May 28, 1946.

8. Ibid.

9. Ibid., June 11, 1946.

10. Ibid.

11. Ibid., May 10, 1949.

12. Executive Committee, San Antonio Chamber of Commerce, meeting minutes, April 7, 1950.

13. Water Works Board of Trustees, meeting minutes, March 12, 1951.

14. Board of Directors, San Antonio Chamber of Commerce, meeting minutes, March 13, 1951.

15. Ibid.

16. Lewis W. Gillenson, "Texas' Forgotten People," *Look* 15, no. 7 (March 27, 1951).

17. Board of Directors, San Antonio Chamber of Commerce, meeting minutes, March 27, 1951.

18. W. L. Matthews to Dr. Herbert Hill, February 23, 1951, copy in meeting minutes, Board of Directors, San Antonio Chamber of Commerce, April 10, 1951.

19. Board of Directors, San Antonio Chamber of Commerce, meeting minutes, May 22, 1951.

20. Ibid.

21. Water Works Board of Trustees, meeting minutes, October 13, 1944.

22. Ibid.

23. Water Works Board of Trustees, meeting minutes, December 29, 1947.

24. Water Works Board of Trustees, meeting minutes, Minutes of the Water Works Board of Trustees, October 12, 1949.

25. W. D. Masterson to City Water Board, February 21, 1950, Water Works Board of Trustees Minutes.

26. Black and Veatch Consulting Engineers, "Report on Water Rates: City Water Board, San Antonio," 1959, pp. a, 13, on file in Texana Collection, San Antonio Central Library.

27. Ibid., 15.

28. "Majority Report of the Investment Bankers Committee," in Board of Directors, San Antonio Chamber of Commerce, meeting minutes, October 14, 1952.

29. Ibid.

30. Ibid.

31. Ibid.

32. Water Works Board of Trustees, meeting minutes, December 4, 1951.

33. Ibid., February 8, 1955.

34. On the background of San Antonio city politics in this period, see Good Government League, "In Search of Good Government," Crumrine Inc., San Antonio, 1972.

35. Councilmember Henry B. Gonzalez, quoted in "New Water Row Flares," *San Antonio Light,* March 4, 1955.

36. Editorial, "City Council Bounces Water Bill as Political Football," *San Antonio News,* March 11, 1955.

37. Water Works Board of Trustees, meeting minutes, March 28, 1955.

38. Editorial, "Legislative Time Running Out on Water-Bond Plan," *San Antonio News,* April 19, 1955.

39. Editorial, "Now Is the Time to Face Basic Water-Board Issues," *San Antonio News,* May 13, 1955.

40. City Water Board, "Report, Financing Improvements and Expansion, City Water Board, July 1955," cover letter, p. 2, on file in Texana Collection, San Antonio Central Library.

41. "Much Talk, Little Water Rate Hike Action," *San Antonio Light,* October 11, 1955.

42. Newspaper editorial quoted in Good Government League, "In Search of Good Government," 21.

43. Don Politico, "'Hangover' Follows Vote," *San Antonio Light,* November 30, 1955.

44. "Dads Study 3-Point Water Plan," *San Antonio Light,* January 8, 1956.

45. "Vote on Water Bonds Put Off," *San Antonio News,* January 14, 1956.

46. "Council to Bar Other Issue from Water Bond Election," *San Antonio News,* May 9, 1956.

47. Elmer A. Dittmar, "San Antonio's Water Problem," April 25, 1956, p. 24, in San Antonio Chamber of Commerce meeting minutes.

48. "Don Politico Says," *San Antonio Light,* May 27, 1956.

49. Ibid.

50. Don Politico, "S.A. Voters Show Lack of Trust in City-Run Water Unit," *San Antonio Light,* June 13, 1956.

51. "At Last! Water Progress," *San Antonio Express and News,* May 19, 1957.

52. Board of Directors, San Antonio Chamber of Commerce, meeting minutes, May 14, 1957.

53. Ibid., October 13, 1959.

54. "Water Level at Record Low," *San Antonio Light,* June 13, 1956.

55. Water Works Board of Trustees, meeting minutes, May 25, 1949.

56. Ibid., July 13, 1951.

57. Ibid.

58. Ibid., December 4, 1951.

59. Ibid., August 25, 1952.

60. City Water Board, "Report, Financing Improvements and Expansion," 2.

61. Water Works Board of Trustees, meeting minutes, April 10, 1953.

62. Ibid., August 31, 1953.

63. Board of Directors, San Antonio Chamber of Commerce, meeting minutes, September 24, 1957.

64. Water Works Board of Trustees, meeting minutes, October 9, 1962.

Chapter 8. Establishing "Sole Source" Protection

1. U.S. EPA, Office of Water, Office of Ground Water and Drinking Water, *Designated Sole Source Aquifers Nationally: Fact Sheet with Designated Aquifers and Pending Petitions Listed* (Washington, D.C.: EPA Office of Water, February 1996), 1, 3–4. "Sole source" aquifers occur in Washington (11), Oregon (1), Wyoming (1), California (4), Idaho (3), Montana (1), Arizona (2), Oklahoma (1), Texas (2), Minnesota (1), Louisiana (2), Guam (1), and Hawaii (2); some designated aquifers exist across state borders. For the most recent information on the sole source program, please see the Environmental Protection Agency website at http://www.epa.gov/OGWDW/swp/ssa.html.

2. EPA Office of Water, *25 Years of the Safe Drinking Water Act: History and Trends,* EPA 816-R-99-007 (Washington, D.C.: EPA Office of Water, December 1999).

3. References to the Edwards Aquifer in this chapter refer to the San Antonio segment, which stretches from Bracketville in Kinney County to the southwest of San Antonio up to Kyle in Hays County to the northeast of the city. Water in the San Antonio segment flows from southwest to northeast and discharges in natural springs in New Braunfels and San Marcos. The San Antonio segment is the most productive segment of the aquifer system and the area most commonly known as the Edwards. The Barton Springs segment extends from

Kyle northward to the Colorado River in Austin. The final segment of the aquifer system extends from the Colorado River north into Bell County. The segments of the aquifer are separated geologically. Edwards Underground Water District and Edwards Aquifer Research and Data Center, *Water, Water Conservation and the Edwards Aquifer* (San Antonio: Edwards Underground Water District, 1981), 9–16.

4. Lyndon B. Johnson School of Public Affairs, *Impact of the Safe Drinking Water Act on Texas,* The Safe Drinking Water Policy Research Project, Report no. 21 (Austin: Lyndon B. Johnson School of Public Affairs, University of Texas at Austin, April 1978), 20–25.

5. "Texas Water Quality Board," *The New Handbook of Texas* (Austin: Texas State Historical Association, 1996), 6:442; *San Antonio Express,* November 21, 1975; Fay Sinkin, "Purchase of the Edwards Aquifer Recharge Zone in Bexar County: Questions and Answers," Aquifer Protection Association file, Fay Sinkin Collection, Trinity University Elizabeth Coates Maddux Library, University Archives (hereafter Sinkin Collection); *San Antonio Express-News,* July 26, 1959; "Edwards Underground Water District," *New Handbook of Texas,* 2:803.

6. "The Big Troubles at San Antonio Ranch," clipping from an unknown source, San Antonio Ranch Town file, Sinkin Collection. HUD felt that economic classes could be mixed by attracting the poor with housing, training, and jobs, and the rich with amenities in "new towns."

7. *San Antonio News,* February 4, 1972; *San Antonio Express,* February 1, 1972. The Department of Housing and Urban Development intended for the "New Town" program to encourage the mixing of economic classes by attracting the poor with housing, training, and jobs, and the rich with amenities according to "The Big Troubles at San Antonio Ranch." Local media also referred to the alliance as the Alliance for the Protection of the Aquifer.

8. Wayt T. Watterson and Roberta S. Watterson, *The Politics of New Communities: A Case Study of San Antonio Ranch* (New York: Praeger, 1975), v, 1–2, 43–49; see chapter 2 for more details on the connections between UTSA and Ranch Town development. Roberta S. Watterson worked for San Antonio Ranch developers and Wayt T. Watterson worked in the City of San Antonio planning office. Watterson provides a detailed look at the development of San Antonio Ranch, including the proposed new town in town, and the outcome of the new communities program. The Fifth Circuit overturned the fees order and took jurisdiction for oversight away from Judge Spears during appeals. For information on the ramifications of *Sierra Club v. Lynn,* 502 F. 2d. 43 (5th Cir. 1974), see Val P. Wilson, "Ground Waters: Are They Beneath the Reach of the Federal Water Pollution Control Act Amendments?" in *Environmental Affairs* 5, no. 3 (1976): 545–66.

9. *Commercial Recorder,* July 11, 1974; "A Primer on Water," *Texas Observer,* July 26, 1974, 7; *San Antonio Express-News,* October 5, 1974. Plaintiffs against New Town included the Sierra Club, Citizens for a Better Environment, San Antonio League of Women Voters, and San Antonio American Association of University Women.

10. *San Antonio Light,* October 1 and 12, 1974; *San Antonio Express-News,* October 12, 1974.

11. U.S. Congress, House, Committee on Interstate and Foreign Commerce, Subcommittee on Public Health and Environment, *Safe Drinking Water,* Hearings on H.R. 1093 and H.R. 5454 and H.R. 437, 92d Cong., 1st sess., 1971, Serial 92-24; U.S. Congress, Senate, Committee on Commerce, *Potable Waters,* Hearings on Amendment 410 to S. 1478, 92d

Cong:, 2d sess., 1972, Serial 92-57; U.S. Congress, House, Committee on Interstate and Foreign Commerce, Subcommittee on Public Health and Environment, *Safe Drinking Water,*
Hearings on H.R. 14899, 92d Cong., 2d sess., 1972, Serial 92-85; U.S. Congress, Senate,
Committee on Commerce, *Safe Drinking Water Act of 1973,* Report on S. 433, 93d Cong., 1st
sess, 1973, S. Rept. 93-231; U.S. Congress, House, Committee on Interstate and Foreign
Commerce, Subcommittee on Public Health and Environment, *Safe Drinking Water Act—*
1973, Hearings on H.R. 5368, H.R. 1059, H.R. 5348, and H.R. 5995, 93d Cong., 1st sess.,
1973, Serial 93-11; U.S. Congress, Senate, Committee on Commerce, Subcommittee on Environment, *Safe Drinking Water Act of 1973,* Hearing on S. 433 and S. 1735, 93d Cong., 1st
sess., Serial 93-39; *New York Times,* November 19, 1974.

12. *San Antonio Express-News,* November 3, 1974; *Safe Drinking Water Act: Report,* no.
93-1185, 4, 8. Some of the opposition arose from water works groups, the oil industry, and
state governors. Thomas J. Douglas, "Safe Drinking Water Act of 1974: History and Critique," *Environmental Affairs* 5, no. 3 (1976): 501–43.

13. *Cong. Rec.,* November 19, 1974, 36366, 36394–5; Congressional Quarterly, Inc.,
1974 CQ Almanac (Washington D.C.: Congressional Quarterly, 1974), 425. Opposition to the
amendment centered on the extension of the federal government into local matters and the
avoidance of granting special favors for a local problem. Ironically, conservatives would
eventually complain about local people using federal laws to their advantage. The *Washington Post* believed the SDWA contained "sufficient" precautions against feared bullying by the
EPA (September 24 and November 20, 1974) and the Senate had previously passed a stricter
version of the legislation. *Cong. Rec.,* 36403; *New York Times,* November 20, 1974; Douglas,
"Safe Drinking Water Act of 1974," 518.

14. U.S. EPA, Office of Ground-Water Protection, *Sole Source Aquifer Designation: Peti-
tioner Guidance,* EPA 440/6-87-003 (Washington, D.C.: EPA Office of Water, February 1987),
1–2, appendix B; U.S. EPA, Office of Water, Office of Ground Water and Drinking Water, *Designated Sole Source Aquifers Nationally,* 1; Public Law 93-523, U.S. Statutes at Large, vol. 88,
1660–94. *San Antonio Express,* November 20 and 21, 1974; *San Antonio Light,* November 20,
1974; *San Antonio News,* November 20, 1974. San Antonians speculated that Gonzalez had
specifically targeted Ranch Town with the rider.

15. *San Antonio News,* November 22, 1974; *San Antonio Light,* November 28, 1974; *San
Antonio Express-News,* December 1, 1974.

16. *San Antonio Light,* November 25, 1974; *San Antonio Express,* December 3, 1974.

17. *San Antonio Express,* December 3 and 4, 1974; *San Antonio News,* December 3, 1974;
New York Times, December 4, 1974.

18. *San Antonio News,* December 4 and 6, 1974; *San Antonio Express,* December 5 and
16, 1974; *San Antonio Light,* December 16, 1974; *San Antonio Express,* December 11 and 16,
1974; *Washington Post,* November 20 and December 4, 1974; *Wall Street Journal,* December
4, 1974.

19. *San Antonio Express,* December 18, 1974; *San Antonio News,* December 18, 1974; Ed-
ward V. Cheviot, "The Safe Drinking Water Bill," broadcast December 20, 1974, Television
KMOL TV4 file, Sinkin Collection. Most educational materials pinpointed pollutants and
quality without mentioning the sole-source program (U.S. EPA, *An Environmental Law: The
Safe Drinking Water Act of 1974 Highlights* [Washington D.C.: EPA, July 1975]; U.S. Congress: Safe Drinking Water Act file, Sinkin Collection; "The National Safe Drinking Water
Act," *Texas Town and City* (May 1976): 5, 11]); *New York Times,* November 19, 1974.

20. *San Antonio Light,* May 7 and 9, 1975; *San Antonio News,* May 9, 1975; *San Antonio Express,* May 9, 1975.

21. Thomas P. Harrison II, Regional Counsel, U.S. EPA, to Mrs. William R. Sinkin, March 7, 1975, U.S. EPA: Correspondence file, Sinkin Collection; *Federal Register* 40, no. 242 (December 16, 1975); *Environmental News,* May 14, 1975, U.S. EPA: *Environmental News* file, Sinkin Collection.

22. *San Antonio Light,* May 16, 21, 22, 24, 28, and 29, 1975; *Citizen-News,* May 29, 1975.

23. San Antonio City Water Board, *Drink San Antonio's Water . . . with Confidence* (San Antonio: City Water Board, c. 1975), San Antonio City Water Board file, Sinkin Collection; *New Braunfels Herald,* May 29, 1975; *San Antonio Light,* May 30, 1975.

24. *San Antonio Light,* June 4 and 5, 1975; *San Antonio Express,* June 5, 1974; *Northside Herald,* June 4, 1975

25. *San Antonio Light,* June 4, 1975; Henry B. Gonzalez, "Statement of Henry B. Gonzalez, Member of Congress, to the Environmental Protection Agency, June 4, 1975," U.S. EPA: Statement of Henry B. Gonzalez, Congressman file, Sinkin Collection; "Statement of Texas Attorney General's Office Regarding Designation of Edwards Aquifer: San Antonio, Texas: June 4, 1975," U.S. EPA: Statement of Texas Attorney General's Office file, Sinkin Collection.

26. *San Antonio Express,* June 5, 1975; *New Braunfels Herald,* June 12, 1975; *San Antonio Light,* June 5 and 19, 1975.

27. *San Antonio Express,* June 22, 25, and 26, 1975; *San Antonio Light,* June 25, 1975; *San Antonio News,* June 27, 1975.

28. *San Antonio Express-News,* July 19, 1975; *San Antonio Express,* July 23, 1975; *San Antonio News,* July 23, 1975.

29. *Environmental News,* December 12, 1975, Correspondence: Sohn, Robert file, Sinkin Collection; *San Antonio Express-News,* December 13, 1975; *San Antonio Light,* December 13, 1975; *Federal Register* 40, no. 242 (December 16, 1975).

30. U.S. EPA, Office of Water, Office of Ground Water and Drinking Water, *Designated Sole Source Aquifers Nationally,* 5–18; Claudia Copeland, *Legislative History of the Safe Drinking Water Act: Together with a Section-by-Section Index* (Washington D.C.: Library of Congress, February 1982); Lyndon B. Johnson School of Public Affairs, *Impact of the Safe Drinking Water Act on Texas,* 14–20. The U.S. EPA Office of Water's *Fact Sheet: Drinking Water Regulations under the Safe Drinking Water Act* (Washington D.C.: EPA, May 1990) provides an overview of regulations between 1974 and 1986 and 1986–90. Attention focuses on surface water and the various chemicals and other pollutants regulated. For up-to-date information please see the EPA Office of Ground Water and Drinking Water websites at the following addresses: <http://www.epa.gov/earth1r6/6wq/swp/ssa/effects.htm> and <http://www.epa.gov/ogwdw/swp/ssa.html>. Information cited from the latter was last updated July 3, 2000.

Chapter 9. Sitting Down at the Table

1. *San Antonio Express-News,* August 24, 1994.

2. John A. Folk-Williams, *Western Water Flows to the Cities: A Sourcebook* (Covelo, Calif.: Island Press, 1985).

3. Roger Fisher and William Ury, *Getting to Yes: Negotiating Agreement Without Giving In* (New York: Viking Penguin, 1991).

4. Citizen's Working Group, *Final Report,* April 6, 1998 (San Antonio: San Antonio Water System, 1998).

5. For a more detailed historical treatment of the controversy see John Donahue, "Water Wars in South Texas," in *Water, Culture, and Power: Local Struggles in a Global Context*, ed. John M. Donahue and Barbara Rose Johnston (Covelo, Calif.: Island Press, 1998), 187–208.

6. Current groundwater policy in Texas dates from 1904 and is based on the "English rule" of free capture, according to which property owners could pump water from beneath their land as long as they did not waste it. With advances in hydrology and pumping technology, the law of free capture was challenged in the Texas Supreme Court in 1999 (*Sipriano v. Ozarka Spring Water Co.*). In a split decision the Court upheld the doctrine of free capture, indicating that it preferred the Texas Legislature to discuss the merits of a "reasonable use" doctrine.

7. An acre-foot of water is the amount of water that could stand in one acre of land at a depth of one foot. One acre-foot is equal to 325,851 gallons and can supply a family of five for a year. In 1993 the University of Texas Bureau of Economic Geology calculated that the aquifer holds up to 215 million acre-feet of water, four times what was estimated in 1978 (*San Antonio Express-News*, October 13, 1993, and July 22, 1994). The question remains as to how much of the water is economically recoverable.

8. R. W. Maclay, "Stratigraphic Subdivisions, Fault Barriers, and Characteristics of the Edwards Aquifer, South Central Texas," in *Aquifer Resources Conference Proceedings: Geological and Managerial Considerations Relating to the Edwards Aquifer of South Central Texas* (San Antonio: Trinity University, Division of Science, Engineering and Mathematics, and the South Texas Geological Society, 1988), 8.

9. Total aquifer discharge includes pumping but also spring flows. Spring flows, primarily in Comal and Hays Counties, account, on the average, for 54 percent of total aquifer discharge.

10. The GBRA represents the economic interests of Hays and Comal Counties to the east of San Antonio. As mentioned earlier, the springs that feed the Comal and Guadalupe Rivers are major tourist attractions and the water from the springs, used for hydroelectric generation, and sold to downstream industrial users, is an important source of income for the GBRA. The GBRA brought suit against the U.S. Fish and Wildlife Service for failing to enforce pumping limits that would maintain the springs flowing and the endangered species alive. Comal Springs in New Braunfels begins to go dry when the aquifer drops to about 622 feet above sea level. While it may seem strange that the springs would go dry with so much water in the aquifer, they are at the upper end of the formation, and so are not a gauge of the quantity of water at lower levels to the west.

11. Donahue, "Water Wars in South Texas," 193.

12. Sidney Plotkin, *Keep Out: The Struggle for Land Use Control* (Berkeley: University of California Press, 1987), 137.

13. The "water activists" had come out of the Homeowner's Taxpayer's Association (HTA) which sees itself as a citizen's group holding the line of tax increases by limiting spending by city government. Several had their origins in an earlier successful drive (1985–86) to defeat a referendum to fluoridate the city's water. Their opposition to fluoridation was less a spending issue and more an issue of perceived government intrusion into the private sphere.

14. *San Antonio Express-News*, August 28, 1993.

15. Ibid., November 23, 1993.

16. Ibid., October 25, 1993.

17. *North Central Sun, San Antonio Express-News,* March 16, 1996.

18. Mayor's Citizens Committee on Water Policy, "Framework for Progress: Recommended Water Policy Strategy for the San Antonio Area." Final Report of the Mayor's Citizens Committee on Water Policy submitted to the San Antonio City Council on January 23, 1997, 12.

19. Ibid., 13.

Chapter 10. Preservation of San Antonio's Built Environment

1. Charles B. Hosmer Jr., *Preservation Comes of Age: From Williamsburg to the National Trust, 1926–1949* (Charlottesville: University of Virginia Press, 1981), 289.

2. Lewis F. Fisher, *Saving San Antonio: The Precarious Preservation of a Heritage* (Lubbock: Texas Tech University Press, 1996), 503–4.

3. *An Evaluation of Expansion Opportunities for the Henry B. Gonzalez Convention Center* (Washington, D.C.: Urban Land Institute, 1995), 8–18.

4. William J. Murtagh, *Keeping Time: The History and Theory of Preservation in America* (Pittstown, N.J.: Main Street Press, 1988), 27; Fisher, *Saving San Antonio,* 40, 60–61, 59–60.

5. Wallace Evan Davies, *Patriotism on Parade: The Story of Veterans' and Hereditary Organizations in America, 1783–1900* (Cambridge: Harvard University Press, 1955), 353.

6. Hosmer, *Preservation Comes of Age,* 275.

7. Lewis F. Fisher, *Crown Jewel of Texas: The Story of San Antonio's River* (San Antonio: Maverick Publishing, 1997), 24–27; Fisher, *Saving San Antonio,* 2–9, 210–11.

8. Robert J. Mullen, *Architecture and Its Sculpture in Viceregal Mexico* (Austin: University of Texas Press, 1997), 215.

9. Frederick Law Olmsted, *A Journey Through Texas* (New York: Dix, Edwards, and Co., 1857), 148–59.

10. Richard Everett, "Things in and about San Antonio," *Frank Leslie's Illustrated Newspaper* 7, no. 163 (January 15, 1859), 1.

11. Donald E. Everett, "San Antonio Welcomes the 'Sunset'—1877," *Southwestern Historical Quarterly* 65 (July 1961): 47–50.

12. *Texas Sun,* February 1878, in Everett, "San Antonio Welcomes the 'Sunset,'" 47–48.

13. Richard Harding Davis, *The West from a Car-Window* (New York, 1892), in Donald E. Everett, *San Antonio: The Flavor of Its Past, 1845–1898* (San Antonio: Trinity University Press, 1975), 2.

14. Fisher, *Saving San Antonio,* 349.

15. "Passing of the Chili Stands," *San Antonio Daily Express,* June 9, 1901; James Newcomb, unpublished typescript, 982, in Everett, *San Antonio,* 2.

16. Charles B. Hosmer Jr., *Presence of the Past: A History of the Preservation Movement in the United States Before Williamsburg* (New York: G. P. Putnam's Sons, 1965), 36–37.

17. "The Alamo," *San Antonio Daily Express,* January 16, 1877.

18. Hosmer, *Presence of the Past,* 105.

19. Fisher, *Saving San Antonio,* 40–42.

20. Ibid., 46–47.

21. L. Robert Ables, "The Work of Adina De Zavala," master's thesis, Mexico City College, 1955, cited in Fisher, *Saving San Antonio,* 45.

22. Fisher, *Saving San Antonio,* 55–56.

23. L. Robert Ables, "The Second Battle of the Alamo," *Southwestern Historical Quarterly* 70, no. 3 (January 1967): 372–413.

24. *San Antonio Express,* February 4, 1912, 25-B.

25. *San Antonio Express,* April 21, 1912, 27-B.

26. Fisher, *Saving San Antonio,* 105–7.

27. *San Antonio Light,* May 26, 1912, 35.

28. *San Antonio Express,* July 28, 1912.

29. Fisher, *Saving San Antonio,* 75.

30. William H. Wilson, *The City Beautiful Movement* (Baltimore: Johns Hopkins University Press, 1989), 1–5.

31. Fisher, *Crown Jewel of Texas,* 21–25.

32. *San Antonio Express,* Sept. 8, 1912, 1.

33. Fisher, *Crown Jewel of Texas,* 26–29.

34. Ables, "The Work of Adina De Zavala," 32.

35. Ables, "The Work of Adina De Zavala," 12. Some latter-day revisionists attribute De Zavala's lack of progress to discrimination because of her Hispanic surname. This argument, on close inspection, appears quite doubtful. Although three of her four grandparents were of Anglo origin, Miss De Zavala took special pride in her Spanish Mexican heritage and spoke openly of her grandfather's contribution to Texas independence. In fact, notes Ables, "It is an anomaly in the history of the State of Texas that a woman of Spanish-Mexican ancestry should have such an intense desire to preserve and illuminate Texas history while many of her Anglo contemporaries did little or nothing." She may have offended those with whom she crossed swords in preservation conflicts, but when it came to the pure study of history she was accepted in the highest ranks of established statewide historical organizations. (Ables, "The Work of Adina De Zavala," 1.)

36. Fisher, *Saving San Antonio,* 97.

37. Ibid., 109.

38. Ibid., 78–81, 125.

39. Ibid.

40. "Mary Rowena Maverick Green," *The New Handbook of Texas* 3, ed. Ron Tyler (Austin: Texas State Historical Association, 1996), 315; Fisher, *Saving San Antonio,* 95.

41. *San Antonio Express,* March 19, 1924, 22.

42. Fisher, *Saving San Antonio,* 94, 147–48.

43. Ibid., 148–51.

44. Ibid.

45. Hosmer, *Preservation Comes of Age,* 3.

46. Paul Goeldner, comp., *Texas Catalog: Historic American Buildings Survey* (San Antonio: Trinity University Press, 1975), 1–4.

47. Ron Tyler, ed., *The New Handbook of Texas* (Austin: Texas State Historical Association, 1996), 5, 1099; Fisher, *Saving San Antonio,* 156, 158–60.

48. Fisher, *Saving San Antonio,* 158–59, 175.

49. Ibid., 159–60.

50. Ibid., 151, 166.

51. Ibid., 161–62, 169.

52. Hosmer, *Presence of the Past*, 281, 572; Elizabeth D. Mulloy, *The History of the National Trust for Historic Preservation* (Washington, D.C.: Preservation Press, 1976), 8.

53. Fisher, *Saving San Antonio*, 203–5.

54. Ibid., 199–202, 205.

55. *San Antonio Light*, July 18, 1939, 1; Richard B. Henderson, *Maury Maverick: A Political Biography* (Austin: University of Texas Press, 1970), 199–200; Hosmer, *Preservation Comes of Age*, 205–6.

56. Hosmer, *Preservation Comes of Age*, 289.

57. Fisher, *Saving San Antonio*, 232–33.

58. Ibid., 135–36; Fisher, *Crown Jewel of Texas*, 56–58.

59. Fisher, *Crown Jewel of Texas*, 68–69.

60. Ibid., 70.

61. *San Antonio Express*, Oct. 9, 1953, 14; Fisher, *Saving San Antonio*, 261.

62. *San Antonio Express*, Oct. 23, 1953, 5.

63. Fisher, *Saving San Antonio*, 283–84.

64. *San Antonio Express*, March 29, 1970, 1-H.

65. Fisher, *Saving San Antonio*, 323–33.

66. Ibid., 245–50.

67. *The New York Times*, April 5, 1968, 50.

68. Fisher, *Saving San Antonio*, 348, 364.

Chapter 11. Elusive Balance

1. Quoted in Vicki Vaughan and Patricia Konstam, "Cement Plant's Old Life Is Recast," *San Antonio Express-News*, June 7, 1996. The representative added that "Storefronts, and not parking lots will be visible from the streets. Most buildings will be finished on all sides, and loading docks will be concealed." This turned out to be less than the truth. The site had been vacant since 1985, when the cement plant relocated.

2. The self-presentation of Naples, Florida, as an ideal blend of greenery, pedestrian pathways, and shops can be clearly identified on the town's official website at <http://www.naples.com>.

3. Patricia Konstam, "Developers' Ecology Awareness Praised," *Express-News*, March 21, 1997; see also "Starting September 1, Two Partners Plan to Begin a Year Long," *Express-News*, June 7, 1996.

4. David Anthony Richelieu, "Quarry Shows Its Backside to Neighbors," *Express-News*, July 20, 1997; Richelieu, "Quarry Problems Loom: Huebner Oaks Gets Nicer," ibid., December 21, 1997; Mike Greenberg, "Déjà vu Design: Alamo Quarry Market Intended to Inspire Strolling and Shopping, Founders in Sea of Asphalt," ibid., February 15, 1998. Only along the northern—and, to a much lesser degree, the eastern—boundaries of the market are there even hints of what could have been, with some attempt to blend landscaping, trees, and large, outward-facing windows on shops to produce a harmonious and inviting aspect of the market site. The western boundary, on the other hand, all too visible from the highway, reveals the Alamo Quarry Market in a far less attractive guise of a vast parking lot, screened off only by "restaurant row," a boundary wall of structurally similar chain resturants.

5. Anne Morris, "Survival Stories: Tough, Colorful Plants at Commercial Sites Weather Heat, Drought," *Express-News*, July 15, 2000.

6. For the history of the cement plant, the accompanying quarry, and the community of Cementville, see Char Miller, "Concrete Ends," *Texas Observer,* August 16, 1996, 23.

7. The quote is actually from the plan's workshop on urban design, in which sixty-five "planners, architects, landscape architects, urban designers, engineers, environmentalists, and interested downtown stake holders" participated. Though the resolutions specifically referred to the downtown area, the language and rhetoric are the norm for area design and planning programs, *Downtown San Antonio: A Strategic Plan for Entering the 21st Century* (1997), 23.

8. The state of Texas is typical in defining landscape architecture as the development of land areas "where—the principal purpose—is to arrange and modify the effects of natural scenery for aesthetic effect, considering the use to which the land is put." It includes "arrangement of natural forms, features, and plantings, including the ground and water forms, vegetation, circulation, walks, and other landscape features to fulfill aesthetic and functional requirements." *Regulation of the Practice of Landscape Architecture* (Austin: The Board, 1983), 1. The pamphlet is a reprint of article 249c of *Vernon's Texas Civil Statutes.*

9. Anne Whiston Spirn, *The Language of Landscape* (New Haven: Yale University Press, 1998), 11. Columnists discussing dissatisfaction with the Alamo Quarry asserted, for their part, that the final product was at least partly salvaged by the attempt to situate the development as part of a historical and symbolic flow: "Longtime residents of Alamo Heights," one wrote, "may have regarded the cement plant as an eyesore, but it was their eyesore, part of the distinctive culture of the place." Greenberg, "Déjà vu Design."

10. Lewis F. Fisher, *Saving San Antonio: The Precarious Preservation of a Heritage* (Lubbock: Texas Tech University Press, 1996), 14–22. The site was "discovered" in 1691; see also T. R. Fehrenbach and others, *The San Antonio Story* (Tulsa: Continental Heritage, 1978), 13–21; the latter work, issued by the San Antonio Chamber of Commerce, suffers from a relentlessly upbeat tone that, ironically, ultimately becomes a bit depressing, but the opening sections are relatively straightforward. Michaele Thurgood Haynes, *Dressing Up Debutantes: Pageantry and Glitter in Texas* (Oxford, N.Y.: Berg, 1998), offers a brief but fascinating cultural history of San Antonio, 15–28.

11. To be sure, a number of Hispanic Texans fought with the Alamo defenders against Santa Ana. This fact was largely (and deliberately) ignored during the nineteenth- and most of the twentieth-century celebrations of the battle.

12. Doyce House, *City of Flaming Adventure: The Chronicle of San Antonio* (San Antonio: Naylor Co., 1949), 184.

13. Quoted in Haynes, *Dressing Up Debutantes,* 25. In relations between Tejanos and their Anglo and German rivals, she notes, "there was still an underlying feeling of acquisition or Manifest Destiny, rather than accommodation."

14. See Fisher, *Saving San Antonio,* 13–14. The rhetoric of San Antonio's boom era lives on in a certain type of San Antonio history; the Chamber of Commerce's *The San Antonio Story* is exemplary in this regard; see, for example, 114–39. For T. R. Fehrenbach, the primary author of the book, San Antonio obtained the best of old worlds—progress plus a sort of "timelessness": "The present never quite assimilated the past in San Antonio, just as no ethnic group ever entirely assimilated any other. . . . The new flowed amid the old, while the old embedded itself in the new, in a process which continued" (131, 133).

15. See Fisher, *Saving San Antonio,* 42–87.

16. The La Villita project is described, with site plans, in *The Restoration of La Villita: A Report of Progress, Aims, and Historic Significance, November 1939* (San Antonio: City of San Antonio, 1939), with remarks by Mayor Maverick. See also Fisher, *Saving San Antonio,* 198–205. The business/booster-oriented *Story of San Antonio* typically acknowledges the La Villita project (and even the role of Maverick), only to go on to state flatly, "In the great debacle of the national Depression, a long period of relative stagnation set in. As the surrounding agrarian countryside suffered, business declined. . . . No new business buildings were erected and the skyline remained unchanged for a full generation"—unlike, the account stresses, Dallas and Houston. The authors of the narrative are preparing the reader for the formation of the business-led Good Government League and (as the reader learns) an era of reform, modernization, and growth.

17. There are few good sources on the River Walk—see Vernon G. Zunker, *A Dream Come True: Robert Hugman and San Antonio's River Walk* (Seguin, Tex.: V. G. Zunker, 1994), for some information; Caroline Shelton's *San Antonio, The Wayward River* (San Antonio: Trinity University Press for the Paseo del Rio Association, 1979) contains only a minimal text, with a foldout watercolor reproduction of the walk itself. For the restoration campaign, see Fisher, *Saving San Antonio,* 181–98.

18. Robert P. McAusland, "Introduction," to *The Art of Landscape Architecture,* ed. Dennis Drabelle (Washington, D.C.: Partners for Livable Places, 1990), 5; Michael Laurie, *Introduction to Landscape Architecture* (New York: American Elsevier, 1976), 9.

19. Typically, *The San Antonio Story* presents this in the most positive terms: see especially 179–81. For a partial corrective, see Kemper Diehl and Jan Jarboe, *Cisneros: Portrait of a New American* (San Antonio: Corona Publishing, 1985), 52–56. This account critiques the GGL from the viewpoint of a mayor who challenged it (on occasion) as city council representative (and later mayor). A brief attempt at a "balanced" critique of San Antonio politics, focusing on the GGL period and its end, is Chris Williams, "'Bat Roosts' to Term Limits: S.A. Government Evolved from Days of Rampant Vote-Buying," *Express-News,* July 4, 1999. See also John Booth et al., eds., *The Politics of San Antonio: Community, Progress, and Power* (Lincoln: University of Nebraska Press, 1983), and especially a study of the community organizers who helped to break the GGL's power, Citizens Organized for Public Service: Joseph Daniel Sekul, *The C.O.P.S. Story: a Case Study of Successful Collective Action* (San Antonio: n.p., c. 1984). An examination of the relationship between the economic development, demographic growth, and political power of Dallas, Houston, and San Antonio is Char Miller and David Johnson, "The Rise of Urban Texas," in *Urban Texas: Politics and Development,* ed. Char Miller and Heywood Sanders (College Station: Texas A&M Press, 1990), 3–29; Heywood Sanders, "Building a New Urban Infrastructure: The Creation of Postwar San Antonio," in *Urban Texas,* ed. Miller and Sanders, 154–73.

20. See Fisher, *Saving San Antonio,* 272–73.

21. Examples of bleak and sterile developments abound. The city's largest junior college, San Antonio College, began construction of a new, northside campus in 1951. The result is a campus with a number of interesting (and some rather pedestrian) buildings scattered across a barren site.

22. The Japanese Tea Garden then became the Chinese Sunken Garden; the word "Chinese" was gradually dropped in most usage from the 1950s on. In 1984 a somewhat refurbished site was officially renamed the Japanese Tea Garden, though the concert area of the

site remains the "Sunken Garden Theater." Basic information on this site can be found on the web, at www.ci.sat.tx/sapar/japanhis.htm. See also Emily' Spicer, "Japanese Tea Garden's Name a Casualty of War, Ideology," *Express-News*, July 6, 1999.

23. See John Leeper, "Introduction," in *The Maron Koogler NcNay Art Institute: A Museum of Modern Art. Selective Catalogue* (San Antonio: McNay Art Institute, n.d.), xi–xiv; also Dan Goffard, "McNay Museum a Showpiece for City," *Express-News*, February 18, 1992.

24. On SAMA's acquisition of the brewery, which had been closed since 1925, see *The San Antonio Museum of Art: The First Ten Years* (San Antonio: San Antonio Museum of Art, 1991), 5–7.

25. Current plans for the future expansion of the SAMA complex do envision a final orientation to the riverfront, with picnic tables and an artificial island in midstream.

26. Spicer, "Japanese Tea Garden's Name a Casualty of War, Ideology," notes, "In recent years, dry weather has left the garden ponds bone dry, graffiti has marred the rock walls with obscenities, and a lack of funding has kept the grounds from their full lush potential." If anything, this is an understatement.

27. On Cementville, see Miller, "Concrete Ends," *Texas Observer*, 23; Thelma Garza, "Cementville, Texas," *Express-News*, September 12, 1995.

28. Susan Yerkes, "St. Anthony Draws Friends and Faithful," *Express-News*, February 24, 1996.

29. Spirn, *Language of Landscape*, 252–53; Donald Horne, *The Great Museum: The Re-Presentation of History* (London: Pluto Press, 1984), 29–31. To be fair, Spirn does not agree in the main with Horne's wholesale condemnation of the process in question; for her, there is a necessary flow and change "over the course of a century, of history, the nature of the authority it confers, and the role of historic preservation." That is exemplified in her discussion of Disney's Magic Kingdom (236–39).

30. Horne, *The Great Museum*, 110–12.

31. Umberto Eco, "Travels in Hyperreality," in his *Travels in Hyperreality: Essays* (New York: Harcourt, Brace, Jovanovich, 1983), 10. Eco also emphasizes the substitutive role of these recreations: using the example of the (now-defunct) Museum of Living Art in California, he argues that the philosophy is not "We are giving you the reproduction so that you will want the original," but rather "We are giving you the reproduction so you will no longer feel any need of the original" (19).

32. The architect O'Neil Ford argued that attempts to restore the "original" La Villita site inevitably ran afoul of the changing nature of the original over time. The goal was to provide a broad exemplar of regional architecture. Fisher, *Saving San Antonio*, 204–5.

33. The debate about development policies erupted (if only sporadically) in the 1997 mayoral election, in which Howard Peak (a member of the City Council and eventual winner) accused Mayor Bill Thornton of being subservient to city developers: see, for example, Cindy Tumiel, "Peak Hits Thornton on Development Ties," *Express-News*, April 22, 1997; Patrick Driscoll, "Commentary," *Express-News*, April 30, 1997.

34. See a sample of newspapers articles on the issue: Dan Goddard, "Public Arts Funding Takes Center Stage," *Express-News*, December 29, 1996; Joy Williams, "Persistent Protesters Don't Like the Scent of 'Percent for Art,'" *Express-News*, July 16, 1996; Chris Williams, "City Wants Time to Mull Art Alternative," *Express-News*, August 1, 1997; Williams, "Big Arts Agencies Take Brunt of Budget Cutbacks," *Express-News*, September 13, 1997.

35. See Williams, "Persistent Protesters Don't Like the Scent of 'Percent for Art'"; Mike Greenberg, "Council Rejects 'Percent for Art,'" *Express-News*, July 21, *Express-News* columnist Roddy Stinson typified opponents' arguments: see "More Goo-Goo News," *Express-News*, May 18, 1966.

36. For a review of the ordinance and the debate over its effectiveness, see Rudoph Bush, "Tree Rules Fail to Stop Bulldozers," *Express-News* supplement for North-Central San Antonio, May 5, 1999. The single meeting of the committee is discussed in Chuck McCullough, "Tree Committee Disbanded after Only One Meeting," *Express-News*, August 5, 1998.

37. Bush, "Tree Rules Fail to Stop Bulldozers"; for controversies about the ordinance's effect, see, for example, "First Test of Tree Ordinance," *Express-News*, November 14, 1997; Amy Dorsett, "Tree Ordinance Faces First Test: City Moves Ahead with Investigation of Tree Cutting," *Express-News*, November 19, 1997.

38. The Huebner-Oaks shopping center on the city's far north, for example, was eventually to be praised by local analysts, largely in comparison to the Alamo Quarry Market, for its scattered pathways, superior landscaping, its shade, and unified architectural style. See David Anthony Richelieu, "Suburban Chic Village Lifestyle at Huebner Oaks," *Express-News*, March 2, 1997; Richelieu, "Quarry Problems Loom."

39. Greenberg, "Déjà vu Design."

40. See Morris, "Survival Stories."

41. Bonnie Pfister and Vicki Vaughn, "InverWorld Affiliates Face Suit," *Express-News*, July 14, 1999; Vicki Vaughn, "PowerHouse Café's Owners Close Doors: Plug Pulled on PowerHouse," *Express-News*, July 3, 1999.

Afterword

1. Sidney Lanier, "San Antonio de Bexar," in *Sidney Lanier: Florida and Miscellaneous Prose*, ed. Philip Graham (Baltimore: Johns Hopkins Press, 1945), 202.

2. Ibid., 233–35, 239–41.

3. Ibid., 202.

4. Roy Bragg, "Climate, Geography Set the Stage for Flooding Disaster," *San Antonio Express-News*, October 28, 1998, 1A; Chuck McCullough, "Cibolo Creek Cleanup Expected to Start Soon," *San Antonio Express-News*, March 24, 1999, 5H; Christine Kremer and David F. Zane, "Storm-Related Mortality in Central Texas, October 17–31, 1998," Bureau of Epidemiology, Texas Department of Health, Austin, February 1999, accessible at <http://www.tdh.state.tx.us/injury/st_storm.htm>.

5. See chapters 8 and 9 in this volume for background; Char Miller, "Water Torture," *San Antonio Current*, July 24–30, 1997, 10–13; Jerry Needham, "SAWS to Add Land for Water Storage," *San Antonio Express-News*, May 17, 2000, 8B; "SAWS Mulls Options for New Sources," March 18, 2000, 1, 6B; Susan Combs, "Water Rules Must Consider All Texans' Needs," *San Antonio Express-News*, February 28, 2000, 5B; Char Miller, "Water, Money, Power Flows to Agriculture," *San Antonio Express-News*, March 10, 2000, 5B; Nate Blakeslee, "Smoke and Water," *Texas Observer*, August 20, 1999, 8–13; Zeke MacCormack, "Medina Residents Bash Bexar Thirst," *San Antonio Express-News*, March 10, 2000, 7B; "Cibolo Reservoir Dispute Is Boiling," March 7, 2000, 1, 4B.

6. Ralph Maitland, "San Antonio: The Shame of Texas," *Forum*, August 1939; Owen P. White, "Machine Made," *Collier's*, September 18, 1937; Lewis W. Gillenson, "Texas' Forgot-

ten People," *Look* 15, no. 7 (March 27, 1951); Char Miller, "Slumming: San Antonio's Legacy of Shame," *Texas Observer*, April 11, 1997, 8–12; Donald L. Zelman, "Alazan-Apache Courts: A New Deal Response to Mexican American Housing Conditions in San Antonio," *Southwestern Historical Quarterly* (October 1983): 122–50; Robert B. Fairbanks, "Public Housing for the City as a Whole: The Texas Experience," *Southwestern Historical Quarterly* (April 2000): 403–24; Stephen Brook, *Honkytonk Gelato: Travels Through Texas* (New York: Atheneum, 1985), 146–47.

7. See the relevant portions of chapters 3–7 in this anthology for discussions of the convergence of political and environmental factors in determining the city's economic viability and public health.

8. On civil defense employment on San Antonio's bases, see David R. Johnson, "The Failed Experiment: Military Aviation and Urban Development in San Antonio, 1910–1940," in *Martial Metropolis: U.S. Cities in War and Peace*, ed. Roger T. Lotchin (New York: Praeger, 1984), 89–108; Sherry Sylvester, "Bexar Wages among Lowest of Big Counties," *San Antonio Express-News*, July 21, 2000, 1, 11A; only San Bernadino County (Calif.) posted lower wages than Bexar County.

9. Mexican American women were prominently involved in unionization: Julia K. Blackwelder, *Women of the Depression: Caste and Culture in San Antonio, 1929–1939* (College Station: Texas A&M University Press, 1984), 130–51; Richard A. Garcia, *Rise of the Mexican American Middle Class: San Antonio, 1929–1941* (College Station: Texas A&M University Press, 1991), 54–67; Selden C. Menefee and Orin C. Cassmore, *The Pecan Shellers of San Antonio: The Problem of Underpaid and Unemployed Mexican Labor* (Washington, D.C.: GPO, 1940), 50–51.

10. Minutes of Board of Directors, Chamber of Commerce, February 11 and 25, 1941; Johnson, "The Failed Experiment," 89–108; Robert Landolt, *Mexican-American Workers in San Antonio* (New York: Arno Press, 1976), chap. 5; Garcia, *Rise of the Mexican American Middle Class*, 202–3, 302–3; Richard J. Harris, "Mexican-American Occupational Attainments in San Antonio: Comparative Assessments," in *The Politics of San Antonio: Community, Progress, and Power*, ed. David R. Johnson, John A. Booth, and Richard J. Harris (Lincoln: University of Nebraska Press, 1983), 53–71; Char Miller, "Sunbelt Texas," in *Texas Through Time: Evolving Interpretations*, ed. Walter L. Buenger and Robert A. Calvert (College Station: Texas A&M University Press, 1991), 295–98; a critique of this assumption about progress in the local Hispanic community is Rodolfo Rosales, *The Illusion of Inclusion: The Untold Political Story of San Antonio* (Austin: University of Texas Press, 2000).

11. Blackwelder, *Women of the Depression*, explores the complex character of patriarchy and paternalism that dominated San Antonio's public arena and domestic spaces, 3–11, 25–42, 75–89.

12. Char Miller and David R. Johnson, "The Rise of Urban Texas," in *Urban Texas: Politics and Development*, ed. Char Miller and Heywood Sanders (College Station: Texas A&M University Press, 1990); Miller, "Sunbelt Texas," 279–309; Harvey L. Molotch, "The City as Growth Machine," *American Journal of Sociology* (September 1976): 309–30; John R. Logan and Harvey L. Molotch, *Urban Fortunes: The Political Economy of Place* (Berkeley: University of California Press, 1987).

13. David R. Johnson, "'Frugal and Sparing': Interest Groups, Politics, and City Building in San Antonio, 1870–1885" (33–57); Miller and Johnson, "The Rise of Urban Texas"

(22–29); and Heywood Sanders, "Building a New Urban Infrastructure: The Creation of Postwar San Antonio" (154–73); all in *Urban Texas,* ed. Miller and Sanders. Not until the mid-1950s, with the advent of the Good Government League, a reform machine with substantial business backing, did San Antonio begin to mimic the more successful planning agendas of Dallas and Houston.

14. *San Antonio Express-News,* February 13, 1941, 12A; February 17, 1941, 1A; February 25, 1941, 2A; Minutes of the Board of Directors of the Chamber of Commerce, February 11 and 25, 1941; Johnson, "Failed Experiment," 103–5; instead of airplane manufacturing plants, the Chamber further advocated the creation of a "municipal advertising campaign" to tout San Antonio as one of the nation's "progressive cities" and the expansion of a nascent convention business: *San Antonio Express-News,* February 9, 1941, 2A, 4A; February 20, 1941, 6; February 25, 1941, 1.

15. "Venereal Disease Control," in *Public Health Survey of San Antonio, Texas, with Particular Regard to Tuberculosis and Venereal Disease Control* (Washington, D.C.: U.S. Public Health Service, 1939), 1–2.

INDEX

Ables, L. Robert, 210
aesthetic quality of landscape, 43–44
acequias (irrigation ditches), 5, 49. *See also* irrigation
African Americans/blacks, 102, 103, 110, 245; enfranchisement of, 104, 108, 113; homicide rate for, 107, 111, 112, 116; and park development, 92–93, 96–98; political machine of, 93–95, 104, 260*n*28; upward mobility of, 115
Agency for Toxic Substances and Disease Registry (ASTR), 136
agriculture, 26, 27–28, 59; Spanish colonial, 47, 48–50. *See also* irrigation
Air Force Bases, 122, 123–26, 135, 137. *See also* military and environment; *and specific base*
Alamo, 10, 201, 205–8, 226, 228
Alamo Area Council of Governments, 174
Alamo Cement Company, 231–32, 234
Alamo City, the, 37
Alamo Monument Society, 206
Alamo Quarry Market, 11, 222–25, 231–35, 236–38, 275*n*4
Alarcón, Martín de, 49
Aldalve, Rafael, 183
Alinsky, Saul, 114, 185
Anglo-Americans, 109, 226, 242; as immigrants, 41, 59–60, 65, 76
annexation, 8, 114, 157
Apache nation, 51, 63, 65–66
Applewhite reservoir, 166, 187, 195; opposition to, 9–10, 182, 185–86

aquatic species, 184–85
aquifer contamination, 134. *See also* Edwards Aquifer; groundwater contamination
Aquifer Protection Association (APA), 173, 185
architecture, 211. *See also* historical preservation; landscape architecture
Army Corps of Engineers, 166, 167
artesian springs, 6, 29, 30–32
artesian zone, 33, 171
arts funding, 235–36
Ashe junipers (*Juniperus ashei*), 26, 27
At Home in Texas: Early Views of the Land (Doughty), 41
Atlantic Coastal Plain, 29–30
Atomic Energy Commission (AEC), 135
Austin Chalk, 28
Ayres, Atlee B., 218

Baca, Antonio, 54
Backland Prairie Biome, 127
Baker, Victor, 35, 36
Balcones Canyonlands, 25
Balcones Escarpment, 18, 23, 28–32
Barreiro, Francisco Alvarez, 44
Barshop, Sam, 185
Bartholomew, Harland, 217–18
Bartlett, Terrell, 152
Base Realignment and Closure program (BRAC), 134
bat caves, 27
bear hunting, 64–65